HERSTORY

Women Who Changed the World

HERSTORY

Women Who Changed the World

Edited by Ruth Ashby and
Deborah Gore Ohrn

Introduction by Gloria Steinem

VIKING

To my daughter, Rebecca
—R.A.

Dedicated to my mother, Evelyn Dilts Gore, and my aunt Peggy Dilts Herz,
who served as role models.
—D.G.O.

VIKING
Published by the Penguin Group
Penguin Books USA Inc., 375 Hudson Street, New York, New York 10014, U.S.A.
Penguin Books Ltd, 27 Wrights Lane, London W8 5TZ, England
Penguin Books Australia Ltd, Ringwood, Victoria, Australia
Penguin Books Canada Ltd, 10 Alcorn Avenue, Toronto, Ontario, Canada M4V 3B2
Penguin Books (N.Z.) Ltd, 182–190 Wairau Road, Auckland 10, New Zealand

Penguin Books Ltd, Registered Offices: Harmondsworth, Middlesex, England
First published in 1995 by Viking,
a division of Penguin Books USA Inc.

3   5   7   9   10   8   6   4

Copyright © Byron Preiss Visual Publications, Inc., 1995

Introduction copyright © Gloria Steinem, 1991, 1995

All rights reserved

A Byron Preiss Book

Book Design: Heidi North
Associate Editor: Kathy Huck
Assistant Editor: Robin Ambrosino

Special thanks to Stephanie Hutter, Hope Innelli, Vicky Rauhofer, Cary Ryan, Shelly Perron,
Susan Korman, Diana Ajjan, Megan Miller, and Michael Mendelson.

Front cover images: Eleanor Roosevelt, AP/Wide World Photos; Frida Kahlo detail, reproduction
authorized by the Instituto Nacional de Bella Artes and the Harry Ransom Humanities
Research Center at the University of Texas at Austin; Toni Morrison, © Kate Kunz; Corazon
Aquino, AP/Wide World Photos.

Back cover images: Queen Hatshepsut detail, The Metropolitan Museum of Art, Rogers Fund
and Edward S. Harkness Gift, 1929 (29.3.2); Joan of Arc, AP/Wide World Photos; T'su-
hsi detail, Fogg Art Museum/Harvard University Art Museums, Bequest of Grenville L. Winthrop; Sarah Winnemucca, Nevada Historical Society.

Grateful acknowledgment is made to the following authors, agents, and publishers for the use
of copyrighted material. Every effort has been made to obtain permission to use previously
published material. Any errors or omissions are unintentional.

AMS Press, New York: Excerpt from *Diaries of Court Ladies of Old Japan. The Belknap Press of
Harvard University Press and the Trustees of Amherst College:* Selections from *The Poems of
Emily Dickinson* edited by Thomas H. Johnson; copyright 1951, by President and Fellows of
Harvard College, copyright © renewed by President and Fellows of Harvard College, 1983.

Library of Congress Catalog Card Number: 94-61492

ISBN 0-670-85434-4

Printed in U.S.A.

Set in 12 point Garamond Adobe

Without limiting the rights under copyright reserved above, no part of this
publication may be reproduced, stored in, or introduced into a retrieval
system, or transmitted, in any form or by any means (electronic, mechanical,
photocopying, recording, or otherwise), without the prior written permission
of both the copyright owner and the above publisher of this book.

Page 299 constitutes an extension of this copyright page.

C O N T E N T S

THE DAWN
PREHISTORY TO 1750

FROM REVOLUTION TO REVOLUTION
1750 TO 1850

CONTENTS

THE GLOBAL COMMUNITY
1890 TO THE PRESENT

CONTENTS

Seeking Out the Invisible Woman

by Gloria Steinem

One recent night while switching TV channels, I happened onto *Amadeus,* the movie based on Mozart's life. I'd seen it before but without noticing it had obliterated Nannerl, Mozart's older sister. Only learning a little about women's history had introduced me to this other Mozart. Like him, she had been a child genius. Together, they traveled the courts of Europe performing at the command of their father. Until she was sent home to marry at fifteen or so, they were each other's only companions. In fact, we don't know whether some compositions attributed to Amadeus might really have been Nannerl's, as some musicologists speculate. Nonetheless she was to become a teacher of other musicians. Only from her brother's letters do we know he considered her the really talented one.

On that same night, through the century-skipping magic of television, I came upon *The Right Stuff,* a movie about the first United States astronauts. This time, I had not even a remedial history book to tell me what I was missing, but thanks to Joan McCullough's cover story in *Ms.* magazine, I was painfully aware of the on-screen absence of twenty-five female pilots who had been given the same tests as John Glenn and Alan Shepard. Thirteen had passed with flying colors. Indeed, one of them, Jerrie Cobb, had entered the program with twice as many air miles as John Glenn and emerged lucid from hours in a sensory deprivation tank that left one male astronaut crying and imagining he heard barking dogs. This first Mercury Program found that women in general were more resistant to radiation, less subject to heart attacks, and better able to endure extremes of heat, cold, pain, noise, and loneliness. Since women also weighed less than men in general and required less food and oxygen, they could have saved a lot of tax-payers' dollars in the very expensive per-pound business of launching a capsule into space. Nonetheless, this female success came as such a shock to NASA that its all-male officials simply decreed: no women. When two women candidates, Jerrie Cobb and pioneer helicopter pilot Jane Hart, fought back by organizing a congressional hearing on this ban in 1962, John Glenn and Alan Shepard testified that women were unqualified because they had not met the jet-test requirements. (Never mind that women were not eligible for the military program that could have given them such experience.) A NASA spokesman was quoted as saying, "Talk of an American spacewoman makes me sick to my stomach." As Jerrie Cobb said after the subcommittee let NASA's no-women rule stand, yet failed to question its expensive training program for a chimp named Glenda: "Millions for chimps, but not one cent for women!"

Watching *The Right Stuff* so many years later, I wondered: What was wrong with including the true story of female astronauts? Would women's possession of "the right stuff" turn it into "the wrong stuff"?

I think the answer was a resounding yes. In 1963, I interviewed those first male astronauts about their history-making flight, and also about the Soviets' launching of a woman astronaut. A NASA spokesman referred to the latter event as "just a publicity stunt." The astronauts themselves compared her to their trained chimp. At the time, I hadn't questioned them about the fate of our thirteen female astronaut candidates for a simple reason: I didn't know they existed. If reported by the press at all, they had been trivialized and downplayed as "Astrotrix" and "Spacegals."

There's one more turn of the screw that tells the difficulty of recording women's history of the recent past, much less of past centuries. When Sally Ride—an activist who made it very clear that only a massive women's movement had made her selection possible—was scheduled to become the first woman in space, I invited Jane Hart to travel with me to the event at Cape Canaveral in Florida. I hoped that reporters would remedy history by interviewing her as a "backgrounder." Unfortunately, few were interested in Jane or those obscure, heroic thirteen. None cared about their continuing exploits. After raising eight children, for instance, Jane had sailed a small boat around the world. Jerrie Cobb had flown medical supplies, paid for by money she collected, in her own single engine plane up the Amazon River in Brazil to distribute to Indian tribes. Each woman had gone on trying to be the explorer and history-maker she was born to be. Yet most people still think that Sally Ride was the first U.S. woman qualified to be an astronaut.

Do these two examples surprise you? If so, brace yourself for more surprises and for anger at the incompleteness of our educations. All you have to do is spend a few hours with feminist historians like Gerda Lerner and Marilyn French, or study pre-patriarchal religions, or discover the power women had in the Dark Ages but lost in the "Renaissance" when misogynist classical texts were resurrected to oppose them, or read of African warrior queens who fought colonial invaders, or Native American "councils of grandmothers" who chose male chiefs and decided the issues of war and peace. In contrast, the few women who show up in history books are likely to be the mothers or wives of famous men. From a patriarchal point of view, they are playing the "right" roles, and they are also likely to be of the "right" color, class, age, sexuality, or part of the world. Perhaps the slogan on a current button sums it up best. "The truth will set you free. But first, it will make you mad."

Nonetheless, the truth *will* set you free. Looking at the world *as if women mattered* provides a long overdue understanding of how and why events take place. Men can learn that they needn't separate themselves from women—or from supposedly "female" qualities within themselves—to make history. Women can learn they have powers and talents that are released by self-authority, esteem for one's self, and respect for one's group. Both women and men benefit from the blossoming of the female half of the world.

But right now, there is still a reason why studies show, even among young women who have been the valedictorians of their high schools, intellectual self-esteem tends to diminish with every year of higher education. Once in college, female students see texts in which fewer and fewer women are visible, and are expected to obey forms of authority in which women are more and more rare. What we are learning is: *Our place.*

Human history isn't accurate or complete without women's history. It's for all year, every year, and must be integrated into every course. But even reading one book that describes the world *as if women mattered* can change the rest of your life.

PREFACE

In July 1993, a group of archaeologists working in southern Siberia found the mummy of a two-thousand-year-old woman. About eighteen when she died, she was dressed in an elegant white silk blouse, red skirt, and white stockings. Around her left arm coiled a wreath of intricate blue tattoos. Together with the dishes, mirror, and horses' harnesses with which she was buried, the tattoos identify her as a princess and probably a priestess.

That is all we know about Lady, as the archaeologists have dubbed her. Although she was a person of importance in her own society, this is probably all we will ever know. True, she will help scholars find out more about the nomadic Scythian culture in which she lived. But we will never learn her real name, or whom she fell in love with or why, or what she thought about as she rode her horse across the Siberian steppes on a lovely spring morning. We will never know her as a real person.

But, you may object, she's been dead for centuries; of course we can't *know* her. On the contrary, we become acquainted with people we've never met all the time, not just in the newspapers or on TV, but through biographies. The biographer relies on the relics of yesterday—on birth and death certificates, wills, contracts, tax rolls, letters, faded photographs, whatever is available—to bring back personality from the past. Making sense of these fragments of a life requires considerable art and ingenuity. "How," exclaimed writer Virginia Woolf before embarking on the biography of a friend, "can one make a life of six cardboard boxes full of tailors' bills, love letters, and old picture postcards?"

At least Woolf had access to the cardboard boxes. The further back in time we go, the harder it can be for a biographer to assemble enough evidence to recreate a whole existence. For societies like Lady's that had no written language—for what we call prehistory—it is nearly impossible to create portraits of individual people.

When the editors of this book first conceived of the *Herstory* project, we wanted to bring together biographies of women from all times and places. Our first criterion in chosing our subjects had to be availability of information. Naturally, this criterion posed limitations. There were probably Bainouka queens in Africa before the arrival of the Europeans, but since they lived in a preliterate society, there are no written records of their lives.

Even for literate societies, information about individuals can be scant. Generally, better records have been kept of rulers than of their subjects. Traditionally, only some groups of woman—such as queens and warriors—have been considered important enough by historians to deserve much attention. Also, until recently, only women of the upper classes have been literate—i.e., able to write the letters, diaries, etc. that would let us remember them. That is one of the reasons why in the first section of the book you will find that many of the biographical subjects are members of either royalty or the elite. These women also come from ancient and early modern societies with well-developed written records.

Yet, even for queens, biographical information differs in scope and accuracy. We know little about the ancient British queen Boudica—who lived in a preliterate society—except what Roman historians can tell us. The life of Queen Elizabeth, ruler of Renaissance England, is revealed in thousands of contemporary sources as well as in her own poems and letters. Yet, still, we can only guess at her private emotions, such as what she really felt about the fascinating earl of Essex. We understand much more about Queen Victoria, born three centuries later. In addition to official records and memoirs, we have her daily diary, which she kept dutifully from age thirteen to her death. We need no longer, as with Boudica or Elizabeth, depend on idealized descriptions or portraits to show us what Victoria looked like. Stern, plump, commanding, she materializes before us in dozens of photographs. A primitive "moving picture" made at the end of her life even preserved the pomp and circumstance of her sixtieth anniversary on the throne.

Our second criterion for including a subject in this book was that she had to exert great influence, in her own and subsequent times. Some choices were obvious, like Cleopatra or Joan of Arc or Golda Meir. Others were more difficult. Who can say whether Isadora Duncan or Martha Graham has been more important to modern dance? Or whether Toni Morrison or Alice Walker better represents the voice of the late twentieth-century African-American writer?

No one, of course. Our final list of 120 women, then, is hardly definitive, merely suggestive. The women presented here stand for thousands of exceptional women throughout the ages. They are *exceptionally* exceptional not only because of their accomplishments but also because they managed to survive centuries of exclusion from history books.

Until recently, historians—the official keepers of the human record—have all been male. As a result, "history" has been written from men's point of view, and primarily about their own achievements. Women historians working today have noted women's virtual invisibility in official history. I decided to test this finding before writing this essay.

When I discovered I would be editing a book spanning all of human history, I searched my bookshelves to find anything that would help. *Man's Journey Through Time*, published in 1974, seemed to offer the kind of grand overview I was looking for. But the book's cover and title merely confirmed my suspicions. All the little black-and-white illustrations on the jacket depicted men: the Greek statue of the discus thrower, a knight on horseback, Napoleon on horseback, soldiers in World War I, a male astronaut in a spacesuit. In the book itself, only 30 women, compared to about 640 men, had been picked to represent all women throughout history—and of these, 20 are queens, including four wives of King Henry VIII!

This is the kind of history of "great men and great wars" about which a character in Jane Austen's *Northanger Abbey* (1818) complained: "I read it [history] a little as a duty, but it tells me nothing that does not either vex or weary me. The quarrels of popes and kings, with wars and pestilences, in every page; the men all so good for nothing, and hardly any women at all—it is very tiresome."

Of course, women have always been in *actual* history—the progress of human events—as opposed to official history. As the groundbreaking historian Mary Beard asserted, "Woman *is* and *makes* history." But until recently, we did not have access to that history. Periodically, some writers like the medieval feminist Christine de Pizan would try to praise great women of the past and make their lives available to all readers. But these reevaluations were invariably forgotten.

Only with the women's liberation movement in the 1960s and the subsequent establishment of women's studies programs in schools and colleges did we start to tell the story of humankind from our point of view. The ultimate aim of women's history is not to exclude half the human population but to include the half that has been left out. As might be expected, history looks very different from the interior of a Greek matron's house than it does from the council chamber of the male citizen; from the medieval kitchen than from the battlefields of the Crusades.

Traditional historical periods have a different significance for women too. What did the Golden Age of Greece or the Renaissance mean to women living in those times? Since we wanted to avoid traditional periodization, in *Herstory* we have divided history into three broad categories: from prehistory until 1750 and the widening of opportunities for women in Europe; from 1750 to the beginnings of the international women's movement in the 1890s; and the twentieth century.

In order to help readers place individual women in the context of their times, we have preceded each group of biographies with a short historical survey. Naturally, much has been left out. But since in such a short space it is impossible to relate how all women of all times and all places lived and worked, we have just touched on representative cultures. What was life like for women in Egypt in 2000 B.C.? In Mexico in 1500? In America in 1960?

Above all, we have sought to introduce to you some unforgettable women. They speak to us across the divide of centuries and continents, from the courts of China and the towns of medieval Europe and the primeval forests of the Americas. And through their words and deeds, they realize the prediction of the Greek poet Sappho some twenty-five centuries ago: "I say that even later someone will remember us."

Ruth Ashby

The
Dawn
Prehistory to 1750

The Dawn
Prehistory to 1750

Somewhere in Africa about forty thousand years ago, a woman appeared who looked just like us. She walked upright and had a high forehead, large brain, and sparse body hair. She spoke a language and used tools. She was—for the first time—fully human.

Venus of Willendorf, *c. 25,000 B.C.*
Prehistoric female figurines may represent fertility or Mother goddesses.

She and her mate were modern *Homo sapiens*, the product of millions of years of evolution. Like their most recent hominid ancestors, they were hunter-gatherers. That is, they survived by collecting plants, insects, and small animals and by hunting large animals. Before c. 100,000 B.C., when weapons able to kill large game were developed, males and females probably performed the same food-gathering tasks. Afterward, their roles diverged.

Our first female would have been a natural forager, able to balance the tasks of gathering nuts or berries with the need to breast-feed and care for her young. The male, meanwhile, would have been better suited for hunting large prey, a task that would be hindered by the presence of infants. But the two roles—forager and hunter—would have been equally necessary for survival, and equally respected. Society would have been egalitarian—neither sex would have had more authority than the other.

Our ancestors would always have known where and at what times of year certain local plant foods could be found. Then one day, while out foraging, a quick-witted Neolithic female might have noticed that plants grew from little seeds. Later, others would have discovered that they could stick seeds in the ground themselves and control where the plants would grow. In short, they would have discovered agriculture.

Sometime between 10,000 and 7000 B.C. in Southeast Asia and Southwest Europe, people—most likely females—began to cultivate crops. The nomadic lifestyle of the hunter-gatherer disappeared. Now it was necessary to protect the crops and then to store the grain after it was harvested. Communities began to stay in one spot and build permanent dwellings.

Then came a development that altered the relationship between men and women for a long time to come. People began to domesticate cattle and sheep and other animals and use them for plowing, for food, and for clothes. Hunting became less important, and men took over agriculture and the herding of animals. Women, it is believed, developed the art of spinning and weaving flax and wool into cloth. For the first time, woman's duties kept her within the home, while the man remained outside. The livestock and the land became his.

Individuals started to accumulate private property. Those who through luck or skill managed to raise extra crops and livestock could barter their surplus for more goods and services. An unlucky farmer might have nothing to trade but his own labor. With such simple beginnings, the hierarchy of wealth and status that we call the class system began. Scholars disagree about what came first: the subordination of one class of men to another or the subordination of women to men. Certainly, the second is closely connected to the first. If a wealthy man wanted to pass his possessions onto his children, he would have to make sure his children were his own. The strict laws against female adultery and the seclusion of females began as an attempt to ensure the legitimacy of offspring and establish lines of inheritance.

Early records also show that women and children were often used as a medium of exchange—to pay off debts or to cement alliances. Ultimately, male heads of households could consider not only plows and oxen but also women and children as their possessions. And thus patriarchy was born.

Patriarchy—the domination of women and children by men—has been a feature of nearly all human societies for five thousand years. (Relatively egalitarian hunter-gatherer societies seem to be the exception to this rule.) Patriarchy was established gradually over a few thousand years, and not, we can imagine, without much resistance. Yet by the "dawn of civilization"— the beginning of recorded history—in Egypt and Mesopotamia in 3000 B.C., inequality between men and women, higher and lower classes, and free and slave populations was well established.

Patriarchy is by no means monolithic. It has not taken the same form in all times and places throughout history, though common features can be observed. Nor has it ever meant that women were powerless, or necessarily subjugated. No system that has given us Queen Hatshepsut, Florence Nightingale, and Gabriela Mistral can be described as always oppressive. But the persistence of patriarchy has meant that women have been historically disadvantaged—restricted from access to education, politics, religion, science, the arts, any sphere of activity not associated with their alloted roles as child-rearers and housewives. And—although child rearing is one of the most important of human responsibilities—woman's restriction has been justified on the grounds that she is intellectually and morally subordinate to man. The greatest historical injustice of patriarchy is not that it kept woman in the home but that it labeled her as inferior for being there.

Was there ever a time in human history when women were dominant over men? Probably not, scholars have decided. There is no clear evidence that *matriarchal*, as opposed to egalitarian or patriarchal, societies ever existed.

Nonetheless, women's status within the general framework of patriarchy has varied greatly from culture to culture. As you read through this book, you may measure women's status by noting: (1) their ability to inherit, own property, and conduct business; (2) their ownership of their own bodies and sexuality; (3) their access to the wider world, through education, politics, professions, etc.; (4) their participation in institutionalized religion.

THE ANCIENT WORLD

To illustrate the great diversity in cultural attitudes toward women, let's take a quick tour of some ancient civilizations:

Ancient Egypt (3100–30 B.C.)

Insofar as one can generalize about a culture that lasted for three thousand years, Egyptian women seem to have enjoyed nearly equal rights with men. Possessing full adult status, they could inherit and bequeath property. A woman could sell in the marketplace and work in the fields and even be called up for enforced labor service to the state—which she no doubt hated as much as any man. Powerful women could be priests and hold religious office and, as queens, rule kingdoms—sometimes jointly with their husbands. Or rare occasions, women, such as Queen Hatshepsut, could rule alone. Egyptian society was so unusual that when the Greek historian Herodotus visited it in mid-fifth century B.C., he sputtered, "The Egyptians themselves, in their manners and customs, seem to have reversed the ordinary practices of mankind. For instance, women attend market and are employed in trade, while men stay at home and do the weaving." This last is an exaggeration—but a telling one.

Ancient India

In the Vedic Age (1500–300 B.C.), women seem to have held

Young Egyptian girl bearing funeral gifts. Painted wood, c. 2,000 B.C.

high status: they could be scholars or teachers and even composers of Vedic (religious) hymns. Over the ensuing centuries, as power passed from local kinship groups to centralized states and hierarchical castes (classes) were strengthened, women lost their earlier prestige. By the Gupta period (A.D. 22–528), the Laws of Manu decreed: "In childhood, a female must be subject to her father, in youth, to her husband, and when her lord is dead, to her sons; a woman must never be independent." By the year 1000, the practice of suttee (widows voluntarily being burned alive on their husbands' funeral pyres) was encouraged for the highest castes.

China

Except for the Egyptian, Chinese civilization has endured longer than any other in history. It has also given birth to the most systematic oppression of women. When the philosopher Confucius (c. 551–479 B.C.) set down the principles of order, harmony, and hierarchy that were the basis of that civilization, he also determined the destiny of women for two and a half thousand years.

Confucianism is based on the cult of ancestor worship, in which ancestors are traced from father to son. In the traditional Confucian family—three to five generations of males under one roof—women existed merely to produce sons who would one day be ancestors. In her lifetime, a woman was subject to the Three Bonds of Obedience: to her father when young, to her husband when married, and to her sons when widowed. As a girl she was sold into marriage by her parents and had little or no contact with her birth family after that. A perpetual outsider, bound to submission and servility, she had no property, no authority, no education, and no way out save through suicide, which was not uncommon. Woman's one hope was to bear male children and eventually derive authority from her grown sons.

Her extremely low status led to the most notorious examples of Chinese misogyny: the frequent killing of female infants, or infanticide; the selling of girls into concubinage; and foot binding. No large-scale assault was made on these ancient abuses until the Chinese Communist Revolution of 1949.

Classical Greece (c. 480–338 B.C.)

Fifth-century Athens, as we all know, was the cradle of modern democracy. Citizens could vote, hold office, and serve on juries—male citizens,

Greek women weaving and working wool. Frieze, c. 560 B.C.

that is. Female citizens, like resident aliens, slaves, and children, could not participate in the workings of the *polis*, the city-state. Their role was to keep the home and bear the children. They were so secluded that it's unclear whether they were even allowed to attend the daylong dramatic performances that were the crowning glory of the Golden Age.

What's worse, Athenian society was terribly misogynistic. The following pronouncement by the philosopher Aristotle is mild in comparison to the antiwomen invectives of other writers: "The male is by nature superior, and the female inferior; and the one rules and the other is ruled; this principle, of necessity, extends to all mankind."

As eventually the ancient civilizations of the Mediterranean world faded away, in their place came two new religions that would change the course of history—but not really for women.

CHRISTIANITY

Christianity spread like wildfire throughout northern Africa and southern Europe in the first four centuries A.D. With its promise that "the last shall be first," the new religion appealed especially to the powerless—to the lower classes, slaves, and women. Thousands of women took an active role as missionaries and martyrs. Whereas traditional Judaism separated women in the synagogues and forbade them to study the Torah, Christian women could attend services with men and, as deaconesses, were even allowed to baptize and teach female converts. Above all, they were acknowledged as the spiritual equals of men: "There is neither Jew nor Greek, there is neither bond nor free, there is neither male nor female: for ye are all one in Christ Jesus" (Gal. 3:28).

Early Christianity did not lose its patriarchal roots, however. The letters of the apostle Paul specify that the husband is the head of the wife as Christ is the head of the husband and of the Church (I Cor. 11:3; Eph. 5:22–23). Furthermore, Paul revealed an uneasiness about marriage and female sexuality that, together with the recommendation of chastity for all, contributed to the Church's growing distrust of women.

ISLAM

Muhammad (A.D. 570–632) founded Islam (Arabic for "submission to the will of Allah") when he received his call to be prophet at age forty. Within a century after his death, Moslems had conquered most of the southern and eastern Mediterranean coastline. Like Christianity, Islam was born of the deeply patriarchal traditions of the ancient Near East. And as with Christianity, its faith is spiritually egalitarian.

In the early days of Islam, women like Muhammad's wife A'isha took part in the holy war, becoming disciples for the new religion and going out to the battlefield to tend the wounded or even to fight. Early Islamic women prayed in mosques and some became religious scholars.

In his holy book, the Koran, Muhammad exhibited some concern for the rights of women. He limited the number of wives a man might take to four (and only if they were all treated equally), guaranteed female inheritance rights, and gave married women the right to control their property. Over the following centuries, however, a body of Islamic law grew up that in most instances was more restrictive for women than the Koran itself. The Koran, for instance, stipulates that adulterers of both sexes be whipped, but Islamic law says that only women adulterers should be stoned to death. Women were more secluded by their families, and veiling was enforced. No longer was it customary for women to take part in the public prayers in mosques. As in Christian cultures, a more systematic body of laws meant more restrictions for women.

THE MIDDLE AGES

The Roman Empire, which once spanned Europe and the Mediterranean world from Britain to Byzantium, finally expired in A.D. 476. In the tumultuous centuries that followed—what used to be called the Dark Ages (c. 476–1000)—Europe was buffeted by foreign invasions and internal power struggles. For a time, the newly established monasteries and convents became islands of relative peace. Double monasteries, where men and women were in retreat together, were especially popular. There, monks and nuns read classical and Christian books in the original Greek and Latin, copied manuscripts, and taught students. The abbesses who usually ran these monasteries were women of great learning and influence.

In the feudal world of the early Middle Ages, where family was paramount, noble women as well as men could exert great power. They were rulers, military leaders and judges, defenders of castles and managers of estates. As many scholars have pointed out, women were not to enjoy such varied opportunity again until the twentieth century.

Much of their influence withered during the High Middle Ages (1000–1300). When the church in Rome decreed that the clergy could no longer marry and that lay (nonchurch) people could no longer appoint bishops and other church officials, women lost some of the little influence they had in religious matters. Another factor was that in order to keep their property intact, the great families began to bequeath it to their elder sons and will it away from their daughters. Lastly, when the first great medieval universities were founded, they excluded women.

Medieval scholars and clergy alike debated woman's true nature. On the one hand, women were held to be weak, ignorant, and licentious. Just as Eve had tempted Adam to eat of the forbidden fruit in their Garden of Eden, so, clergymen argued, women ever since had been more susceptible than men to temptation and evil. Books on wicked women—especially wives—were extremely popular. Not only women but also some men realized the unfairness of these accounts. As the Wife of Bath justly notes in Geoffrey Chaucer's *The Canterbury Tales*, everything depends on one's point of view:

> By God, if women had written stories
> Like those the clergy keep in oratories,
> More had been written of man's wickedness
> Than all the sons of Adam could redress.

Unfortunately, few women had either the education or the authority to answer criticisms of their sex.

On the other hand, the popular cult of the Virgin Mary celebrated her as the second Eve: she had erased Eve's sin by saving the world through her son, Jesus Christ. Pious, chaste, and submissive, Mary became a role model for many women, especially mothers. Women were also praised by medieval poets, who sang songs of love at the aristocratic courts.

In any event, ordinary men and women probably had little time to listen to either celibate clergymen or romantic poets. For people of the middle and lower classes, marriage was a partnership in which husband and wife depended on each other to survive. Not only did women raise the children and keep the house, they often pursued an occupation as well. They might work in their husbands' businesses as drapers or brewers or weavers or even run their own shops, as unmarried women or widows were permitted to do. Some women, like the painter Judith Leyster, joined predominantly male craft guilds. Peasant women tilled the soil alongside their husbands. If they held their own land, they might have to work it themselves.

THE RENAISSANCE

The Renaissance saw the rebirth of classical learning throughout Europe and a new respect for individuality, education, and civic virtue. The philosophy of humanism emphasized the freedom and marvelous adaptability of man. Its most famous expression was Pico della Mirandola's "Oration on the Dignity of Man" (c. 1486): "O highest and most marvelous felicity of Man! To him it is granted to have whatever he chooses, to be whatever he wills."

Man, perhaps. But how about woman?

Unfortunately, the Renaissance inherited the misogyny of the classical world along with its learning. Liberal, educated humanists still regarded women as somehow incomplete. "When a woman is born, it

Raphael's Mother and Child Enthroned *portrays ideal motherly love. Alterpiece panel, c. 1505.*

is a defect or mistake of nature and contrary to what she would wish to do," authoritatively declared the Italian writer Baldassare Castiglione. As inferior beings, most women were barred from the new learning. Some of the most privileged women—the daughters of educated men and noble families—did have an education equal to a man's. But women who wanted to live a life of the mind, like the Mexican intellectual Sor Juana Ines de la Cruz, usually found themselves under attack.

Women did participate in the arts—they were musicians or singers or dancers in the new court ballet. They acted in the Italian commedia dell'arte (but not on the English stage, where all Shakespeare's characters were played by males). And they painted, specializing in portraiture or, like the Dutch artist Rachel Ruysch, in still lifes. Few, like Artemisia Gentileschi, attempted the large-scale figure paintings that could earn them the most money and prestige.

No matter what their achievements, women who stepped outside their accepted role were regarded as unusual, possibly freakish, certainly undesirable. "A woman's intellect is normally feebler . . . than [that] of a man," intoned the French archbishop François de Fenelon. "Women should not govern the state or make war or enter the sacred ministry." And that was that. Except, of course, that many of the most successful monarchs of the next three centuries were women: Isabella I (1451–1504) of Spain, Catherine de Médicis (1519–1589) of France, Elizabeth I (1533–1603) of England, and Catherine the Great (1729–1796) of Russia. They ruled their countries with a firm hand, despite the mutterings of those who thought they were upsetting the natural order.

THE REFORMATION

In 1517, Martin Luther successfully defied papal authority, and the Protestant Reformation—the attempt to reform the Christian Church—was under way. Among other things, Luther tried to rehabilitate marriage, by denouncing clerical celibacy and the assumption that it was better to be a virgin than be married. He praised "the pious, god-fearing wife," while being quick to remind his flock that the man was still head of both wife and family.

Although a few women did become preachers, all in all, Protestantism did not bring a substantial improvement in the status of women. The most

*Twenty-seven women and men stood trial during the Salem witchcraft
frenzy of 1692. Painting by T.H. Matteson, 1855.*

important lasting effect the Reformation had for most females might have
been the beginning of widespread reading instruction for girls as well as
boys so they could read the Bible in their own language. In the eighteenth
and nineteenth centuries, it would be women's new literacy that would
finally give them a voice of their own.

The years of the Reformation also coincided with the witchcraft persecutions. From about 1500 to 1700, more than a hundred thousand
people in Europe were denounced as witches and put to death, usually
at the stake. About eighty percent of them were women. The panic raged
throughout Protestant and Catholic countries alike, peaking in Germany,
Austria, Switzerland, and Poland. It spread across the Atlantic to Salem,
Massachusetts, where in 1692 nineteen people were hanged and one
pressed to death.

Why did the mania flourish during the years of the Protestant Reformation? By questioning age-old religious certainties, the Reformation ushered

in a new age of turmoil. Religious and civil wars deposed kings and destroyed churches. People looked for the one true faith, only to find evidence of heresy. They needed scapegoats and found them in the village wise-women, who could, it was thought, concoct a potion to heal the sick or ease the pain of pregnancy—or kill an infant or cripple a cow. Under torture, these women confessed to the most outrageous acts: copulating with the devil, flying on a broom or pitchfork, talking to toads. The women thus accused were usually old, single or widowed, and eccentric—and utterly powerless.

The witchcraft persecutions still stand today as the most heinous crime against women in European history.

CONQUEST AND REBELLION

In 1492, Christopher Columbus sailed into the West Indies and inaugurated the European invasion, conquest, and settlement of the Western hemisphere. In the resulting clash of cultures, whole peoples were destroyed, and those individuals or groups that survived were changed forever. How (and whether) indigenous women adapted or rebelled depended in large part on their status in their own society. Here are some examples:

Aztecs

When Hernán Cortés and the Spanish arrived in 1519, Mexico was ruled by the predatory Aztec empire. It demanded regular tribute and labor from outlying villages, including males and females to be sacrificed, and females were captured to be concubines or slaves. By the time the Indian woman La Malinche was given to Cortés, she had already been given in concubinage twice. Naturally, neither she nor other Indian women had any loyalty to the Aztecs. In the early days, some Indian women were able to take advantage of the conquest by marrying Spanish soldiers. Their offspring were recognized as inheritors of the conquistadors and became part of the elite of the new society. But the mestizos, the illegitimate offspring of Spanish and Indians, slipped further down the class ladder, followed by Indians and black slaves. Thus the class system of South America and Central America even today was determined in part by the choices women made—or were forced to make—in the first years of the conquest.

Incas

The Inca and Andean society the Spanish discovered when they invaded Peru in 1532 was hierarchical but was based on reciprocal relations between men and women. Property, land, and surnames were inherited through parallel male and female lines—from father to son and mother to daughter. There were female as well as male gods, and female and male religious organizations. Since the Spanish brought with them a system whereby all women were legal minors, they gave men legal rights over their wives' property and refused to recognize women's organizations.

Barred by the conquerors from their traditional economic, religious, and political roles, women often rebelled and practiced their own religions. The Spanish, believing that women were especially susceptible to the devil's influence, charged these women with witchcraft. One woman who was accused of being a sorceress cried out, "Now don't you see, the universe has turned inside out; for we are being persecuted." To escape, some women fled to high tablelands called *puna*. In Andean society today, the *puna* are still the women's territory, the place where they defied colonialism and the destruction of their culture.

North America

The hunting-gathering societies of North America, especially those along the eastern shore, were usually egalitarian. Algonquian women, for instance, were farmers, traders, sachems (tribal leaders), and healers. In Iroquois and Cherokee societies, women could appoint or depose tribal sachems. Most Indian women retained ownership of their own property when they married and kept their children if they divorced. Divorce was usually a relatively simple procedure for both men and women. In many communities, such as the Navajo, Indian woman enjoyed additional authority because their children inherited both their family identity and their property through their mother's rather than their father's line.

When the Europeans tried to Christianize or colonize these peoples, they found resistance. For instance, the Jesuit missionaries who tried to convert the Montagnais-Naaskapi on the St. Lawrence River realized that to make the Indians into proper, pious Christians, they would have to introduce the idea of male dominance. Only if males controlled women could they keep women from forming premarital sexual unions or leaving their husbands

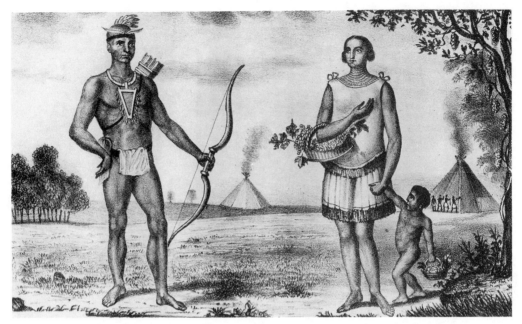

An eighteenth-century view of an idealized North American Indian family.
Europeans typically ignored women's roles as farmers, traders, and healers.

when they were dissatisfied. But the Indians resisted, and to this day, despite conversion, the Montagnais remain strongly cooperative and egalitarian.

By the end of the seventeenth and beginning of the eighteenth centuries, European nations ruled all of the Americas, and European influence was already spreading, tentaclelike, across the rest of the world. In Europe itself, a small band of radical thinkers articulated a new belief in human progress, individual liberty, and the responsibility of a government to its people. Their ideas would have revolutionary consequences in the next two hundred years as the poor, the oppressed, the disenfranchised—and women too— took up the banner of liberty and fought for their rights.

Ruth Ashby

Queen Hatshepsut

(Years of reign: c. 1486–1468 B.C.)

"Now my heart turns to and fro, in thinking what will the people say, they who shall see my monument in after years, and shall speak of what I have done."
—Inscription on obelisks at Karnak

In three thousand years of ancient Egyptian civilization, only five women ruled as pharaohs in their own right. Of these, the most successful was Hatshepsut, who reigned for more than twenty years.

The daughter of the pharaoh Thutmose I of Egypt, Hatshepsut married her half-brother, Thutmose II, in accordance with royal custom. When Thutmose II died, Queen Hatshepsut's nephew, Thutmose III, was next in line for the throne. Since he was too young to govern, Hatshepsut ruled in his place. When Thutmose III came of age, Hatshepsut refused to give up her power: she proclaimed herself pharaoh alongside her nephew.

To strengthen her title to the throne, Hatshepsut claimed to have the divine approval of Egypt's great god Amon-Re. She said she dreamed that Amon-Re was really her father and that when she was born, he proclaimed: "Welcome my sweet daughter, my favorite, the King of Upper and Lower Egypt—Hatshepsut. Thou art king, taking possession of the Two Lands."

Even though she was a woman, Hatshepsut wanted to make sure that she looked exactly the way a pharaoh should. Therefore, many statues of her show her wearing male clothing—a kilt, headdress, and false beard, the traditional symbols of royalty.

Throughout her joint reign with Thutmose

Queen Hatshepsut. Statue, c. 1480 B.C.

III, Hatshepsut wielded the real power. She increased trade with the Nubians, encouraged agriculture, developed mining in the Sinai Desert, and brought peace and prosperity to Egypt. In the ninth year of her reign, she sent cargo ships to the land of Punt, probably the present coast of Somalia. The ships returned laden with rare and precious merchandise: ebony, ivory, cinnamon, incense, myrrh, and baboons.

Energetic Queen Hatshepsut loved to build beautiful monuments. The temple she had dedicated to herself at Deir el-Bahri is still considered one of the masterpieces of Egyptian architecture. She also erected four pink granite obelisks in Amon-Re's temple at Karnak, with gold and silver peaks that glowed for miles in the sun. On the obelisks, she had stonecutters carve inscriptions describing events in her life.

When Hatshepsut died, Thutmose III, under his aunt's thumb for so long, took his revenge. He defaced and overturned Hatshepsut's monuments and tried to erase her name from the records. The inscriptions Queen Hatshepsut left on her pillars and temples have been recovered, however, and remain as permanent testimonies to a powerful pharaoh.

Lyn Reese

Sappho

(c. 610–c. 640 B.C.)

Although they are

Only breath, words
which I command
are immortal

Legends, myths, and controversy surround Sappho, the greatest woman poet of ancient Greece. Little is known of her life, except what her poems tell us. And all her poems, except one, exist merely in fragments.

Sappho was born toward the end of the seventh century B.C. on the island of Lesbos, in the Aegean Sea. Despite their low status in classical Athens a century later, women on Lesbos were well educated and highly valued. Sappho grew up in an aristocratic family, had three brothers, and was married. She probably also had a daughter: "I have a lovely child, whose form is like / Gold flowers, my heart's one pleasure, Cleis. . . . "

Anything else about her life is mere conjecture. After her death, legends grew up that she was the teacher of a cult of young girls and that she had committed suicide by throwing herself off a cliff for the love of a sailor named Phaon. Neither story has ever been substantiated. Nor has the report that her poetry was lost because Christian popes and emperors burned it for its erotic content. It is more likely that her work disappeared because of centuries of neglect during the early Middle Ages.

What remains are fewer than seven hundred lines out of an estimated five hundred poems. Sappho wrote lyric poetry, short, intense expressions of personal feeling, as well as more formal dirges and choral hymns. Together with the work of other lyric poets such as her contemporary Alcaeus, her poetry represented a break with the heroic epic tradition of Homer.

Despite her marriage, Sappho addressed her erotic poetry to women. This poetry became notorious later on—especially during the Victorian Age—for its homosexual content. Lesbos, the island of Sappho's birth, has given us the word *lesbianism.*

Poetry in Pieces

Although Sappho's poems are often missing whole lines, the beauty of her poetry remains.

It's no use

Mother dear, I
Can't finish my weaving
                                    You may
blame Aphrodite

soft as she is

she has almost
killed me with
love for that boy

Fresco from Herculaneum, believed to be Sappho, c. 100 B.C.

There were other women poets in ancient Greece, and many of them were considered to be among the best poets of the day. None of them, however, was as celebrated as Sappho, whom Plato called the "tenth muse." Twenty-five centuries later, enough of her poetry has survived to continue to inspire poets today.

Deborah Gore Orhn

Aspasia

(c. 420 B.C.)

"Your great glory is not to be inferior to what God has made you, and the greatest glory of a woman is to be least talked about by men, whether they are praising you or criticizing you."
—Funeral oration, c. 430 B.C.

The famous oration, spoken by Pericles during the Peloponnesian War, advised women not to draw attention to themselves. But Aspasia, who is believed to have written this oration for her longtime companion, didn't take her own advice. Instead, the most famous woman in classical Greece became known for her learning and outspokenness.

In fifth-century B.C. Athens, female citizens were kept mainly at home, busy with their household chores, while men were allowed to take part in politics and other public activities. Slave and foreign-born women were less confined, but they were neither as respected nor as protected as female citizens. One group of noncitizens were high-class courtesans called *hetaerae*. These women were educated and paid to accompany men to places where other women could not go—to lectures, parties, or the theater. Aspasia was one of the most talented of the hetaerae.

Born in Miletus in Asia Minor, where women's roles were somewhat less restricted, Aspasia learned to read, write, and play music while still a girl.

When she came to Athens, her scholarship and mastery of the art of conversation brought her to the attention of Athens's most popular political leader and orator, Pericles. Although she was a foreigner and therefore could not marry Pericles, Aspasia moved in with him in the mid-440s B.C. after he divorced his wife.

In time, Aspasia bore Pericles a son. Pericles's love for Aspasia was so great that he kissed her at the doorway of their home every day when he left and again when he returned, thus offending conservative Athenian citizens.

Because of her association with Pericles, Aspasia became quite powerful. She opened a school in which she lectured on philosophy and taught the proper way to debate. She even invited female citizens to attend along with their husbands. It is believed that her courses were attended by the most prominent men in Athens, including Pericles, the philosopher Socrates, and the playwright Euripides. Her house became a center of intellectual discussion.

Socrates especially admired Aspasia. Some say that he learned his famous method of teaching and learning, the so-called Socratic method, from her.

Aspasia used her position as a non-Greek to speak against laws that restricted women to their home. She told Athenians that marriage should be an encounter between two equals, each of whom should adapt to the needs of the other, and she championed the education of women.

Not surprisingly, many Athenians disliked Aspasia. Even if she had not been a hetaera, she was too controversial to be a respectable woman. Her ideas on the relations between the sexes were considered especially shocking. Aspasia was accused of "impiety" and "indecency." Some irate citizens claimed that Pericles listened too much to Aspasia's advice on foreign affairs and that she even wrote his speeches. Pericles, in tears, was forced to defend himself and Aspasia in a public court. His arguments cleared her of the charges, but his own reputation was tarnished because of his association with her.

After Pericles died, Aspasia married Lysicles, an ignorant sheep dealer who rose to some prominence in Athens, thanks to her influence. Aspasia continued to talk and teach and perhaps to write. But none of the original writings of the best-known woman of fifth-century Athens have survived.

Lyn Reese

Cleopatra

(69–30 B.C.)

Cleopatra, queen of Egypt, is one of the most glamorized figures in history. She has been portrayed as a playful seductress who used her powers of beauty and sexuality to get what she wanted. What is not often acknowledged is that she was also a very good ruler.

Cleopatra was the daughter of Ptolemy XII, king of Egypt. Her family was Macedonian Greek, descended from one of the generals of Alexander the Great, who had conquered Egypt in 332 B.C. It was the custom of the time for sisters and brothers within the ruling family to marry each other to strengthen the family line. It was not unusual, therefore, for eighteen-year-old Cleopatra to marry her ten-year-old brother when their father died. As Ptolemy XIII and Cleopatra VII, they ruled Egypt from 51–47 B.C. They came to power during a difficult period. There were food shortages during most of their reign because the Nile had stopped overflowing and crop production was down. In addition, the rivalry between Egypt and Rome was a constant threat to Egypt's power.

Cleopatra. Marble bust, c. 31 B.C.

Though it was considered unusual for a woman to have political ambitions, Cleopatra enjoyed her power and wanted more. She would allow no one to stand in her way. When the chief minister tried to oust her from power, she asked Julius Caesar, the Roman general and statesman, to intervene. He was so charmed by Cleopatra that he ordered her restored to the throne, and in the ensuing battles, the chief minister was killed.

When Ptolemy XIII was also killed in 47 B.C., Cleopatra married Ptolemy XIV, another brother, who became her coruler. She followed Caesar to

Rome—cruising up the Nile in a luxurious barge laden with food, wine, and jewels—and moved into his villa. Their idyllic love affair ended when Caesar was murdered on March 15, 44 B.C. (the Ides of March) by those who envied his power. When a civil war broke out after Caesar's death, Cleopatra left Rome and returned to Egypt.

Before Ptolemy XIV reached the legal ruling age of fourteen, Cleopatra—thirsty for more power—had him poisoned. Soon after, Marc Antony, a supporter of Caesar, visited Cleopatra. The two married in 36 B.C. and together had three children. Cleopatra convinced Antony to order the death of her sister in order to ensure her sovereignty, and she named her son as coruler.

The Romans, who always considered Cleopatra to be an outsider, did not like her ambition and set out to end her reign. Octavian (later Augustus), Caesar's heir, defeated the Egyptian fleet at Actium in 31 B.C., and Octavian was made emperor of Rome. Antony was told that his wife had died and promptly killed himself. Cleopatra, however, was actually alive and had been taken prisoner by Octavian. Rather than be "exhibited in his triumph" as he entered Rome, Cleopatra killed herself by the bite of a poisonous snake. In 30 B.C., Egypt became a Roman province.

Despite her hunger for power, Cleopatra was devoted to her country. She was a patron of the arts and sciences and was extremely popular with her Egyptian subjects. The Greek historian Plutarch wrote in his biography of Cleopatra, "Her form, coupled with the persuasiveness of her conversation, and her delightful style of behavior—all those produced a blend of magic."

Judy Gitenstein

The Trung Sisters

(d. A.D. 42)

Some historians believe that were it not for the courageous acts of the Trung sisters, who led what is considered to be the first national uprising against the Chinese, there might not be a Vietnamese nation today.

Trieu Au goes to battle on an elephant.
Vietnamese print.

From 111 B.C. to A.D. 221, the region we now call Vietnam was ruled by the Han Dynasty of China. The Trung sisters, Trung Trac and her younger, constant companion, Trung Nhi, were born to a powerful Vietnamese lord. Despite China's imposition of Confucian family values, which prescribed female obedience, Vietnam was remarkably liberal with regard to women's rights. Women benefited from hereditary rights through their mothers' lineage, and they could become political leaders, judges, and traders.

For more than one hundred years, the Vietnamese people did not actively oppose Chinese rule. Around A.D. 39, however, some of the Vietnamese lords and chiefs were beginning to feel threatened by the Chinese. At this time, Trung Trac was married to Thi Sach, a powerful Vietnamese lord. When a Chinese commander killed Thi Sach in order to frighten the restless Vietnamese back into submission, Trung Trac and Trung Nhi decided that it was time for rebellion.

The Trung sisters organized tribal lords and an army of men and women. They trained thirty-six women, including their mother, to be generals; in fact, many of the names of the uprising's leaders that are recorded in temples are those of women. Legend says that in order to encourage the people to support the rebellion, the Trung sisters committed various acts of bravery, such as slaying a ferocious people-eating tiger. They then used the tiger's skin as paper on which they inscribed a proclamation urging the people to follow their lead against the Chinese.

The Trung sisters led their eighty-thousand-strong army to attack and defeat Chinese forces at the governor's home and other key sites. The Vietnamese victory allowed them to lay claim to a province extending from Hue into southern China, and the Trung sisters were proclaimed co-queens.

They established their royal court in Me-linh, an ancient political center in the Hong River plain. The queens abolished the taxes imposed by the Chinese and tried to restore a simpler form of government that reflected traditional Vietnamese values.

The Trung sisters ruled until A.D. 42, when the Han emperor sent Chinese forces to recapture the region. The queens and their people fought

Trieu Au

The Trung sisters were not Vietnam's only warrior heroines. After the collapse of the Han dynasty, Trieu Au, a peasant skilled in the ways of war, marshaled forces against the Chinese occupation. In A.D. 248, dressed in golden armor and riding an elephant, she led her army into battle. After a courageous fight, her army was defeated, and Trieu Au committed suicide rather than surrender. Like the Trung sisters, she is honored in temples and remembered for her words of defiance: "My wish is to ride the tempest, tame the waves, kill the sharks. I want to drive the enemy away to save our people. I will not resign myself to the usual lot of women who bow their heads and become concubines."

valiantly against the Chinese. One close comrade of the sisters was a woman named Phung Thi Chinh, who was assigned to lead one of the armies. Legend says that she fulfilled her mission despite her pregnancy and delivered her baby on the front. Surrounded by soldiers, she hoisted her newborn infant on her back and, with a sword in each hand, carved her escape through the enemy!

The Vietnamese troops were badly defeated by the Chinese. Popular belief holds that the Trung sisters chose the traditional Vietnamese way of maintaining honor—they committed suicide by drowning. When Phung Thi Chinh learned of the sisters' act, she too took her own life. Throughout history, the Trung sisters have been idealized as heroines who led the first national revolt against the Chinese. Temples have been built in their honor, and they are celebrated each year with a national holiday.

Lyn Reese

Boudica

(C. A.D. 25–62)

"The gods will grant us the vengeance we deserve! Remember why we are fighting today—then you will win this battle, or die. That is what I, a woman, will do—let men live in slavery if they will!"
—Speech to her troops, A.D. 62

It must have been quite a vision: riding a chariot on the battlefield with fiery red hair down to her knees, a strong frame and voice to match, Boudica bellowed a cry to her invaders: "Better masterless poverty than prosperous slavery! The Romans are hares and foxes trying to rule over dogs and wolves."

Boudica rides into battle with her two daughters. Bronze statue by T. Thornycroft, cast in 1902.

Boudica, whose name means "victory" in the Celtic language, was the leader of the Iceni tribe who led her troops against the invading Romans and their Briton allies. The Romans invaded Britain for the first time under Julius Caesar in 55 B.C., departed soon thereafter, and came back again in A.D. 43, when the Briton tribes rebelled and were subdued.

One of the tribes that surrendered was the Iceni, who lived in East Anglia, today the region of Norfolk and Suffolk, England.

Boudica was born into a royal family and married Prasutagus, king of the Iceni tribe, with whom she had two daughters. At the time of the second Roman invasion, when King Prasutagus submitted to the Romans, he struck a deal that allowed him to remain in his kingdom as regent. King Prasutagus was very wealthy, and upon his death in A.D. 60, he named the

Roman emperor as his coheir, along with his two daughters and Boudica. This bequest would have given half his property to his family, half to the emperor, and succession as regent to Boudica.

However, the Romans refused to recognize Boudica's right to the kingdom and planned to conquer the Iceni. They began to plunder the kingdom. They confiscated the property of the Icenian nobles, and plotted to take the regency away from Boudica. The Romans wanted all of Britain—its land, people, and valuable gold and silver Celtic jewelry.

When Roman officials came to inventory Boudica's assets, she was flogged and her two daughters were raped. Infuriated, Boudica began recruiting an army and planned a revolt. She organized some 120,000 soldiers, half Iceni and half Trinovantes, from the tribe to the south. The army amassed light chariots, bronze and iron weapons, and fine iron swords.

Boudica made her attack while the Roman governor, Suetonius Paulinus, was fighting rebels in Wales. Her army sacked and burned the Roman-controlled cities of Camulodunum (Colchester), Londinium, and Verulanium (St. Albans). It is estimated that in Londinium alone, some seventy thousand Romans, Britons, and foreigners were massacred. When news of the rebellion and massive devastation reached the governor, he immediately sped back east.

As soon as Suetonius could gather his troops, the Roman force attacked Boudica's weary, overconfident army. The Britons were defeated—it is estimated that eighty thousand died—and Boudica fled to her kingdom. There she and her daughters probably ended their lives by taking poison. Death was more inviting than slavery to the Romans.

Boudica had brought the invincible Roman legions to near disaster, and neither the British nor the Romans forgot her. "Moreover, all this ruin was brought upon the Romans by a woman, a fact which in itself caused them the greatest shame," as the second-century historian Dio Cassius wrote. Romans went on to rule in Britain for another four hundred years, and Boudica passed into legend—as queen, as patriot, and as British warrior.

S. Suzan Jane

Hypatia

(c. 370–415)

Hypatia is the most famous of the women philosophers and mathematicians of the ancient world. Though we know little about her life, it is clear that she was a gifted scholar who made major contributions in her fields.

Hypatia was the daughter of Theon, the Alexandrian geometrician and philosopher who taught at the Museum, an institute of higher learning in Alexandria. An unusually liberated father, Theon educated his daughter in geometry, mathematics, and astronomy. She was quick to master any subject. The ecclesiastical historian Socrates, who was her contemporary, later wrote, "After being educated by her father, Hypatia came to surpass both contemporary and later intellectuals in mathematical knowledge."

Hypatia was also tutored by the most celebrated scholars of her day in the philosophies of Plato and Aristotle. Soon Theon was referring to her as "his philosopher-daughter," because students from all over the world came to Alexandria University to hear her lecture. Though Hypatia was a woman among men, her tremendous erudition and unswerving composure, as well as her reputation for chastity, earned her great respect.

Only the titles of Hypatia's scholarly works survive today. We know she wrote treatises on algebra, geometry, and the movement of the planets. She also questioned many of the received beliefs of her day, even in religion, and attempted to create a reawakening of reverence for the Greek gods and goddesses. Stressing the importance of the feminine aspects of culture, she argued that the worship of female goddesses enhanced the influence and power of women.

Through her teachings, Hypatia attracted people from many backgrounds and gradually became a political force that threatened the power of the emerging Christian Church. Her views and position earned her a powerful enemy in Cyril, the bishop of Alexandria.

When Hypatia was asked to be an advisor to the government, Bishop Cyril grew more irate. Knowing he could not easily denounce her in public, he organized a group of fanatics to murder her on the way to her weekly lecture at the university. Hypatia was pulled from her chariot, dragged into the cathedral of Alexandria, and brutally murdered. Then her body was burned. Books she had written were pulled from libraries and burned as well. Cyril was determined to eradicate every trace of Hypatia's critical mind.

In the centuries after her death, Hypatia was remembered primarily as a pagan martyr. Yet a few of the letters her students wrote to her survive, alluding to some of her scholarly accomplishments. One of them, for instance, suggests that she was the scientist who invented instruments to measure the specific gravity of liquids. Today, though we can only speculate about the exact nature of her accomplishments, we recall Hypatia as the first outstanding woman scholar in history.

S. Suzan Jane

Empress Theodora

(c. 497–548)

"For a king, death is better than dethronement and exile."
—c. 532

A peasant girl orphaned at the age of four, Theodora seemed destined to a life both brief and full of drudgery. Yet she became one of the greatest rulers of the age.

Theodora was born in Constantinople, then part of the Byzantine Empire, as the Roman Empire was called in the eastern Mediterranean. Already beautiful by the age of fifteen, she began working as a dancer and actress. Such work was considered disreputable, almost as bad as prostitution, but there were few other ways for women to earn a living. Unhappy with the social stigma associated with entertaining, Theodora left the theater for the more acceptable profession of spinning wool.

Soon after, Theodora caught the attention of the emperor's nephew Justinian. The two fell in love, and their relationship changed her life forever. Under Constantinopolitan law, marriage across classes was strictly prohibited;

Empress Theodora and her court. Mosaic, 547.

but Justinian, determined to marry his love, used his position in the royal family to have the law changed.

In the year 527, Theodora and Justinian were crowned empress and emperor of the Byzantine Empire. A highly intelligent woman, Theodora became a powerful force in the kingdom, and she dedicated herself to improving women's lives. Having come from the peasantry herself, she understood the plight of lower-class women, whose lives offered nothing but poverty and hard work.

Theodora created many important laws to protect women's rights. They included the death sentence for rape; protection of women in divorce cases; the right of women to inherit property and keep their dowry; protection from abusive husbands; the right to teach Christianity; and prohibitions against the practice of selling children into slavery to pay off parental debts. Theodora also purchased the freedom of many girls who had been sold into prostitution or slavery. Women's rights and their position in society had never been so protected or respected.

Theodora's influence was not limited to her own kingdom. Foreign emperors regularly sought her advice, and diplomats negotiated foreign policies with her. In 532, Theodora's courage and wisdom saved the dynasty. When two factions plotted a coup against Justinian and riots broke out, Theodora persuaded her husband to stay in Constantinople rather than flee the city. Heeding Theodora's counsel, Justinian stood his ground and sent his loyal troops into battle. The coup was thwarted and Justinian's sovereignty remained intact.

In 548, Empress Theodora died of cancer, leaving Justinian to rule for another two decades. Although no notable legislation was passed during the remainder of his life, Theodora and Justinian's joint rule left an enormous legacy of contributions to women's rights.

S. Suzan Jane

Wu Chao

(625–705)

Wu Chao, the first woman to rule as emperor in Chinese history, never let anyone stand between her and the power she sought. Forced into the life of a concubine, she used every means possible to rise to power, eventually ruling over all China during the T'ang dynasty.

The daughter of a Chinese general, Wu Chao was born in 625. When she was thirteen, her beauty was noticed by the emperor, who requested that she enter the palace as a concubine. Wu Chao served Emperor T'ai Tsung until his death in 649. Following Chinese tradition, she then retired to a Buddhist convent, though it was a stay that did not last for long.

The heir to the throne was Kao Tsung, who immediately brought Wu Chao back to the palace as his concubine. Within six years, she bore the emperor his first son, and three more sons and a daughter followed. Wu Chao was dissatisfied with her status as a concubine, however, and she systematically plotted her rise in the imperial household.

Setting out to destroy the empress, Wu Chao accused her of sorcery and of plotting to kill the emperor. Wu Chao strangled her own daughter in her cradle and then accused the empress, who was childless, of murdering the baby, since she was the last one seen playing with the infant. This was enough to cause the emperor to dismiss the empress, and he replaced her with Wu Chao.

Enchanted with Wu Chao and plagued by illness, Kao Tsung eventually allowed her to take over his entire administration. She gained the support of a group of Buddhist monks who identified her as a prophet and as the incarnation of Buddha. This proclamation was a great boost to Wu Chao's popularity with the people and to her ability to hold power. Despite religious support, however, Wu Chao was ruthlessly ambitious and a harsh ruler. She readily disposed of any concubines, statesmen, or even family members who posed a threat to her reign. She entrusted government affairs to the best men she could find, and they in turn were extremely loyal to her.

Whatever her methods, Wu Chao did achieve significant diplomatic success during her rule. China defeated Korea in war, and through negotiations, she convinced Korea to become an ally of China. She instituted a reform program that reduced taxes, decreased military operations, and increased agricultural production. She replaced the government's aristocratic military control with a more scholarly meritocratic bureaucracy, called for the construction of magnificent buildings in the capital, and promoted Chinese culture and arts.

When Kao Tsung died in 683, Wu Chao exiled her son Chung and his wife and governed China with her son Jui. Since Jui was a weak and incompetent ruler, his mother effectively retained power. Wu Chao retired in 690 and recalled Chung to become the rightful emperor. Ten months later, she died at the age of eighty.

For more than fifty years, Wu Chao maintained power in a country where traditionally women had very low status. The question remains of what was more significant about her reign: her contributions to the T'ang dynasty or her ruthless political tactics. Despite her personal ambition and methods of maintaining power, her contributions to the T'ang dynasty were considerable.

S. Suzan Jane

Murasaki Shikibu

(c. 978–1030)

"Pretty and coy, shrinking from sight, unsociable, fond of old tales, conceited, so wrapped up in poetry that other people hardly exist, spitefully looking down on the whole world—such is the unpleasant opinion that people have of me. Yet when they come to know me they say that I am strangely gentle."
—Murasaki's diary, c. 1007–1010

A lady of the Japanese imperial court, Murasaki Shikibu is the author of *The Tale of Genji*, widely regarded as the first novel ever written. Though we know little about Murasaki's life, we can tell from the diary she kept for a short two years that her gift was recognized and rewarded even in her own time.

Between 950 and 1050 in Heian Japan, the most important writers were women, and much of what we know today about upper-class life in those far-off times comes from detailed descriptions found in women's diaries, novels, and poems. Murasaki Shikibu was one of the stars of this remarkable world, where well-to-do women were allowed to pursue their artistic and literary interests more freely than in later centuries.

Murasaki Shikibu was born the daughter of a provincial governor of good family. Apparently, her literary abilities were evident early in her life. When he discovered her interest in literature, her father, also a scholar, lamented that she had not been born a boy. He did allow her to study with her brother, however, and she quickly surpassed even her father in knowledge and literary skills.

Murasaki Shikibu married a distant relative when she was in her early twenties. Her only daughter, who later became a well-known author in her own right, was born in 999. After the death of her husband in 1001, Shikibu was brought to court by the imperial family, who had heard of her brilliant mind and writing talent.

In Heian times, poetic talent was particularly highly regarded. Chinese

A Poetry Competition

Members of the imperial court were often called upon to compose a poem spontaneously, as this excerpt from Murasaki Shikibu's diary demonstrates:

...I can see the garden from my room beside the entrance to the gallery. . . . The Lord Prime Minister is walking there. . . . He peeps in over my screen! His noble appearance embarrasses us, and I am ashamed of my morning [not yet painted and powdered] face. He says, "Your poem on this! If you delay so much the fun is gone!" . . . and I seize the chance to run away to the writing-box, hiding my face—

> Flower-maiden in bloom—
> Even more beautiful for the bright dew,
> Which is partial, and never favors me.

"So prompt!" said he, smiling, and orders a writing-box to be brought [for himself].
His answer:

> The silver dew is never partial,
> From her heart
> The flower-maiden's beauty.

was the language of serious learning, but women wrote in their native Japanese because they were forbidden to use the higher-status language of scholarship. The narratives, poems, and romances that women like Murasaki Shikibu recorded in everyday language were widely circulated and very popular with the Japanese people.

Clearly, this was a fine time to be a poet at the imperial court. A withdrawn, thoughtful person, Shikibu was not, however, always fond of the frivolities of court life. In the diary she kept for two years, for instance, she described a court-sponsored drawing competition as a "moment in the history of our country when the whole energy of the nation seemed to be concentrated upon the search for the prettiest method of mounting paper scrolls!"

Murasaki Shikibu's best-known work, *The Tale of Genji*, is a very long prose romance—running to fifty-four chapters—about complications in the life of a prince called Genji. Like many court ladies, Shikibu was a keen observer of the social arts and attitudes of the upper class. *The Tale of Genji* is unusual, however, because it provides a deeper look into the motivations and inner lives of its characters. Although the work has a more rambling structure than novels today, it has been called the world's first novel because of the realism of its characters and situations.

Little is known about Murasaki Shikibu's later life. She may have retired from court to seek seclusion in a convent at about the age of fifty.

Lyn Reese

Sultana Razia

(Years of reign: 1236–1240)

Sultana Razia was the only woman ever to sit on the throne of Delhi, India. Her people were Moslems of Turkish descent who first invaded northern India in the eleventh century. Like other Moslem princesses, she was trained to lead armies and administer kingdoms if necessary.

When Razia was young, her father, the sultan of the city and lands around Delhi, noted that Razia had a remarkable talent for politics. He thus chose her, rather than one of his sons, to be his successor. To those who objected, he said: "My sons are devoted to the pleasure of youth, and not one of them is qualified to be a king. After my death you will find that there is no one more competent to guide the state than my daughter."

After the sultan's death, the emirs, or nobles, opposed letting Razia become sultan since she was a woman and had brothers who could rule. In order to maintain the peace, Razia gave up the throne, asking all to swear allegiance to her stepbrother Ruknuddin. As her father had predicted, Ruknuddin led a life of pleasure, neglecting the affairs of state.

Realizing that Ruknuddin was an ineffective leader, some emirs had second thoughts about letting Razia rule. Ruknuddin's mother attempted to kill Razia but failed. Dressed in red robes, Razia called everyone to a mass meeting and told them of the plot. Disgusted with Ruknuddin's rule, the people demanded that Razia become their sultan. In 1236, she ascended the throne.

Razia turned out to be a very capable ruler. Using her absolute authority, she succeeded in establishing peace and order, decreeing that trade be encouraged, roads built, trees planted, and wells dug. She also supported poets, painters, and musicians and had schools and libraries constructed. Her interest in the arts was not surprising since Razia was an educated woman who wrote poetry and could recite the Koran, the holy book of Islam.

Razia frequently appeared in public without a veil, wearing the tunic and headdress of a man. She held open meetings to conduct the affairs of state. These liberal actions bothered some of the emirs. Razia also made enemies when she tried to abolish a tax imposed on the Hindus, people of a different faith who had been conquered by the Muslims. Some officials saw the tax as a way to remind the Hindus that they were subjects, and Razia was opposed to this discrimination.

The emirs were also troubled by the special favors the sultana gave to Jamal Uddin Yaqut, a man who was not of Turkish blood. She made Jamal master of horses, a high position that by tradition had been enjoyed only by nobles of Turkish descent. Jamal became Razia's constant advisor and companion and may have been her lover.

Jealous of Razia's attention toward Jamal, one of the governors, Altunia, rebelled. With Jamal by her side, Razia led her troops on a long march against Altunia. Weakened by the march and outnumbered by the rebel armies, Razia's forces were defeated. Jamal was killed, and Razia was taken prisoner. In Delhi, the emirs seized the opportunity of her imprisonment to have one of her half brothers proclaimed sultan.

In order to save her kingdom, Razia married her captor, Altunia, and in 1240 rode forth with him to take back the throne of Delhi. Halfway to Delhi, they were defeated by the much stronger forces of the new sultan. Both Razia and Altunia died in the battle, and a tomb for Razia was built on the banks of a river near Delhi. Soon the tomb became a place where people gathered to remember Delhi's only female ruler and ask for her blessing.

Lyn Reese

Christine de Pizan

(c. 1365–c. 1430)

"There is not the slightest doubt that women belong to the people of God and the human race as much as men and are not another species or dissimilar race, for which they should be excluded from moral teachings."
—The Book of the City of Ladies, 1405

Today, it seems odd that anyone would have to argue woman's humanity. Yet in Europe during the Middle Ages, it was generally agreed that women were inferior to men, if not altogether evil. The one woman who was learned and brave enough to champion her sex with her pen was France's first woman of letters—Christine de Pizan.

Born in Venice, Christine was the daughter of Tommaso de Pizan, a doctor and astrologer, and his wife. When Christine was four, the family moved to Paris, where her father became astrologer at the court of Charles V. Christine grew up in a scholarly environment, and though she received no formal education, her father tried to encourage her intellectual interests.

As was customary, Christine was married by the time she was fifteen to a young notary named Etienne de Castel. Her marriage was very happy, but after just ten years of marriage, Etienne died of the plague. The twenty-five-year-old widow was left alone with three children (one died soon thereafter), a mother, and a niece to support. She then devised a plan of self-education, reading history, poetry, and the sciences. She wanted to write and needed a broad base of knowledge to be taken seriously.

Pizan made her literary debut in poetry, which was much admired by the French court. Eventually, she became the most successful female professional writer of the Middle Ages. Her works were many and varied: love poems, allegories, prose histories, and instructive pieces. Her *Book of Three Virtues* (1405), on the proper roles for women of different classes, had been published in three editions by 1563. Christine earned the patronage of kings and princes and was able to place her children in advantageous positions.

Christine de Pizan leads the way to the City of Ladies. From The Book of the City of Ladies, *1405.*

Above all, Pizan stood up for women. In her *Book of the City of Ladies*, she describes sitting in her library and reading one misogynist book after another. How could so many learned men be wrong about women? she wonders. Then "Reason, Rectitude, and Justice" appear before her and urge her to defend women. After relating the stories of exemplary women throughout history, Pizan argues against women's inferiority. Women are as virtuous as men, she concludes, and if they were educated, they would be as learned as well.

After the French were defeated at Agincourt in 1415, Pizan retired to a convent at Poissy. Her last known poem celebrated her contemporary, the brave and tragic military leader Joan of Arc:

> Ah, what honor to the feminine sex!
> Which God so loved that he showed
> A way to this great people
> By which the Kingdom, once lost,
> Was recovered by a woman,
> A thing that men could not do.
>
> —"The Tale of Joan of Arc," 1429

Ruth Ashby

Joan of Arc

(1412–1431)

"Even little children repeat that oftentimes people are hanged for having told the truth."
—Defense at her tribunal, 1431

When Joan of Arc was thirteen years old, she claimed she heard the voice of God in the garden of her father's home. The voice told her that she had been chosen to help Him and to do great, even superhuman things. Three years later, she said she heard Saint Michael, Saint Catherine, and Saint Margaret tell her to help the dauphin, the eldest son of the French king. The dauphin was being kept from the throne as a result of France's conflict with England, now known as the Hundred Years War. Joan decided to go to the dauphin, first cutting her hair short and donning men's clothing for the journey since it was neither safe nor proper for young women to travel alone. When she arrived, she was able to identify the dauphin immediately, even though he wore peasant's clothing to disguise himself from his enemies.

Joan was so sincere and sure of her purpose that, believing she was a young man, the dauphin gave her his troops to command. In May 1429, Joan pushed the English out of the city of Orléans, and in June

Joan of Arc romanticized, wearing long hair and a skirt. French, nineteenth century.

she defeated the English at Patay. Joan received much acclaim, and the dauphin was crowned King Charles VII at the city of Reims.

A few months later, Joan tried to protect Paris against the English, but this time she did not succeed. In the spring of 1430, she was captured and sold to the English by Philip of Burgundy. Enclosed in an iron cage so small that she could not stand, and with her neck, hands, and feet bound with chains, she was taken to be tried at the church court at Rouen, France.

Imprisoned in the castle of Rouen, Joan was brought before the court to answer to twelve charges. They included those of witchcraft and heresy, that is, denying the authority of the Catholic Church. She was also charged with the crime of wearing men's clothing, which she continued to do even though she no longer disguised the fact that she was a woman. She felt that wearing pants rather than a skirt protected her from the sexual advances of the male guards who slept in her cell.

Joan strongly denied the charge of heresy. Her guidance came directly from God, she claimed, the very highest authority of the Catholic Church. The court disagreed, saying that the voices she had heard were not those of God but those of the devil. With this, they condemned Joan to death.

Joan of Arc, the Maid of Orléans, was burned at the stake on May 30, 1431. She was nineteen years old. Charles VII, the king Joan had risked her life to see crowned, had done nothing to defend her during her imprisonment and trial. Not until twenty years later did Charles order an inquiry. In 1456, the old verdict was annulled and Joan's name was cleared.

Joan of Arc has inspired many stories, legends, and works of art through the centuries, most notably George Bernard Shaw's 1923 play, *Saint Joan.* It was published three years after Joan was canonized by Pope Benedict XV. Today, this French martyr and military heroine has come to symbolize French nationalism. Her feast day of May 30 is a national holiday, a day to remember Joan's loyalty, bravery, and ultimate sacrifice.

Judy Gitenstein

Queen Isabella I

(1451–1504)

"One king, one law, one faith."
—Motto of Queen Isabella I

C alled the Catholic Queen and the Law and Order Queen, Isabella of Castile entered into a marriage alliance that formed the largest and most powerful empire in Europe. Her devotion to religion and politics won her great popularity with the Spanish people, who viewed her as a symbol of their country's unity and purpose.

Isabella was the only daughter of Juan II, ruler of the kingdoms of Castile and León in Spain. After her father died, she was raised by her mother while her half brother Enrique IV took over as king of Castile. Isabella was tutored by monks, learning poetry, music, philosophy, sewing, and horseback riding.

When Isabella was old enough to marry, she and Enrique disagreed sharply about her future husband, whom Enrique had already chosen for her. Determined to make her own decision, Isabella argued for her marriage to her second cousin, Ferdinand. The couple met secretly and realized that their marriage would hold great political potential. She would inherit Castile, while he was in line to inherit Aragon. Together, they could consolidate their kingdoms and their power.

Despite Enrique's resistance, Isabella and Ferdinand married in 1469. In 1479, after Enrique died, Isabella became queen of Castile. She and Ferdinand ruled Castile and Aragon separately, but jointly they held Spain, the largest kingdom in Europe.

An ambitious ruler, Isabella promoted education, religion, and the arts. Under Enrique's rule, nobles who attained individual power had considered themselves "kings" of their own estates. Isabella ended this feudal anarchy and restored royal authority, prohibiting the building of new castles, burning older ones, and rescinding individual noblemen's privileges.

Isabella was a very devout Catholic, and sensing religious diversity around her, she decided that it was necessary to impose religious orthodoxy. She helped support the Spanish Inquisition, which relentlessly persecuted Christian heretics, especially converted Jews, who held the greatest economic and cultural influence in the land. The inquisition began in 1483 and led to the expulsion of Jews from Castile in 1492. During these years of terror, Jewish funds were seized, heretics were burned at the stake, and thousands died. Isabella's troops also attacked Granada, where the Moors too were considered a threat to Christianity. Despite her pregnancy, Isabella supervised the battles. When victory was declared in 1492, Isabella claimed, "I have caused great calamities and depopulated towns, lands, provinces, and kingdoms, but I have acted thus from love of Christ and the Holy Mother."

Following the conquest of Granada, Isabella agreed to finance Christopher Columbus's quest to find a passage to the Far East and India. Eager to gain wealth for Spain and to spread Christianity, Isabella was unaware of the great event about to unfold: the discovery of the New World.

In a country that revered the Virgin Mary, the dignified and gracious Isabella was seen as possessing an admirable combination of piety and femininity. She bore five children and was devoted to her country's progress. In 1494, the pope rewarded Isabella's and Ferdinand's religious zeal with the title *Los Reyes Catolicos* (the Catholic Monarchs), a role they took very seriously. The most influential queen in Spanish history, Isabella I died on November 26, 1504.

S. Suzan Jane

La Malinche

(c. 1500–c. 1527)

La Malinche, also known as Marina and Doña Marina, was a woman of historical contradictions. An invaluable aide to Hernán Cortés in his conquest of Mexico and his enslavement of the Aztecs, she is also regarded as the "Mexican Eve," the mother of the mestizo people.

La Malinche was born a princess in the village of Viluta, Mexico, in the early 1500s. Her wealth and social status enabled her to become educated— a privilege not available to daughters of less powerful parents. But during

Xaltelolco.

La Malinche translates while Cortés receives Aztec emissaries. Codex, sixteenth century.

a period of war, she was either sold or captured, then resold by the Mayans as a slave to the Aztecs. Her privileged life ended, replaced by one of hardship and drudgery.

However, La Malinche's beauty, intelligence, and ability to speak many languages set her apart from other slaves and proved to be valuable assets when Hernán Cortés led the Spanish expedition to Mexico. When Cortés landed in 1519, he had two missions: to conquer the land and seize its riches for Spain, and to convert the Indians to Christianity. La Malinche was part of the tribute sent to Cortés in the vain hope of stopping his march of conquest. Cortés recognized La Malinche's verbal and intellectual abilities, and he promised her freedom if she became his ally and helped him establish good relationships with the Indian peoples of Mexico.

As a slave, La Malinche had little choice but to agree. She rode with Cortés, accompanying him on all his expeditions. Initially, Cortés doubted La Malinche's loyalty, but his worries subsided when La Malinche told him about the Aztec leader Montezuma's plot to ambush Cortés and his troops. Cortés called for an immediate attack on the Aztecs living among the Spanish, and the Aztecs lost most of their best warriors.

In the following years, La Malinche continued to support Cortés. Through her persuasion, she helped Cortés assemble an army of Mexicans to fight against the Aztecs. Eventually, she was even able to convince Montezuma himself essentially to become a prisoner of the Spaniards, giving them free reign in the Aztec capital, Tenochtitlán. But in a chaotic skirmish, Montezuma died, stoned by his own people, and the Aztecs launched an all-out attack against the Spaniards.

Though much of the Spanish army was lost in their night flight from the city, La Malinche and Cortés escaped unharmed. Cortés regrouped his soldiers and launched a massive counterattack. On August 13, 1521, Tenochtitlán fell, and with it the Aztec empire.

The Spanish immediately began rebuilding the city that La Malinche and Cortés had won. In 1522, La Malinche bore Cortés's son, beginning the ethnic group of people called the mestizos. Of mixed Spanish and Indian blood, this group populates most of Mexico today. Cortés gave La Malinche enough land and gold to secure her comfort and asked that she continue to serve as his interpreter in a crusade to Honduras. In 1527 (or early 1528), shortly after returning from Honduras, La Malinche died.

Without doubt, the success that Cortés attained in Mexico can be directly attributed to La Malinche's service to him. The Aztecs whom La Malinche betrayed were not her own people, yet all the Indians of Mexico were eventually conquered by the invaders she helped support. La Malinche witnessed the end of an old civilization and the rise of a new and became symbolic mother to the new ethnic group that prevails in Mexico to this day.

S. Suzan Jane

Catherine de Médicis

(1519–1589)

"I hope to show that women have a more sincere determination to preserve the country than those who have plunged it into the miserable condition to which it has been brought."
—Letter to Ambassador of Spain, 1570

First as the wife of King Henry II of France and then as queen regent for her sons, Catherine de Médicis wielded enormous political power in a treacherous and turbulent age.

Catherine was born into the powerful Medici family in Florence, Italy. Her mother, Madeleine de la Tour d'Auvergne, was a Bourbon princess who died fifteen days after Catherine's birth. Her father, Lorenzo de' Medici, duke of Urbino, died five days later. Catherine went to Rome to live with her granduncle, Pope Leo X. When she was just five years old, the search for a suitable husband began. Nine years later, she married the duke of Orléans, who was to become Henry II, king of France.

The young Catherine threw herself into the role of political wife. She learned Greek, mathematics, astronomy, hunting, and dancing, and tried to live up to the motto on her marriage crest: I BRING LIGHT AND SERENITY. Her accomplishments were admired by all but her husband, however. By the time he was crowned king in 1547, he had taken a mistress, and Catherine was forced onto the sidelines of court life. Henry's reign, and Catherine's life in his shadow, lasted until 1559, when Henry was killed in a jousting match.

Catherine's three sons, Francis II, Charles IX, and Henry III, would succeed their father on the throne of France. Catherine maintained a strong influence over her children, overseeing their education and marriage alliances. After Francis died in 1560 and Charles was crowned king at the age of ten, Catherine, as queen regent, held the real power. Even when Charles reached legal ruling age, he remained dominated by Catherine.

Catherine ruled during a time when Europe was plagued by religious and political turmoil, and monarchs who did not take sides were viewed as weak rulers. Many opposed her Edict of Toleration, scorning her for her apparent neutrality in the war between the Protestants (the Huguenots) and the Catholics. In fact, Catherine plotted with other Catholic leaders to rid France of the Huguenots. In 1572, she convinced Charles to order the Massacre of Saint Bartholomew's Day, in which seventy thousand Huguenots were killed throughout France.

Charles IX died in 1574, and finally Catherine could name her favorite son, Henry, to be crowned king. This time, Catherine did not try to overrule her son. The two had a close relationship, and Catherine did Henry's bidding, including making long diplomatic trips on his behalf.

Henry III died of a stab wound in 1589, and Catherine passed away shortly thereafter. Despite her dominating rule and efforts at religious "cleansing," Catherine left a legacy of artistic patronage. During her life, she had ordered the construction of a new wing of the Louvre and planned the Tuileries Palace, whose gardens remain today among the most beautiful spots in Paris.

Judy Gitenstein

Queen Elizabeth I

(1533–1603)

*"I am come amongst you . . . being resolved . . . to lay down for my
God, and for my kingdom, and for my people, my honour and
my blood, even in the dust. I know I have the body of a weak
and feeble woman, but I have the heart and stomach of a king,
and of a king of England, too."*
—Address to her troops at Tilbury, August 9, 1588

The Spanish Armada was on its way. English troops stood massed on the shore, waiting for the expected invasion. Wearing a silver breastplate and carrying a truncheon, Queen Elizabeth rode into camp to encourage her men. The speech she gave that day stirred the soldiers to new heights of patriotic fervor. It also dramatized the great paradox of her forty-five-year reign: in a century of bitter antifeminism, the greatest European "king" was a woman.

Elizabeth Tudor was born on September 7, 1533, the daughter of King Henry VIII and his second wife, Anne Boleyn. When Anne subsequently failed to give Henry a son, Henry had her beheaded. Elizabeth was not quite three.

The princess grew up away from court in her own household. She received an excellent classical education of the sort ordinarily reserved for boys. Besides learning history, rhetoric, and philosophy, she became fluent in Greek, Latin, French, and Italian. Her tutor, Roger Ascham, wrote of her when she

*Queen Elizabeth. Portrait by an anonymous
painter, sixteenth century.*

was sixteen, "Her mind has no womanly weakness, her perseverance is equal to that of a man, and her memory long keeps what it quickly picks up."

Elizabeth needed all her good judgment to navigate the shoals of religious politics. When her sickly brother, King Edward VI, died in 1553, her older sister, Mary, became queen. Mary was a zealous Catholic, eager to return Protestant England to the true religion. As a Protestant, Elizabeth was suspected of plotting against her sister. Yet she prudently kept up the appearance of complete loyalty. When Queen Mary died in 1558, England joyously welcomed a new Protestant monarch.

Elizabeth was twenty-five when she ascended the throne. It was assumed the young queen would marry. She needed an heir; otherwise the next in succession was Mary Queen of Scots, a Catholic with strong ties to the French throne. For the next twenty years, the princes of Europe vied for Elizabeth's hand. Yet the negotiations always fell through. Most likely, Elizabeth did not want to share her power. Also, any marriage might have brought more political entanglements than advantages.

The Royal Treatment

In the sixteenth century, before haute couture or women's magazines, members of the nobility set the style in fashion. One of the most influential trendsetters was Queen Elizabeth. In fact, she set the look of the era, popularizing the use of white makeup. Unfortunately, this facial paste contained white lead, a dangerous substance that proved lethal for some users.

The Virgin Queen also helped promote the farthingale and the bum-roll. The farthingale was a petticoat made up of underwire hoops. The bum-roll was a rounded bustle placed just below the waist. When worn together, they made women look shapely around the hips and ultranarrow at the waist. Encased in these heavy undergarments, a fully dressed woman could measure as wide as four feet at the hips—making grand entrances through doorways extremely difficult.

If Elizabeth could have followed her heart, she would probably have married Robert Dudley, later earl of Leicester, with whom she was in love. But Dudley had many enemies and an uncertain reputation. So Elizabeth remained single. Throughout her reign, she used the promise of alliance through marriage as a lure to keep on good relations with other countries. At home, the cult of the Virgin Queen married to her kingdom gradually grew up, and Elizabeth encouraged it.

Elizabeth was an extremely popular queen and used her intelligence and charm to woo court and commoner alike. Every summer, she set off on a royal "progress" through the countryside so her devoted subjects could catch a glimpse of her.

Elizabeth's great goals were to keep her country solvent and out of war. She was notoriously tightfisted, but then, her monarchy was one of the poorest in Europe, and she was dependant on a reluctant Parliament to raise taxes. Her thrift kept England from going bankrupt.

Just as important, in an era of great religious strife and persecution on the Continent, Elizabeth managed to steer England on a middle course throughout much of her reign. Although the country was officially Protestant, she tolerated Catholics and Puritan extremists as long as they remained absolutely loyal to the crown.

England was finally forced into war in 1588, when Spain's King Philip II launched the Invincible Armada to attack England. The fleet of 130 ships was routed by English fire ships in the English Channel. England was triumphant.

The defeat of the Armada was the high point of Elizabeth's reign. Her last decade had its share of troubles too. In the 1590s, the country went through a period of bad harvests and depression, and Elizabeth's popularity suffered accordingly. She also had to deal with Mary Queen of Scots. After being forced to abdicate the Scottish throne in 1568, Mary fled south and was put under house arrest in England. Elizabeth finally put Mary to death in 1587 when she discovered Mary had plotted against her life.

Elizabeth's final challenge was the rebellion of her favorite courtier, the earl of Essex. When he tried to raise an army against his queen in 1601, Elizabeth was forced to execute him for treason.

For most of her life, Elizabeth was extremely healthy. As she grew older, she hid her advancing years behind a thick face mask of white paste and powder. But age was not to be denied. Some months before her death, Elizabeth's coronation ring had to be sawed off her finger because it was too tight. On March 24, 1603, Elizabeth proclaimed King James VI of Scotland as her successor and died. The Elizabethan Age was over.

Ruth Ashby

Mary Queen of Scots

(1542–1587)

"In my end is my beginning."
—Motto of Mary Queen of Scots

From the moment she was born, Mary Queen of Scots caused controversy. The only daughter of Mary of Guise and James V of Scotland, she succeeded to the Scottish throne when she was only a few days old and was crowned queen at nine months. As the granddaughter of the sister of King Henry VIII of England, Mary was also the next heir to the English throne after the king's own children.

King Henry VIII wanted to marry the girl to his son, Edward, in hopes of someday joining the two kingdoms together. Mary's mother, who was French and Catholic, favored an alliance with France. Partly as a result of Henry's "rough wooing"—English military incursions into Scotland—the proposed alliance with England failed and Mary was engaged to Francis, the heir to the French throne. At age five, she sailed to France.

Mary spent thirteen years at the French court, the happiest years of her life. She was raised as befitted a future queen of France. A bright, happy girl, Mary grew tall (five feet eleven inches) and slim. Many considered her a beauty. Though not as intellectually gifted as her cousin Elizabeth of England, she read Latin, Spanish, and Italian and was especially fond of French poetry.

Unfortunately, her future husband, Francis, was a sickly boy. They were married on April 24, 1558, when Mary was fifteen and Francis fourteen. King Henry II died soon thereafter, and the young couple became king and queen of France. But Francis died within two years and at age eighteen Mary was left a widow.

She decided to return to Scotland. Although Catholic in a land of Protestants, Mary was at first quite popular. Her charm, gaiety, and obvious wish to please gained her many supporters. She also showed great tact with Protestant extremists, promising to conduct Catholic mass only in private and never to interfere with the religion of her subjects.

Her choice of husband was the first step in her undoing. In 1565, she fell in love with Henry, Lord Darnley, and married him despite the disapproval of both Queen Elizabeth of England and the Scottish court. Darnley, a good-looking but vain and foolish youth, quickly proved himself unfit to be king. He was one of a group of nobles who murdered David Rizzio, the queen's secretary, in her presence. Mary was pregnant at the time but survived to bear a son, James.

Darnley himself was murdered on February 9, 1567, when a house he was in exploded. The events surrounding the bomb plot have remained mysterious, but it seems certain that the nobles who planned it did so without the queen's knowledge. Then, believing that she was acting with the approval of her nobles, the queen married one of the conspirators, the earl of Bothwell, on May 15, 1567. Unfortunately, the marriage implicated her in her husband's murder, and Mary was forced to abdicate the throne in favor of her son. She escaped imprisonment and sought sanctuary in England.

Mary was under house arrest in England for nineteen years. Queen Elizabeth, once sympathetic to her cousin, was now embarrassed by her. Mary was extremely unpopular in Protestant England. She posed an ever-present threat, being not only the closest heir to the English throne but also a Catholic with strong ties to France and Spain. Her enemies sought to portray her as a foreign traitor. Unfortunately, Mary was fond of intrigue and desperate to regain her freedom.

At last, after it was proven that Mary was involved in the Babington Plot to murder Elizabeth, the queen was forced to have her put to death. On February 8, 1587, Mary was beheaded at Fotheringay Castle. She was dignified and calm when she died. When the executioner held her head up for the onlookers to see, the red wig came off to reveal the gray hair beneath. Though only forty-four years old, Mary had become an old woman in captivity.

When Queen Elizabeth died, Mary's son became James I of Great Britain. He built his mother a tomb in Westminster Abbey, the last resting place of English royalty. All the kings and queens of Great Britain from James I onward have been descended from Mary Queen of Scots.

Ruth Ashby

Artemisia Gentileschi

(1593–c. 1652)

"This will show your lordship what a woman can do."
—Letter to Don Antonio Ruffo, August 7, 1649

A rtemisia Gentileschi spent a lifetime proving that a woman painter could prosper in the male-dominated art world of the Italian Renaissance. Today, she is remembered as the first really important woman painter in the history of Western art.

Born in Rome, Artemisia was the daughter of the noted artist Orazio

Artemisia Gentileschi, Judith and Maidservant with the Head of Holofernes, *c. 1625.*

Gentileschi, a follower of the realist painter Caravaggio. Orazio made sure that his talented daughter had the training to be a fine artist. In 1611, he hired his colleague Agostino Tassi to teach Artemisia perspective. When Artemisia was seventeen, Tassi raped her, and Orazio took him to court. Despite a prolonged trial in which Artemisia was tortured by thumbscrew to test whether she was telling the truth, Tassi was acquitted.

The scandal established Artemisia's reputation as a "loose" woman. Shortly thereafter, she married a relative of one of her few supporters and moved to Florence. We know almost nothing about her married life, but we do know she had at least one daughter.

In 1620, Artemisia Gentileschi left Florence for Rome, where she enjoyed the patronage of the grand duke, perhaps at the request of her father. She also set up her own studio and received commissions for portraits and figure paintings. By 1630, she had settled in Naples, where she painted mostly allegories and religious subjects for the nobility and the Church.

Gentileschi specialized in large figure paintings, usually based on stories from the Bible or Greek mythology. Her favorite subjects were heroic women, such as Esther, Judith, Susannah, Mary Magdalene, and Diana. These women are portrayed as strong, solidly built, and vigorous. Gentileschi must have prided herself on her handling of the female nude.

She was especially well known for painting the story of Judith, a legendary Hebrew widow who cut off the head of the enemy leader Holofernes to save her city. Gentileschi gave this popular subject a new and sometimes graphic realism, concentrating on Judith's strength and determination.

From her correspondence with various patrons during the 1640s, we learn that Gentileschi was aware that women artists faced special challenges. Yet in her lifetime her artistic reputation was good enough to enable her to support herself and her family. In a letter to a patron written just a few years before her death, she reveals her supreme confidence in her own ability: "You will find the spirit of Caesar in the soul of this woman."

Ruth Ashby

Judith Leyster

(1609–1660)

For two hundred years after her death, the Dutch master painter Judith Leyster was all but forgotten. Her reputation was revived in 1893, when experts discovered that a painting attributed to the famous artist Frans Hals bore her distinctive signature: *JL* attached to a star. It was a pun on her name, Leyster (lodestar, or leading star). Since then, art historians have found more than twenty of her portraits, still lifes, and domestic scenes. Today, she is acknowledged as the leading woman painter of the Dutch golden age.

The daughter of a weaver, Judith Leyster was born in Haarlem, Holland. She started painting when she was young, probably between the ages of thirteen and fifteen. Perhaps she studied in the workshop of Frans Pietersz de Grebber, whose daughter was also a painter. She may also have studied with Frans Hals, Haarlem's most successful artist. Leyster's choice of subject matter and style often reflect Hals's influence.

An early observer noted that Leyster painted with "good, keen sense." By age twenty-three or twenty-four, Leyster was sufficiently accomplished to join Haarlem's Guild of St. Luke. Guild membership provided training, some financial security, and the right to teach apprentices. Leyster soon established her own workshop and took on two pupils. She had become a "master" painter.

Like many of her fellow artists, Leyster sold most of her paintings to collectors on the "open market." A

Judith Leyster, Self-Portrait, *c. 1630.*

craze for collecting—art, porcelain, tulips—swept Holland in the seventeenth century. Now painters no longer had to depend on wealthy patrons or the Church for commissions. Instead, Leyster and others could concentrate on a certain type of painting and sell their work at public sales or directly to collectors.

Leyster especially excelled at genre paintings—scenes of people in everyday situations. Her paintings are dramatically lit, often by only one candle. She picked popular subjects: people having a good time, drink-

Rachel Ruysch

Judith Leyster's fellow artist Rachel Ruysch (1664–1750) was at the forefront of the enormously popular genre of still-life painting in the Dutch golden age. Born in Amsterdam to Frederick Ruysch, a professor of anatomy and botany, and Maria Post, Rachel revealed her artistic talent at an early age. When she was fifteen, she entered the workshop of a noted flower painter, where she created her earliest known work: detailed studies of flowers, fruit, and insects.

Ruysch painted carefully arranged still-life compositions. Yet her paintings are not "still" at all. They vibrate with life and energy. Flowers swirl across the canvas in sinuous, S-shaped patterns; fruit explode with vitality. Rachel Ruysch must have possessed extraordinary energy. In addition to bearing and raising ten children, she completed nearly one hundred signed paintings in the sixty-eight years of her artistic career.

ing, dancing, playing the fiddle or the flute. Sometimes she portrayed women at home doing domestic chores, sewing, or caring for children. One of her most famous works, *The Proposition* (1631), shows a woman rejecting a man's advances. The young woman, bent over her sewing, completely ignores an older man who holds out a handful of coins to her, presumably the payment he would give her for sexual favors. Her calm self-sufficiency clearly marks this as a subject painted from a woman's point of view.

Most of Leyster's works were painted between 1629 and 1635. In 1636, Leyster married fellow artist Jan Meinse Molenaer, moved to Amsterdam, and had five children. Like many woman artists, she did little painting after her marriage. Instead, she seems to have competently managed her household and administered her husband's business affairs. It seems that even by the time she died, her name was eclipsed by that of her husband. Only in the twentieth century did Haarlem's "leading star" begin to shine again.

Ruth Ashby

Sor Juana Ines de la Cruz

(1651–1695)

"Who has forbidden women to engage in private and individual studies? Have they not a rational soul as men do? . . . I have this inclination [to study] and if it is evil I am not the one who formed me thus—I was born with it and with it I shall die."
—Letter to Father Nuñez, 1681

Sor (Sister) Juana was considered one of the foremost intellectuals of her day as well as one of the greatest women poets of Mexico. Her devotion to learning began early in life. In her writings, she recalled that she "burned with the desire to know" at the young age of three. Juana would follow her sister to school, and she learned to read before anyone knew what she was doing. As she grew up, she studied everything she could, including the Latin and Aztec languages, mathematics, logic, history, and classical literature.

When she was just seven years old, Juana heard about a school in Mexico City that taught the sciences. She pleaded with her mother to be allowed to dress in boy's clothes and attend, but her mother refused. Finally, her family sent her to the city to live with an aunt and uncle and study Latin. When Juana turned thirteen, the viceroy of Mexico and his wife, perhaps impressed by Juana's intellect and charm, invited her to stay with them at the palace. There Juana enjoyed attending parties and engaging in worldly discussions. She wrote poetry, songs, and plays, and her intellect became so well known that when she turned fifteen, forty university professors gave her a comprehensive oral examination. She impressed them all with her wealth of knowledge.

Juana's desire for education remained unfulfilled, however. Her family urged her to marry, but she refused. She knew that the only way she could continue to study would be to enter a convent. In 1669, she became Sor Juana.

The convent Sor Juana joined was very active. She served as its record keeper and accountant, and she continued to collect and read books and meet with her intellectual friends for lively discussions and debates. Gradually, her library grew to contain at least four thousand volumes, the largest collection in Mexico at that time. By her late thirties, she had published three volumes of poetry and was celebrated as a great poet.

In 1690, Sor Juana wrote a criticism of a sermon delivered by a well-known Jesuit priest. When the bishop of Puebla read her commentary, he rebuked her for pursuing secular learning and asked her to give up her writing and devote herself to religious literature.

Sor Juana wrote a moving reply to the bishop, revealing the circumstances in her life that had led to her devotion to study. She claimed that her drive to learn was beyond her control, and she defended the right of women to pursue a scholarly life: "God has given me the gift of a very profound love of truth. Since I was first struck by the lightning flash of reason, my propensity for learning was so strong . . . that neither outside censure nor my own second thoughts . . . have been able to stop me from pursuing this natural impulse."

Despite her spirited response, the bishop pressured Sor Juana to stop writing, and the viceroy and his court no longer defended her. In 1694, because of this relentless disapproval, she renounced her love of books and learning by selling her library, her scientific and musical instruments and art supplies, and by withdrawing from her intellectual friends. She vowed never to write again and performed excessive acts of penance to "redeem" herself. As an epidemic swept through Mexico City, she nursed the sisters who fell ill and died during the epidemic at the age of forty-three.

Lyn Reese

From
Revolution
to
Revolution
1750 to 1890

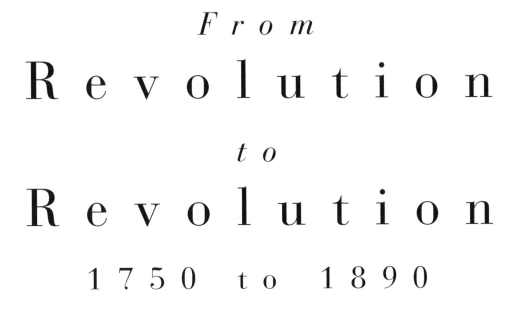

From Revolution to Revolution
1750 to 1890

"Contending for the rights of woman, my main argument is built on this simple principle, that if she not be prepared by education to become the companion of man, she will stop the progress of knowledge and virtue, for truth must be common to all."
—Mary Wollstonecraft

So Mary Wollstonecraft, writing in a London attic in 1791, added her voice to those calling for a new order and a new day. Across the English Channel, the French Declaration of the Rights of Man (1889) asserted that every individual enjoyed the right to "liberty, property, security, and resistance to oppression." Across the Atlantic Ocean, the American Declaration of Independence announced that every man had the right to "life, liberty, and the pursuit of happiness." Were women also thinking individuals just like men? Were women too endowed with inalienable rights?

Wollstonecraft thought so, and in her *Vindication of the Rights of Woman*, she sought to prove that women, who shared with men the gift of reason, also shared with them the responsibility of self-rule. For the Western world, the revolutions of 1776 and 1789 shook up the old order not only of government but of family and society as well. For if all "men" are created equal, then might not slaves and women be created equal as well? If a king who rules without the consent of the governed can be considered a tyrant in his own country, might not a man be considered a tyrant in his home? The whole nineteenth century was an attempt to come to terms with the questions raised by the French and American revolutions.

The uprisings themselves had different consequences for men and women. American women were involved in the agitation that preceded the Revolutionary War—some organized the Daughters of Liberty to boycott British goods—yet they did not serve on citizens' committees or attend the Continental Congress. After the war began, most women carried on the regular business of the colonies, tending farms and keeping shops while their husbands were away. Others marched with both Continental and British armies as cooks, nurses, doctors, laundresses, and companions. Some took their husbands' places in battle, and others, like the intrepid Deborah Sampson, even disguised themselves in men's clothes and joined the army.

Yet women's rights were never even considered when it came time to write a new constitution. Few citizens, either male or female, seemed concerned by the omission. One exception was Abigail Adams, the wife of John Adams, a future president of the United States. She wrote her husband, "In the new Code of Laws which I suppose it will be necessary for you to make, I desire you would Remember the Ladies, and be more generous and favorable to them than your ancestors. . . . Remember all Men would be tyrants if they could." John shrugged off her suggestion and only half-jokingly replied, "Depend on it. We know better than to repeal our Masculine systems." No one in the new country was ready to take up the issue of women.

French revolutionaries were at least more conscious that there *was* an issue. Perhaps this was because women were furiously and publicly involved with the insurrection from its beginning. Women stormed the Bastille and marched on the Palace of Versailles to confront the king, "armed with broomsticks, lances, pitchforks, swords, pistols, and muskets," as one observer recorded. They formed political clubs to debate issues and petition the revolutionary government. One bold woman even wrote *The Declaration of the Rights of Woman,* which she posted on the walls of Paris: "Women, awake! The tocsin of reason is making itself heard the world over. Assert your rights."

In 1793, at the height of the Terror that sent thousands to the guillotine, the government outlawed all women's clubs and excluded women from political activity. It was bad enough that fear and confusion reigned throughout the land; women should not add to it by abandoning their rightful role. "Woman should not leave her family to meddle in the affairs of government," the revolutionaries thundered. By 1804, the backlash was complete: the Napoleonic legal code made it clear that women were legal minors, just like children, criminals, and the insane.

In fact, the French Revolution frightened the ruling elite so badly that all over Europe new civil codes were established to secure the status quo and restrict women. In Prussia, Scandinavia, Switzerland, and Russia, men gained formal legalized control over women. Married women in particular suffered under the new constraints. As guardian of his wife, a Frenchman could read or intercept all the letters she sent or received. The Prussian Civil Code of 1794 stipulated that all women must breast-feed their children—and that the husband, not the wife, should decide how long the breast-feeding was to last!

A devoted wife comforts her bereaved husband in George E. Hicks's Woman's Mission: Companion of Manhood, *1863.*

These legal restrictions went hand in hand with the new seclusion of middle- and upper-class women in the home. The prosperity that resulted from the new manufacturing and trade opportunities of the late eighteenth century created a larger, stronger middle class throughout the United States and Europe. Freed economically from working in outside trades, more women could stay home full-time. Now the "separate spheres" of man and woman became ever more obligatory. As a character in Alfred Lord Tennyson's poem *The Princess* (1847) declared, "Man for the field and woman for the hearth:/ Man for the sword and for the needle she . . ./ All else confusion."

Set apart from the rude hurly-burly of public life, the home became idealized as a haven to which a man might retire after the stress of the day. And the woman was likewise idealized: she was man's helpmeet, his better half, his "angel in the house." She had a duty to mold her children, uplift her husband, and embue the home with the softening influence of her feminine sensibility. By mid-nineteenth century, woman might still be considered physically and intellectually inferior to man, but she was acknowledged as his moral superior.

It might seem paradoxical that, thus imprisoned in the home and stereotyped in popular myth, nineteenth-century women would, for the first time in history, organize for women's rights. How did this happen?

Most important, more women were literate now than ever before. Together with the rise of the middle class had come an increase in literacy and the leisure time to indulge in reading. Women's magazines, offering helpful household hints, verse, romantic stories, and educational articles, appeared throughout Europe and the United States. Eager females rushed into circulating libraries to read the new novel; in England in 1800, three-quarters of novel readers were women.

Nearly as significant, more *writers* were women. Writing offered middle-class women a respectable way to make a living. Authors like Jane Austen and the Brontë sisters in England and Harriet Beecher Stowe and Louisa May Alcott in the United States all wrote to support themselves or their families. They took over the novel of social life and made it their own. Intellectuals like Margaret Fuller also contributed to political and literary journals. Slowly, women made their way into the world of public expression.

Most of these writers were, in Virginia Woolf's words, the "daughters of educated men," mainly clergymen. Only girls with fathers who cared about books had access to learning. Still barred from higher education at the beginning of the nineteenth century, most girls relied on local grammar schools, occasional private tutoring, and girls' boarding or day schools—which usually taught superficial "accomplishments" like music, needlework, and French—for the inadequate instruction they did receive. In both Europe and the United States, access to higher education came slowly. The first European university to open its doors to women was the University of Zürich in 1865, followed gradually by others. Some universities, like Oxford and Cambridge in England, admitted women in the 1800s but would not allow them to receive degrees until after World War I.

In the United States, Emma Willard founded the first academically rigorous secondary school for girls in 1821. This was followed in 1837 by Mount Holyoke Seminary, which later became the first women's college. Educational reformers like Willard and Catharine Beecher believed that the purpose of women's education was primarily to make them better wives, mothers—and teachers of the young. Part of woman's moral mission, they felt, was to instruct the younger generation. Soon young women ventured out across America and Europe to earn their own livings. Teaching and nursing became the first respected professions for middle-class women since the early Middle Ages.

As moral agents, many women also felt they were called upon to make the world a better place. Hundreds—and eventually, thousands—of nineteenth-century women became involved with reform movements that forever changed our idea of what is acceptable in a civilized society. Slavery, prostitution, alcoholism, the callous or brutal treatment of the sick, the indigent, the criminal, and the insane—there was no social evil that women did not try to eradicate. The reform achievements of Sarah and Angelica Grimké, Sojourner Truth, Dorothea Dix, Florence Nightingale, Clara Barton, Carry Nation, Jane Addams, Ida B. Wells-Barnett, and their sisters have never been surpassed.

Reform work taught these crusading women how to organize and how to communicate effectively to a wide audience. More important, it taught them that they could have an effect on society outside the home. Abolition work, in particular, radicalized a generation of American women. It was

The founding mothers of the American women's movement—Elizabeth Cady Stanton and Susan B. Anthony—join forces with a founding father to promote the National American Woman Suffrage Association, January 26, 1896.

A well-to-do woman looks on as her maid demonstrates a washing machine in this late nineteenth-century advertisement. Even when new appliances began to take some of the drudgery out of housework, home care remained women's primary occupation.

when women were forbidden to take part in the World's Anti-Slavery Convention in 1840 that Elizabeth Cady Stanton and Lucretia Mott decided to organize a conference on women. The Seneca Falls Convention of 1848 is considered the formal start of the women's rights movement in America.

In Europe, though individual women had long expressed feminist ideas, women didn't begin to organize until the late 1850s. During the nineteenth century, much of Europe was wracked by wars and revolution as people sought to overthrow foreign rulers or topple their own. With every reestablishment of order came a reaction against reform. Therefore, it was in England, the most stable and prosperous European country at midcentury, that women started to lobby for a variety of issues—including a married woman's control over her own earnings and property, more liberal divorce laws, a woman's right to custody of her children, education, and the vote.

Women in other European countries, encouraged by the American and English examples, began to organize shortly thereafter.

Most of the reforms these liberal feminists advocated affected primarily the middle class. Working-class women had a whole other set of problems. At the end of the eighteenth century, when the Industrial Revolution began, the labor site moved from the farm or home workshop to the factory. There, under often brutal conditions, women and children along with men worked backbreaking fourteen-to-sixteen-hour days. Factory work caused special hardships for women. First, they were separated from their young children, who had to be cared for by somebody else. Next, away from the protection of family, they were often subject to sexual harassment. Also, because women were supposed to be working for "pin money" rather than supporting the family, employers felt justified in paying them one third to one half of a man's salary. Male unions consistently excluded women, whose low-paying, unskilled labor made them more dispensable.

Finally, women were still expected to work a second shift—in the home—after the factory day was done. By the end of the nineteenth century, most industrialized countries had passed labor legislation that reduced women's

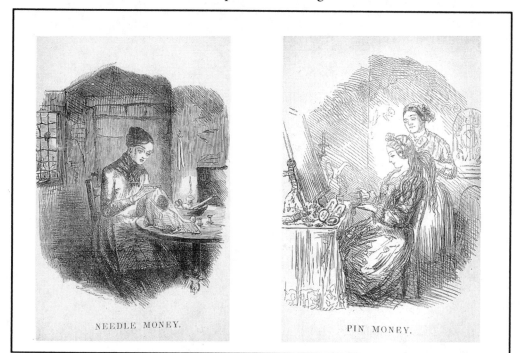

Left: "Needle Money." *Right:* "Pin Money." Punch, *1849. These ironic cartoons contrast a wealthy woman who spends her "pin money" on fashionable ornamentation, with a poor seamstress who earns a meager living with her needle.*

working hours to twelve or ten per day. Most other protective legislation would have to wait until the twentieth century—and still would not end women's double exploitation.

Increased middle-class prosperity also meant that more women hired lower-class domestics to do the hard labor of a household. Nowhere is the age's double standard more obvious than in the contrasting picture of a pampered mistress and her hardworking maid, one serving tea in her elegant drawing room, the other laboring in the kitchen.

IMPERIALISM

In the nineteenth century, European power extended around the world. As one by one the North and South American colonies became independent, European nations extended imperialist rule to much of Africa, Asia, and the Pacific islands. By 1880, European nations were in a race to divide the "undeveloped" land and resources of the world among them. Convinced of their own cultural and racial superiority, Europeans brought with them not only new technologies but also values often utterly at odds with those of the native peoples. The resulting blend of the modern and the traditional, the Western and non-Western, had varied consequences for women. Here are some examples:

British India

The British first acquired an interest in the subcontinent of India in the seventeenth century, when the British East India Company set up a permanent trading base in Calcutta. In 1857, the British crown officially displaced the company and established imperial rule. British officials were dismayed by the nearly utter subjugation of Indian women. Their interest coincided with the work of Indian social reformers (mostly male, since women were both secluded and uneducated), who had been influenced by a Western education and the exposure to new ideas. A number of important reforms were established.

First, suttee, or widow burning, was abolished in 1829 (although in practice the suppression was gradual—there was still a case reported in 1987). Next, in 1856, a law was passed to permit widows to remarry. This act did not immediately change popular custom, since even in 1881 about one fifth of the women in India were widows—and many had been widows since childhood. Then, in 1891, the government passed a bill which set the age of consent for child marriages at twelve. Though these laws were often ignored, they did set important precedents for the twentieth century.

High-caste women were the first to benefit from the movement to educate women; still, by 1907, only 3.6 percent of young females were in school (as opposed to 23.1 percent of males). By the end of the nineteenth century, seclusion restrictions had loosened for some elite women, who appeared for the first time in mixed-sex gatherings.

Unfortunately, lower-caste women may have suffered economically from the effects of British rule, since hand-spun, woven, and embroidered goods were gradually replaced by machine-made goods. Also, in areas with communal property rights, women lost property when the British administration predictably divided property among male heads of households. Uniform laws often ignored the differences among different groups, like Muslim women, who had inheritance rights under Islamic but not local law. All in all, British rule was a mixed bag for women, as it was for all India.

Africa

Until colonialism, women's roles in sub-Saharan Africa were as diverse as African itself. In various societies, women were queens, chiefs, farmers, traders, warriors, landowners, sorceresses, and slaves. Of course men remained dominant. They usually took more than one wife and retained most of the power and wealth for themselves.

Yet, usually, African women enjoyed a certain authority. In many tribes, they maintained their own separate political and economic organizations. Thus, the head of a village would probably have been a male chief, but there might have been a female chief for the women as well. Throughout Africa, women were the primary farmers, and many kept at least part of the income derived from surplus crops. They were also the main traders, and some women were able to become independently wealthy. West African women, in particular, had a reputation as fierce traders.

Colonial rule in most of Africa lasted no more than eighty years, from about 1880 to 1960. Yet those years changed Africa forever.

Predictably, European colonists did not understand the unique position of women in Africa. Using their own social norms as a guide, Europeans consistently recognized and rewarded male chiefs and associations and ignored women-centered activities. Only African males benefited from new educational opportunities, for instance. Worst of all, new laws often robbed women of their economic independence.

Some women fought back. In 1929, Nigerian Igbo women who thought they were going to be taxed unfairly staged a ritualistic "women's war" in front of a colonial office. Waving palm sticks, they danced and chanted songs of ridicule. Because they did not recognize the demonstration as a traditional form of protest, the British fired upon the crowd and killed more than fifty women.

By the end of the nineteenth century, the railroad, the steamship, the telegraph, the telephone, the camera, and even the moving picture had already made the world a much smaller place. More people were educated, more people were prosperous, more people were aware of cultures other than their own. For good or for ill, imperialism had introduced the ideas of Western civilization to places that had changed little in thousands of years. The world was posed for a change. And women were ready.

Ruth Ashby

Catherine the Great

(1729–1796)

"The nation's glory is my own, that is my principle."
—Conversation with Voltaire, 1771

On June 28, 1762, the grand duchess Catherine of Russia was woken by her lover and coconspirator, who said, "Time to rise. Everything is prepared to proclaim you." With that, Catherine got up, dressed in male uniform, and rushed to the capital, St. Petersburg, to overthrow her husband, Czar Peter III. In September, she was crowned empress of Russia, and as Catherine II, she ruled the empire with absolute authority for the next thirty-four years.

The firstborn daughter of a minor German prince, Catherine was born Sophia Augusta Frederica in 1729 in a small Prussian kingdom. Her mother neglected her after giving birth to her brother, and she saw little of her father. When her parents discovered that she had a good memory, however, she was encouraged to learn, and she was taught religion, history, and geography. She was intensely energetic, always more interested in hunting and riding than in conventionally feminine pursuits.

Elizabeth I of Russia chose Sophia to marry her son Peter. Sophia took an immediate liking to Elizabeth, and to please her, she began to prepare for her role as czarina by studying the Russian language. Elizabeth chose Sophia's new Russian name, Catherine, in honor of her mother, Catherine I. Catherine

Catherine the Great, c. 1788

and Peter married in 1744, but the marriage was a disaster from the start. Peter was immature and spent much of his time playing with toy soldiers.

Catherine and Peter's marriage was not consummated, and Elizabeth, fearing that her son was impotent, arranged for Catherine to bear a child by another man. Catherine then took her own lover, an imperial guard officer and war hero named Gregory Orlov, by whom she also had a child.

When Elizabeth died, Peter began a disastrous reign. He continually offended officials of the court and the Church, while Catherine began to build an entourage of supporters through Orlov and his brothers. When Catherine learned that Peter planned to have her arrested so that he could divorce her and marry his mistress, she and Orlov plotted to overthrow him. On a fateful June day in 1762, Orlov spirited Catherine away to an army barracks where the soldiers proclaimed her their savior, and she forcibly took the throne. Peter was imprisoned and probably murdered.

Catherine tried to be a progressive leader. She brought a number of reforms to Russia, such as a more modern code of laws and better education. Yet she allowed her nobles unlimited authority over their serfs, so that by the end of her reign the serfs had less power than ever.

Catherine's reign also saw the expansion of Russia's influence abroad. Taking control in Poland when an uprising threatened to disrupt the country, Catherine ended up dividing Poland with Austria and Prussia. But her intervention angered Turkey, which declared war against Russia in 1768. The war brought Russia victory and new territory bordering the Black Sea. It also resulted in the loss of many men and an increase in foreign debts.

A patron of the arts, Catherine built magnificent palaces and public buildings in St. Petersburg, including the palace now called the Hermitage, where she stored her magnificent collection of art. She also established the Russian Academy for the study of arts and promoted printing and publishing. She herself published a literary magazine, wrote her memoirs, and enjoyed painting, sculpture, and cameo making.

During Catherine the Great's reign, Russia became a world power. When she died in 1796, she left an immense empire and enormous authority to her son, Paul I.

Lyn Reese

Mary Wollstonecraft

(1759–1797)

"Make woman rational creatures, and free citizens, and they will quickly become good wives; that is—if men do not neglect the duties of husbands and fathers!"
—*A Vindication of the Rights of Woman*, 1792

Mary Wollstonecraft is considered by many to be the foremother of the European and American women's rights movements. She lived during the Enlightenment, when progressive thinkers believed that men were born with certain natural rights. Yet many continued to believe that women were by nature inferior to men and did not share those rights. Wollstonecraft challenged such misogynist thinking and ardently maintained that women could be equal to men if given the same educational and economic opportunities.

Wollstonecraft was born near London, England. She grew up watching her father, an unsuccessful middle-class farmer, drink and abuse her mother, and she often tried to defend her mother from his blows. Perhaps because of this abusive relationship, Wollstonecraft learned at a young age to distrust marriage and value independence. In the words of English author Virginia Woolf, Wollstonecraft's life early on became "one cry for justice."

In 1775, Wollstonecraft met some elderly neighbors who allowed her to use their private library to read and study. Through them, she met eighteen-year-old Fanny Blood, an accomplished young woman who became both a mentor and close friend to Wollstonecraft. Wollstonecraft, her sister Eliza, and Fanny Blood decided to open a school for girls in London in 1784.

There Wollstonecraft's circle of friends came to include many people with whom she had lively discussions about education, religion, and other topics. Many of her friends encouraged her to move beyond teaching to writing, and in 1786, she published *Thoughts on the Education of Daughters*. When the school failed, she supported herself financially by taking a job as a governess. Soon she found herself appalled by the upper class's life of privilege and complacency.

Wollstonecraft continued to read avidly and to develop her ideas about the education and rights of women. She was dismissed from her post after ten months and went to work for book and magazine publisher Joseph Johnson in London, doing reviews of books. She wrote a monthly magazine column, which she often used to discuss principles of women's education, to criticize novels that portrayed weak female characters, and to call for more intellectually challenging fiction for women. Her work for the magazine helped lead to the development of more radical ideas, which she expressed in her most famous book, *A Vindication of the Rights of Woman,* published in 1792. In it, she argued that since woman's first duty is to be a competent, knowledgeable mother, she should receive an education equal to man's. She also advocated training single women for adequate employment and viewed marriage as an equal partnership between husband and wife. *Vindication* sold well, sparked much discussion about women's rights, and launched Wollstonecraft's career as a professional writer and celebrity.

In 1792, Wollstonecraft traveled to Paris, then in the throes of the French Revolution. She worked on *An Historical and Moral View of the Origin and Progress of the French Revolution,* and she fell in love with an American, Gilbert Imlay, with whom she had a daughter. When the couple broke up, Wollstonecraft returned to London and resumed her work for Johnson. She mixed with other radical intellectuals and writers, including Thomas Paine, William Blake, and the philosopher William Godwin. Wollstonecraft fell in love with Godwin and they married in 1797. They had a daughter, Mary Godwin Shelley, who would become an author in her own right, publishing the famous novel *Frankenstein.* Wollstonecraft, however, died of a fever shortly after giving birth. She was only thirty-eight years old.

Wollstonecraft's ideas ushered in a new era in feminist thought. She went further than earlier champions of women's rights by arguing that a democratic nation should take active steps to improve the lives of women. The leaders of America's first women's movement, which began in the mid-nineteenth century, were able to build upon the progressive ideas of Mary Wollstonecraft to advance their own cause.

Lyn Reese

Deborah Sampson

(1760–1827)

*"When I entered the hall, I must say I was much pleased at the
appearance of the audience. It appeared from almost every face that
they were full of unbelief—I mean in regard to my being the person
that served in the Revolutionary Army."*
—Diary entry, May 5, 1802

At age forty-one, Deborah Sampson Gannett astounded audiences
throughout New England with tales of her adventures during the
American Revolution twenty years before—when she was a soldier
in the Continental Army. At a time when other young women stayed home
to run households and tend farms, Deborah Sampson had put on a uniform,
picked up a gun, and gone forth to fight for independence.

Deborah was the oldest of the three daughters and three sons of Jonathan
Sampson, a farmer, and Deborah (Bradford) Sampson, a homemaker, in
Plympton, Massachusetts. When young Deborah's father abandoned the
family and went off to sea, her mother was forced to send the children
to live with neighbors and relatives because she was ill and could not
support them.

At age eight, Deborah was sent to live as an indentured servant in Jere-
miah Thomas's household in Middleborough. In return for food, clothes,
and shelter, Deborah was bound to work for the Thomases for ten years.
She ran their household until she was eighteen, when she was free to take
a job as a schoolteacher.

The year was 1779 and the American war for independence against Great
Britain was in its fourth year. While Deborah loved teaching, she also
dreamed of adventure—of traveling across the country, meeting new people,
and earning more money than a poor schoolteacher could make. So she
decided to enlist as a soldier in the army. There was only one problem:
women were not allowed to join the armed forces.

Taller and stronger than most women, Deborah was able to masquerade
as a young man. Wearing men's clothes and using the name Robert Shurtleff

(also spelled Shirtliff), she enlisted in the Fourth Massachusetts Regiment of the Continental Army at Bellingham, Massachusetts on May 20, 1782.

War, however, was not as romantic as Deborah had imagined. Fighting in skirmishes with British forces throughout New England, Sampson witnessed and endured all the horrors of war. Still, she kept fighting. When she was shot in the leg, she even tended to her own wounds rather than risk discovery. Her leg never healed properly as a result. It wasn't until 1783, when she contracted a serious fever in Philadelphia, that doctors discovered her disguise. Despite her illegal enlistment, Deborah was honorably discharged, thanks to her excellent service record. By that time, the war was already drawing to a close, and that same year, the peace treaty was signed in Paris.

Her fighting days over, Sampson returned to Massachusetts, where in 1784 she married a farmer, Benjamin Gannett. They raised three children, and Deborah resumed her teaching career at a nearby school. After stories about her war experiences began to appear in newspapers, Deborah became famous both for her scandalous service and for her accomplishments as a soldier. Soon she was a popular speaker, appearing in her old uniform with its blue coat, white buttons, and leather cap, and lecturing about the horrors of war. While Benjamin stayed home to take care of the farm and the children, Deborah traveled widely throughout New England and New York, becoming one of the first American women to go on the professional lecture circuit.

Deborah's service to her country was recognized by the state of Massachusetts and the federal government, both of which awarded her pensions.

Loreta Velasquez

Like Sampson, Loreta Velasquez (1842–1897) grew up fascinated by stories of glorious battles. The daughter of a Spanish diplomat living in New Orleans, she married a military officer who joined the Southern forces during the Civil War. When her husband was killed, she disguised herself with a fake beard and mustache and a padded jacket, took the name Harry T. Buford, and enlisted in the Confederate Army.

According to her autobiography, "Buford" participated gallantly in the first battle of Bull Run, at Ball's Bluff, and at Shiloh. She reported being appalled and disillusioned by the inhumanity and senseless carnage of war. Recent research has shown that three hundred or more women actively served as soldiers and spies on both sides during the Civil War.

When she died in 1827 at the age of sixty-seven, her children received compensation by a special act of Congress "for the relief of the heirs of Deborah Gannett, a soldier of the Revolution, deceased."

Deborah Gore Ohrn

Jane Austen

(1775–1817)

"I am fully sensible . . . that an historical romance . . . might be much more to the purpose of profit or popularity, than such pictures of domestic life in country villages as I deal in."
—Letter to J. S. Clarke, April 1, 1816

Jane Austen has often been called the first modern novelist. She wrote books about real people living ordinary lives at a time when most popular novels featured impossibly dashing heroes and sentimentalized heroines. In contrast, Austen's social comedies are realistic, yet so full of wit and romance that they are still read and loved by millions of people today.

The seventh of eight children, Jane was born in the village of Steventon, England, to a moderately prosperous middle-class family. Her father was a well educated clergyman who passed his love of books on to his daughter. Jane read voraciously, and through her father's collection, she became acquainted with a wide range of good literature.

Jane Austen led a very quiet life. She never married, although she had several offers. Perhaps she remained single because she was never really in love. But she also seems to have made a conscious decision to remain independent, free to manage her time without the demands of husband and children. After her father died, she lived with her mother and sister Cassandra—keeping house, seeing friends, and visiting the other members of her large family. Her brothers all married, and Austen had many nieces and nephews to keep her company.

Most important, Austen wrote. Her earliest poems, plays, and novels date

Jane Austen

from her teenage years. Even these works poke fun at the society around her, for Austen was a natural satirist.

The novels of Austen's maturity all center around young women—intelligent, perceptive, often witty—who still have much to learn about themselves and their world. Marianne Dashwood of *Sense and Sensibility* (1811), Elizabeth Bennett of *Pride and Prejudice* (1813), and Emma Woodhouse of

Emma (1815) all misjudge their own feelings and those of the young men with whom they are involved. Eventually, these heroines all make the right commitment in love, and the novels end in happiness and harmony.

Jane Austen completed just six novels before her early death at age forty-two. She signed her works "By a Lady," and few outside her immediate family knew she was an author. She took pains to keep her writing a secret. Her nephew later recalled that she used to rely on the creaky door of her sitting room to warn her when visitors were arriving. At the first sound, she would slide her manuscript underneath the blotter of her writing desk.

Jane Austen's books were not very popular when they were first published. Contemporary audiences wanted more drama and sensation in their novels. Austen's reputation grew steadily over the course of the nineteenth century as more and more readers discovered her. Today, Jane Austen is considered one of the greatest novelists of all time.

Ruth Ashby

Emma Willard

(1787–1870)

"The education of females has been too exclusively directed to fit them for displaying the charms of youth and beauty. Though it may be proper to adorn this period of life, yet it is incomparably more important to prepare for the serious duties of maturer years."
—*A Plan for Improving Female Education*, 1819

When Emma Willard began her campaign to reform women's education in America, there were no colleges or high schools for women. Boarding schools for the upper classes stressed female "accomplishments": needlework, music, French, and painting. Educators thought that more difficult subjects like Latin or mathematics would tax women's weak brains and make them unfit for their true vocations as wives and mothers. All agreed that the only goal of female education was to make

Emma Willard

women better companions for men. This was the attitude Emma Willard sought to change by opening up new educational opportunities for women.

Born on a farm in Berlin, Connecticut, Emma Hart was the ninth of the ten children of Lydia Hinsdale Hart and Samuel Hart, who also had seven children from a previous marriage. A political liberal, her father encouraged her to use her mind and often discussed current events and philosophy with the growing girl. Like other farm children, Emma attended the local one-room schoolhouse when she was young. At thirteen, she taught herself geometry and two years later enrolled in the new Berlin Academy.

She was such an apt pupil that by age seventeen she was teaching in the village school. Emma quickly proved herself to be an exceptional teacher. At age twenty, she became the head of a female academy in Middlebury, Vermont. There she met and married Dr. John Willard, an older widower. They were happily married for sixteen years and had one son.

When Dr. Willard had financial problems, Emma opened the Middlebury Female Seminary in her own home. For fear of alarming the more tradition-bound, she would never call her schools "colleges," but she tried to expose her students to a college curriculum. She conducted public oral examinations to prove that females could learn such "unfeminine" subjects as history and mathematics.

The next step, Willard decided, was to found a state-aided school like those open to boys. To this end, she wrote a pamphlet, *An Address to the Public; Particularly to the Members of the Legislature of New-York, Proposing a Plan for Improving Female Education* (1819). Unfortunately, the legislature refused to grant money for her project. But the city of Troy, New York, voted to raise four thousand dollars for a new school to open in September 1821.

The Troy Female Seminary was the first school in America to take female education seriously. Students could take advanced courses in chemistry, philosophy, or physiology as well as receive instruction in good manners and pastry making. Although most girls came from upper-middle-class families, Willard provided scholarships for needy students as well. She also prepared over two hundred women to be teachers before the first teacher training schools opened in the United States.

As a result of her school's success, Willard became widely known and respected. Her best-selling textbooks—in geography, history, and even astronomy—made her wealthy as well. After Dr. Willard's death in 1825, Emma made a second, unsuccessful marriage in 1838. She left her husband after nine months and returned to the Troy Seminary, where she worked on behalf of educational reform until her death at age eighty-four. In 1895, the Troy Female Seminary was renamed the Emma Willard School.

Ruth Ashby

Sacajawea

(c. 1789–c. 1812?)

Legends abound about Sacajawea, a Shoshone who won respect from both Native and European Americans for her skill and courage in exploring the American West. Our best record of her achievements comes from the journals of explorers Lewis and Clark, who believed she was critical to the success of their famous expedition.

Sacajawea was born in about 1789 in what is now Idaho, in the Rocky Mountains. When she was about ten years old, she and several other women and children were taken captive by a war party of Hidatsa Indians. For the next five years, Sacajawea lived as a slave in Mandan Indian villages near the Missouri River. Then she and a friend, Otter Woman, were either purchased or won in a game by a French-Canadian trader named

Sacajawea, her son Pomp on her back, leads the way to the Pacific Ocean. Bronze statue by Alice Cooper, 1905.

Touissant Charbonnier. He married Otter Woman, later taking Sacajawea as his second wife.

In 1804, a United States army expedition called the Corps of Discovery arrived in the Mandan villages. Headed by Meriwether Lewis and William Clark, they had orders from President Thomas Jefferson to explore the land west of the Mississippi, which had just been purchased from France. Charbonnier joined the expedition as an interpreter.

A year later, when the expedition took off, Sacajawea accompanied her husband, taking along their newborn baby, Jean Baptiste, whom Sacajawea called Pomp, which meant "leader of men" in the Shoshone language. Skilled at surviving in the harsh terrain of the Shoshone homeland, she soon became a valuable member of the mission.

Her presence was a comfort to both the white men and the Indians. As supplies dwindled and the trek became more arduous, she kept up the men's morale and taught them how to supplement their diet with local plants. On several occasions, Sacajawea served as interpreter to the Mandan and Shoshone, conveying Lewis and Clark's message of peace and prosperous trade. Although white and Indian relations later became hostile and bitter, Lewis and Clark are still generally well regarded by the tribes they encountered.

At one of the most dangerous junctures of their trip, with supplies nearly gone, the expedition encountered a group of Shoshone led by Sacajawea's brother, Chief Cameahwait. At Sacajawea's urging, Cameahwait provided the horses, guides, and food the expedition needed to cross the Rocky Mountains. It was an extremely difficult trek—one they would probably not have survived without Cameahwait's help. Snow fell and packhorses slipped on the icy trails. The expedition ran out of food, and members were forced to eat horse meat. Finally, the half-starved group reached a tributary of the Columbia River that flowed into the Pacific Ocean. Two months later, in November 1805, William Clark wrote in his journal, "Ocian [sic] in view! O! the joy!"

After the expedition's return, Clark gave a section of land outside of St. Louis to Sacajawea and Charbonnier and offered to educate their son, Pomp. Although accounts are unclear, it is believed that the couple farmed this land for a time, eventually returning to Sacajawea's homeland. One account says she lived until about age twenty-five. Another tradition maintains that she lived until 1884 among the Shoshone of Wyoming and died at age ninety-five, revered by her people.

Today, rivers, mountains, lakes, and even Girl Scout camps are named after Sacajawea. Her exploits have captured the imagination of Indian and non-Indian alike, just as her life joined the worlds of the two peoples.

Deborah Gore Ohrn

Sarah Grimké

(1792–1873)

Angelina Grimké

(1805–1879)

"But perhaps you will be ready to query, why appeal to women *on this subject? We do not make the laws which perpetuate slavery. . . . To this I reply, I know you do not make the laws, but I also know that* you are the wives and mothers, the sisters and daughters of those who do; *and if you really suppose you can do nothing to overthrow slavery, you are greatly mistaken."*
—Angelina Grimké, "Appeal to the Christian
Women of the South," 1836

This remarkable document is the only antislavery work written by a white Southern woman to other Southern women. Its author, Angelina Grimké, had grown up in a slave-holding household in Charleston, South Carolina. Together with her sister Sarah, she traveled north to become an ardent abolitionist and supporter of women's rights. What motivated the Grimké sisters to defy their friends and family and rebel against their upbringing?

Sarah and Angelina were the sixth and fourteenth children of Judge John and Mary Grimké, prominent members of the Charleston aristocracy. Both their large, well run household in town and their plantation in the country depended on the labor of slaves. Twelve years older than Angelina, Sarah realized early the injustices of the slave system. As a child, she consciously defied South Carolina law by trying to teach her maid to read. Yet, when she herself was denied a good education, she felt even more keenly the disadvantages of being born female. To give herself a purpose, Sarah asked to be Angelina's godmother when she was born. For the rest of her life, Sarah was partly a mother to her younger sister.

After going to the North in 1818 to nurse her dying father, Sarah stayed with some Quakers. Three years later, she moved to Philadelphia and joined the Society of Friends. Also disillusioned with the Southern slave culture, Angelina joined her there in 1829.

In the 1830s, the antislavery crusade was sweeping the North. In 1835, Angelina took the first step on the road to activism by writing a letter to abolitionist William Lloyd Garrison, which he printed in his newspaper, *The Liberator*. She followed this with an "Appeal to the Christian Women of the South," which urged Southern women to use their moral influence to denounce slavery and free any slaves they could. Sarah wrote a parallel "Epistle to the Clergy of the Southern States." For these writings, the sisters were threatened with imprisonment if they ever returned to Charleston. They never saw their birthplace again.

Soon antislavery societies were inviting them to speak to small groups of women throughout the Northeast. Angelina, in particular, became known as an eloquent speaker, and men as well as women flocked to her lectures. Her speaking career culminated in 1838 when she became the first female ever to address a state legislative committee in Massachusetts.

Many people were shocked that women would speak before a public assembly. In 1837, a group of Massachusetts ministers wrote a letter denouncing women reformers and preachers. In reply, Sarah wrote her *Letters on the Equality of the Sexes and the Condition of Women* (1838). These letters are one of the first declarations of the rights of women in America.

In 1838, Angelina married fellow abolitionist Theodore Weld, and the sisters' active work as reformers was over. Angelina suffered ill health after the birth of her three children, and Sarah was needed to help her raise them. To earn a living, Sarah and the Welds farmed and ran a successful school.

The Grimké sisters always remained true to their principles, and to the ends of their lives continued to support abolition, women's rights, and later, the rights of freedmen and women.

Ruth Ashby

La Pola

(1795–1817)

"Although I am a woman and young, I have more than enough courage to suffer this death and a thousand more."
—Statement before execution, 1817

A young seamstress from a mountain village, La Pola's idealism and courage made her a national heroine in the South American nation of Colombia. La Pola's real name was Policarpa Salavarrieta. Born in 1795, she grew up with her father, brothers, and a sister in the small village of Guaduas. By the time La Pola was fifteen, she was an independent young woman who worked with her sister as a seamstress and could read and write. But her quiet world would soon be shattered by political upheaval.

Spain had ruled much of South America since the arrival of Spanish explorers in the New World in the fifteenth century. Under Spanish rule, society was divided into three racial groups, which determined access to money and power. The lowest group, composed of Native Americans, blacks, and those of mixed race, could hold only menial jobs. Creoles, or American-born whites, could study law or enter the Church or government but could only hold lower positions. Since the Spanish ruled, Peninsulars, or Spanish-born whites, were the highest-ranking group. They held leadership positions in the Church and government. In the early 1800s, Creoles like La Pola and her family were becoming restless under the Spanish system. Increasingly, they believed that they were entitled to the same opportunities as Peninsulars.

As a teenager, La Pola decided that Spanish rule was wrong. She was influenced by her two older brothers, who were monks in Santa Fé, the regional capital. Their teacher, Friar Diego Padilla, was a powerful opponent of Spanish rule. La Pola's brothers were converted to his beliefs and passed many of his writings on to their sisters in Guaduas.

Then, in 1810, when La Pola was fifteen, the Creoles overthrew the royal government in Santa Fé and set up their own government. For six years, all was peaceful. But the Spanish returned and reconquered Santa Fé in 1816. The new Spanish governor declared martial law. Hundreds of known and suspected Creole revolutionaries were executed without trial.

La Pola decided to resist and joined an underground network. As a seamstress, she was able to move in and out of Spanish homes. As she sewed quietly, the young woman listened closely for news of troop movements or other secrets. She also supported the Creole guerrillas who continued to fight, secretly giving them food and rest at her home.

Because of the accuracy of her reports, she was given increasingly danger-ous assignments. She moved to Santa Fé, where she developed contacts in the Spanish army, urging Creoles who had been drafted to mutiny. But when the Spanish captured spies carrying a list of resistance leaders, La Pola knew that she was in danger. Before going into hiding, she first arranged for the escape of several revolutionaries by bribing the guards at their prison.

Two weeks later, the Spanish found and arrested La Pola. After a brief trial, she was condemned to death by a firing squad at the age of twenty-two. She told a friend, "Don't cry for us, little Lopez. It will be a relief to get away from these tyrants, these wild beasts, these monsters." She was brave and defiant to the end. Two years later, the rebels drove the Spanish from Santa Fé. Today, a statue in Bogotá, the capital of Colombia, com-memorates La Pola as a great patriot.

Elisabeth Keating

Sojourner Truth

(c. 1797–1883)

"That man over there says that women need to be helped into carriages and lifted over ditches and to have the best everywhere. Nobody ever helps me into carriages, over mud puddles, or gets me any best place. Ain't I a woman? Look at me! Look at my arm. I have plowed. And I have planted. And I have gathered into barns. And no man could head me. And ain't I a woman?"
—Akron Women's Rights Convention, 1851

The woman who called herself Sojourner Truth was born a slave in upstate New York sometime at the end of the eighteenth century. She was named Isabella Hardenberg, but her last name was not her own, for slaves were given their masters' names. Her childhood was full of hardship and sorrow. By the time Isabella was born, her mother, Ma-Ma Betts, had already had eleven children die or be sold away.

Isabella had several masters—and last names—when she was young. One of them married her to another slave named Tom, with whom she had at least five children. In 1827, New York abolished slavery, and two years later Isabella went to New York City with two of her children to seek employment as a domestic. While she was there, she joined a spiritual community for two years. Isabella had been deeply religious since childhood.

Finally, she knew her time had come. At the age of forty-six, Isabella renamed herself Sojourner Truth and walked out of New York City on a religious mission. Across Long Island

The dignified Sojourner Truth in her gray Quaker dress and white cap and shawl.

Women and Slavery

Slavery is as old as civilization itself. Slaves built the Egyptian pyramids and the Hanging Gardens of Babylon, the Aztec city of Tenochtitlán and the Great Wall of China. Most slaves throughout history have not been male, however, but female. This is because most males captured in war were killed. Women and female children were kept to be exploited for sexual pleasure and their reproductive capacity as well as for labor.

Because female slaves (especially girls) are the lowest members of the social hierarchy, they have the least power. Like male slaves, females have no claim to their own children, who belong to their owners. But unlike males, females are often at the sexual disposal of their owners or overseers as well as their slave mates, to whom they are rarely legally married.

African slavery in the Americas began in the sixteenth century, when ships first brought African slaves to the Caribbean. It disappeared officially with its abolition in Brazil in 1888. Chattel slavery in Africa has lasted longer, however. From the sixteenth to the nineteenth century, at least two out of every three slaves in sub-Saharan Africa were women, and females fetched a much higher price on the internal slave market than men did. Scholars have suggested that in Africa, women slaves were more desirable than men because it was perceived that they worked harder. Although slavery in Africa was often less harsh than in America because slaves in Africa had a greater chance to assimilate, slaves usually lost their own families and cultures.

For economic reasons, it has proved very difficult to eradicate slavery in some parts of Africa. The last country to abolish slavery was Mauritania in 1980. But human rights groups report that as many as ninety thousand slaves remain in Mauritania and the Sudan. And the majority of them are women and children.

and up to New England she traveled on foot, preaching, singing, and spreading her message of humanity.

Truth joined the anti-slavery community in Massachusetts and met the leading abolitionists of the day. She became a noted speaker at abolitionist and women's rights meetings. Listeners were mesmerized by her commanding presence (she was more than six feet tall) and deep, musical voice. Though she could neither read nor write, Truth had an excellent memory and the gift for putting complex thoughts into clear, everyday language. She had memorized most of the Bible and could quote from it at length. To support herself, she sold copies of the book she had dictated, *The Narrative of Sojourner Truth.* Her motto was "I sell the shadow to support the substance."

When the Civil War erupted, Truth continued to speak out against slavery and went to Washington, D.C., where she met Abraham Lincoln. She worked with the National Freedman's Relief Association to help ex-slaves find employment and a place to live. After the war, she lobbied for their migration to the Midwest.

By the end of her life, Sojourner Truth had become a legend. She died at age eighty-six at her home in Battle Creek, Michigan, surrounded by her surviving children and grandchildren. More than a thousand people attended her funeral.

Ruth Ashby

Catharine Beecher

(1800–1878)

"Let every woman become so cultivated and refined in intellect, that her taste and judgement will be respected . . . so unassuming and unambitious, that collision and competition will be banished . . . then, the fathers, the husbands, and the sons, will find an influence thrown around them, to which they will yield not only willingly but proudly."
—"Essay on Slavery and Abolitionism with Reference to the Duty of American Females," 1837

In nineteenth-century America, Catharine Beecher was the primary spokeswoman for the idea that men and women were meant to perform different roles in society. To men fell the business of politics, war, and commerce; to women, the equally important tasks of nurturing, child rearing, and housekeeping. Yet, Catharine Beecher herself never married and was not a homemaker. Paradoxically, her importance as a writer and an educator lay outside what was then called "woman's sphere."

Catharine was the first of nine children born to the celebrated Congregational clergyman Lyman Beecher and his first wife, Roxana Foote. One of the most influential families of the century, the Beechers also included writer Harriet Beecher Stowe, who was Catharine's sister, and the minister Henry Ward Beecher, who was her brother.

Growing up primarily in Hartford, Connecticut, Catharine was a lively, outgoing girl, always the leader in any social gathering. Like other educated middle-class women, she expected eventually to marry and have children. Yet, when her fiancé died, she decided to use her superb intelligence and energy to create a different kind of life for herself.

In 1823, Catharine and her sister Mary opened the Hartford Female Seminary. It was the first step in Catharine's lifelong crusade to promote women's education in moral virtue, domestic science, and teaching. She believed that through teaching, women could extend their moral influence from the family to the whole of American society. In 1852, she organized the American Women's Educational Association to establish colleges for teacher training.

Beecher's most lasting contribution came with the publication of *A Treatise on Domestic Economy* (1841). In it, she offered practical advice on cooking, cleaning, child rearing, gardening, household medicine, and nutrition. She supplied designs for labor-saving devices to help with housework. For females who nursed sick members of the family at home, she even included illustrations of the systems of the human body. The treatise was reprinted fourteen times before the 1869 publication of the enlarged *American Women's Home,* which Catharine wrote with her sister Harriet.

In her home economics books and other writings, Beecher celebrated women's domestic responsibilities. Whereas some nineteenth-century feminists wanted to expand or change women's role in society, Catharine Beecher wanted to make their traditional role more important than ever. She knew women must be educated to carry out their practical and moral duties as well as possible.

Until the end of her life, Catharine Beecher continued to write and speak about women's health, education, and place in the home. When she died at age seventy-eight, Henry Ward Beecher wrote of his sister: "Her influence was very great. Few persons, even in the ministry, had influenced as many minds as she had."

Ruth Ashby

Dorothea Dix

(1802–1887)

"I proceed, gentlemen, briefly to call your attention to the present
state of insane persons confined within this Commonwealth,
in cages, closets, cellars, stalls, pens; chained, naked, beaten
with rods, and lashed into obedience!"
—"A Memorial to the Massachusetts Legislature," 1843

Dorothea Dix was thirty-nine years old and in poor health when she visited a jail in East Cambridge, Massachusetts, where mentally ill patients were locked up with regular criminals. She was so appalled by the suffering she witnessed that for the next two years she traveled to almost five hundred towns throughout the state and recorded the brutal conditions in which people who were considered insane were kept. It was the start of Dix's lifelong crusade to improve the lot of the mentally ill in North America and Europe.

Dorothea was born in Hampton, Maine, to Joseph Dix, the son of a doctor, and his wife, Mary Bigelow. Dorothea's father was emotionally unbalanced and an alcoholic; her mother, eighteen years older than her husband, suffered from blinding headaches and was unable to care for her children. The family was so unstable that in later years Dorothea would say, "I never had a childhood."

When she was twelve, the family separated and Dorothea and her two brothers were sent to live with her wealthy grandmother in Boston. Soon Dorothea decided that she wanted to devote her life to teaching children, both rich and poor. At fifteen, she started her own school.

Dorothea Dix, c. 1849

Unfortunately, she fell ill with tuberculosis and finally had to abandon teaching. She was recuperating when, in 1841, she began to investigate the situation of the mentally disturbed in Massachusetts. Her findings shocked the public, and in 1843, the legislature passed a bill to provide additional, more humane accommodations for the insane.

This first victory prompted Dix to try for more. Over the next three years, she traveled ten thousand miles across the United States and Canada, collecting statistics on every mentally ill person in every state. Her findings she then presented to the state legislatures. Wherever she went, people were impressed by her high intelligence, earnestness, and devotion to her cause. Throughout her life, Dix was able to found or improve thirty-two hospitals for the mentally ill in this country alone.

In 1854, Dix went to Europe, where she continued to investigate hospitals and encourage a new awareness in the care of the mentally ill. She traveled through eleven countries bearing her message of mercy and understanding.

Because she was so hardworking and effective, Dix was appointed the first superintendent of United States Army nurses when the Civil War broke out in 1861. Throughout the four long years of the war, she directed nurses, organized hospitals, and managed supplies.

Dorothea Dix always remained true to her belief that the mentally ill deserve the same care and compassion as other, more fortunate human beings. When she was eighty-five, she died in Trenton, New Jersey, in a private apartment in the first hospital she had ever built.

Ruth Ashby

Margaret Fuller

(1810–1850)

"We would have every arbitrary barrier thrown down. We would have every path laid open to women as freely as to men."
—"The Great Lawsuit," 1843

Writer, teacher, and feminist, Margaret Fuller was the foremost female intellectual in America during the first half of the nineteenth century. She was born the first child of Timothy and Margaret Fuller in Cambridgeport, Massachusetts. Her father, a lawyer and politician, took early charge of his precocious daughter's education. Extraordinarily bright, Margaret was reading Latin verses by the age of six.

Soon she was studying Greek, German, and philosophy. Yet her rigorous education isolated her from other girls her own age. When she was eleven, her father tried to remedy her social backwardness by sending her to a girls' school. But Margaret had trouble fitting in and spent most of her adolescence at home, teaching her younger brothers and sisters and studying on her own.

Margaret was expected to be first of all a "lady": graceful, deferential, and devoted to her family. Yet, by nature and training she was an intellectual, as eager for achievement as her male contemporaries. Until the last years of her life, Margaret experienced a continual conflict between her dual roles as lady and self-made woman of letters.

A young Margaret Fuller, c. 1830

When her father died in 1835, Margaret helped support the family by teaching in Boston and Providence. She became one of a group of Boston intellectuals who were known as the Transcendentalists. They emphasized self-reliance and the individual's ability to intuit truth through nature.

In 1940, Fuller became editor of the Transcendental journal, *The Dial.* For this, she wrote "The Great Lawsuit," a plea for women's political rights and intellectual fulfillment. Later, she turned the essay into a book, *Woman in the Nineteenth Century* (1845).

Beginning in 1839, Fuller held a series of Conversations for Boston women. She picked broad topics in education, philosophy, mythology, and the fine arts for the participants, who were not used to discussing intellectual matters. Fuller was a brilliant discussion leader, and the Conversations continued for five winters.

In 1844, Fuller moved to New York to write literary and social criticism for Horace Greeley's *New York Tribune.* She sailed to Europe two years later to become America's first female correspondent. After visiting Scotland, England, and France, she settled in Italy in 1847.

There she met a young Italian nobleman, the Marchese Giovanni Angelo Ossoli. They fell in love, had a son, and were secretly married sometime during 1848. With Ossoli, Fuller became caught up in the Italian revolution and ran a soldiers' hospital in Rome. She began writing an eyewitness account of the revolution.

After the Italian republic failed, the Ossoli family set sail for America. Their ship struck the rocks off the shores of Fire Island, New York. All three were drowned on July 19, 1850. Margaret Fuller's manuscript about the Italian revolution has never been recovered.

Ruth Ashby

Harriet Beecher Stowe

(1811–1896)

"I will write something. I will if I live."
—1850

In September 1850, the United States Congress passed the Fugitive Slave Act, requiring all citizens to aid in the capture of runaway slaves. Across the North, people protested. No one was more outraged than author Harriet Beecher Stowe, who was determined to write something about this "miserable wicked fugitive slave business." Many say the book she wrote helped start the Civil War.

Born in Litchfield, Connecticut, Harriet Beecher Stowe was the seventh of the nine children of the famous Congregational minister Lyman Beecher and his first wife, Roxana Foote. The crusading, reformist Beechers were one of the best-known families of the American nineteenth century. Besides Harriet, the Beecher children included educator Catharine Beecher and preacher Henry Ward Beecher.

Known as the "genius" of the family, Harriet was a small, absentminded child much given to daydreaming. She was educated at the local female academy and her

Harriet Beecher Stowe

sister Catharine's Hartford Female Seminary, where she was first a student and then a teacher. She continued teaching in Cincinnati, where the family moved in 1832. There she met and married Calvin Ellis Stowe, a professor of biblical literature, and gave birth to six of her seven children, one of whom died of cholera in 1849.

Stowe's first book was *Primary Geography for Children* (1833). Soon she was publishing domestic stories and sketches of life in New England, some of them collected in *The Mayflower* (1843).

In 1850, the Stowes moved to Brunswick, Maine, where Harriet began *Uncle Tom's Cabin; or, Life Among the Lowly*. Serialized in an antislavery weekly from June 1851 to April 1852 and published in March 1852, the novel was an immediate success. It became the biggest best-seller in nineteenth-century America and was translated into at least twenty-three languages. For decades, it inspired plays, songs, almanacs, toys, wallpapers, and china knickknacks.

By turns dramatic, humorous, and sentimental, *Uncle Tom's Cabin* is a sprawling, romantic novel about the evils of slavery and the redemptive quality of Christian love. The title character, Tom, is a Christlike black slave who resists white tyranny to the death. Stowe wanted to reach the hearts of her audience, and she did. Readers were thrilled when Eliza Harris escaped from slavery across the frozen Ohio River; they cried at the death of saintly Little Eva. Stowe tried to make her "pictures" of slavery so vivid that they would stay with her readers long after they had put down her book.

She was so effective that in 1862 Abraham Lincoln greeted the five-foot-tall author with the words, "So you're the little woman who wrote the book that started this great war!" For those who doubted the authenticity of her account, Stowe published *A Key to Uncle Tom's Cabin* (1853), a collection of documents about slavery.

Now one of the most famous authors in the world, Stowe went on a triumphant tour of England in 1853. She spent the rest of her life writing to support herself and her family. In 1856, she published another, less successful antislavery novel, *Dred: A Tale of the Great Dismal Swamp*. This was followed by numerous short stories and novels, among them *The Minister's Wooing* (1859) and *Oldtown Folks* (1869).

Calvin and Harriet Beecher Stowe eventually settled in Hartford, Connecticut, where she died at age eighty-five. She had used her considerable gifts to help erase the foremost social evil of her day. Few writers have had as much direct effect on their time as did Harriet Beecher Stowe.

Ruth Ashby

Harriet Tubman

(1815–1913)

"There were two things I had a right to, liberty and death.
If I could not have one, I would have the other,
for no man should take me alive."
—Remark on her escape from slavery, 1849

Harriet Tubman, a famous figure in American Civil War history, was a "conductor" of the Underground Railroad, a network of people, black and white, who helped slaves escape from the South into the free North and Canada by offering them safe hiding places and food.

Harriet Green was born into slavery on a plantation on the eastern shore of Maryland, where she worked as a nursemaid, field hand, and cook. The master often criticized her work, and he once hit her in the head with a brick, fracturing her skull. The injury caused Harriet to experience periods of uncontrolled sleepiness and even blackouts for the rest of her life.

In 1844, Harriet married another slave, John Tubman. When the owner of her plantation died in 1849, a rumor circulated that she would be sold to a plantation in another state. It was then that Harriet decided to escape to one of the eighteen free northern states. When she reached the Mason-Dixon line— the boundary between Delaware and Pennsylvania that divided the slave states from the free states—she said, "I looked at my hands to see if I was the same person now [that] I was free. . . . I felt like I was in heaven."

Tubman lived in Philadelphia for one year, working in hotels, saving her money, and thinking about the family and friends she'd left behind. When she heard that her sister and her two children were going to be sold to another plantation, she returned south to engineer their escape. They traveled by wagon, boat, and foot, hiding in barns, shops, and other safe places along the route that became known as the Underground Railroad. Tubman went south once again to free her two brothers, and in 1857, she helped her elderly parents escape. Her husband, John, had remarried in her absence and chose to stay in Maryland.

In the decade preceding the Civil War, Tubman helped more than three hundred people gain their freedom. Although she was a fugitive and considered an outlaw, she always managed to escape her pursuers. Under the Fugitive Slave Act, Tubman knew she could be punished or killed if she was caught, but she also knew that she had to take the risk. Though the Underground Railroad was not really a railroad, Tubman and other conductors used railroad terms and gospel songs as signals of safety or danger. "On my underground railroad I never ran my train off the track and I never lost a passenger," she said.

General Tubman

Harriet Tubman's exploits as conductor on the Underground Railroad gave her the nickname "General Tubman." During the Civil War, she provided real military service as a spy, scout, and nurse for the North. With the help of contacts throughout the South, she was able to obtain Confederate military information for the Union Army. Her most daring adventure was to lead raids against Confederate plantations in South Carolina. In 1863, she rescued nearly eight hundred slaves along the Combahee River. After the war, friends tried to obtain a government pension for her but were unsuccessful.

During the Civil War, which began in 1861, Tubman's knowledge of southern terrain was invaluable to the Union. She was able to gain the trust of black Confederate soldiers and learn their military secrets. Tubman also served as a nurse on the battlefield and at a hospital in Virginia. After the war ended, Congress ratified the Thirteenth Amendment, which abolished slavery in the United States. The Underground Railroad would never have to be used again.

In her later years, Tubman cared for her parents and founded a home for the aged near Auburn, New York. She worked toward establishing African-American schools in the South and was involved in the growth of the African Methodist Episcopal (AME) Church, a powerful organization in the African-American community.

Tubman died in 1913 of pneumonia. Her friend Frederick Douglass, the abolitionist and founder of the American Anti-Slavery Society, summed up Harriet Tubman's life best in a letter to her: "I know of no one who has willingly encountered more perils and hardships to serve our enslaved people than you have."

Judy Gitenstein

Elizabeth Cady Stanton

(1815–1902)

"We hold these truths to be self-evident: that all men and women are created equal."
—"Declaration of Rights and Sentiments," 1848

At the Seneca Falls women's rights convention of 1848, Elizabeth Cady Stanton adapted the Declaration of Independence to the feminist cause. The "Declaration of Rights and Sentiments" declared that there must be an end to discrimination based on sex. It would be 70 years before the Nineteenth Amendment gave women the right to vote, and 120 years before women were widely accepted into most professions. In many ways, the social revolution that Cady Stanton called for in 1848 is still being fought today.

Elizabeth Cady was born to well-to-do parents in Johnstown, New York. Her father, a lawyer and later a United States congressman, often brought her to his law office, where she first learned about the legal discrimination against women. Elizabeth attended Troy Female Seminary (later the Emma Willard School) and in 1840 married Henry Brewster Stanton, a noted abolitionist. She shocked the

Elizabeth Cady Stanton speaking before a Senate committee on women's suffrage, 1871.

Lucretia Mott

When Elizabeth Cady Stanton and Lucretia Mott (1793–1880) organized the Seneca Falls Convention in 1848, Mott had been active in American social reform for nearly forty years. Born into a Quaker community in Massachusetts, at age seventeen she married James Mott, who shared her humanitarian beliefs. Together, they became actively involved with the abolitionist movement, risking their lives to hide escaping slaves in their home. When the American Anti-Slavery Society was formed in 1833 and refused to accept women, Mott helped found the Philadelphia Female Anti-Slavery Society. Petite and gentle in appearance, Mott was an eloquent speaker with a sharp tongue and liberal ideas.

After slavery was abolished in 1863, Mott continued to work for women's rights and voting and other citizenship rights for African-Americans until her death.

presiding minister at the wedding ceremony when she promised to "love, to honor," but not "to obey" her husband.

Participation in the anti-slavery movement introduced Cady Stanton to many of the leading reformers of the day. It also revealed that not even in radical circles were women treated as equals. At the World Antislavery Convention in London in 1840, women were not allowed to be seated with the male delegates. Cady Stanton immediately made a pact with the Quaker feminist Lucretia Mott to hold a women's rights convention when they returned home.

Their cause was delayed eight years while Cady Stanton studied law and history on her own, raised seven children, and ran a household. In 1848, she and Mott organized a convention in Seneca Falls, New York, which was attended by more than one hundred men and women. The American women's rights movement had been born.

In 1851, Cady Stanton met Susan B. Anthony and began an association that lasted for the next fifty-two years. Together they spearheaded the suffragist movement. Cady Stanton, a brilliant speaker and writer, furnished the ideas; Anthony took charge of the organization. They co-founded the National Woman Suffrage Association (later the National American Woman Suffrage Association), of which Cady Stanton was president on and off until 1892.

At the end of the nineteenth century, the women's rights movement had become narrowly focused on the right to vote. Yet, Cady Stanton's feminist concerns were much broader. She wrote and lectured on the reform of marriage, divorce, and property laws, child-rearing practices, religious discrimination, social injustice, and women's rights to their own bodies. The last years of her life were spent writing her autobiography, *Eighty Years and More* (1898), and *The Women's Bible* (1895), a series of feminist commentaries on the Scriptures. At age seventy-four, Elizabeth Cady Stanton could say truthfully, "I get more radical as I grow older."

On November 12, 1895, six thousand people gathered at the Metropolitan Opera House to celebrate Cady Stanton's eightieth birthday. Addressing the crowd, she said, "I am well aware that all these public demonstrations are not so much tributes to me as an individual as to the great idea I represent—the enfranchisement of women." Seven years later, Elizabeth Cady Stanton died at her home in New York City.

Ruth Ashby

Charlotte Brontë

(1816–1855)

Emily Brontë

(1818–1848)

"Women are supposed to be very calm generally, but women feel just as men feel; they need exercise for their faculties and a field for their efforts as much as their brothers do . . . and it is narrow-minded in their more privileged fellow-creatures to say that they ought to confine themselves to making puddings and knitting stockings, to playing on the piano and embroidering bags."
—Charlotte Brontë, *Jane Eyre*, 1847

The story of the brilliant Brontë sisters begins and ends in Haworth, England, on the bleak Yorkshire moors, where Charlotte and Emily's father, Patrick, was the local Anglican clergyman. After their mother, Maria, died in 1821, Aunt Elizabeth Branwell joined the household to help raise the six children.

In 1824, Charlotte and Emily left home to join their two older sisters, Maria and Elizabeth, at a school for clergymen's daughters. Conditions were very harsh, and soon Maria and Elizabeth succumbed to illness and died. Charlotte and Emily were sent home and spent most of their remaining childhood in Haworth. There, in the lonely parsonage set in the desolate countryside, they discovered their lifelong passion—writing.

When Charlotte was ten and Emily eight, their father gave their brother, Branwell, a box of wooden soldiers. Immediately, the children named the little men and began to weave stories around them. For more than the next ten years, Charlotte, Branwell, Emily, and their youngest sister, Anne, lived in the heady world of their imagination, peopled by romantic heroes and adventurous heroines. The four children wrote stories, poems, and plays in tiny booklets about 2¼ by 1¼ inches, in a small, almost indecipherable script. By the time she was fourteen, Charlotte had produced twenty-two miniature volumes of writing.

The family did not have much money, and the girls knew they would eventually have to earn a living. Impelled by a strong sense of duty, Charlotte tried being both a teacher and a governess. Her shyness and extreme sensitivity made it difficult for her to keep any position long. Even more reserved, Emily resigned from teaching after a mere six months.

Their dream was to start a school at Haworth so the family could be together. To prepare themselves, in 1842 Charlotte and Emily traveled to Brussels to study foreign languages. There Charlotte developed a romantic attachment to her teacher, M. Héger, which caused her great pain. When at last the sisters were both back at home, they could find no pupils willing to come to their remote village.

The situation was becoming increasingly desperate. Their father was growing old and blind, and their brother, Branwell, once the bright hope of the family, had become a dissipated alcoholic. Then, in 1845, Charlotte came across some of Emily's poems. Struck by their passion and originality, she sent them to a publisher together with some of her own and Anne's. The poems were published in 1846 under the names Currer (Charlotte), Ellis (Emily), and Acton (Anne) Bell. (The sisters had adopted pseudonyms to keep their identity, and their sex, a secret.) Encouraged by their success, they quickly completed the novels they were working on. Ellis Bell's *Wuthering Heights* and Currer Bell's *Jane Eyre* were both published in 1847.

Anne, Emily, and Charlotte Brontë as painted by their brother Branwell,
c. 1834. He has painted himself out of the picture.

Wuthering Heights met with initial criticism for its dark, brooding subject matter. A tale of obsession and revenge set in the wild moorlands of Yorkshire, it reflects Emily's spiritual intensity and her mystic bond with the natural world. Today *Wuthering Heights* is regarded as one of the masterpieces of English literature.

Jane Eyre, however, was an immediate success. Drawn from Charlotte's own experiences, it is the dramatic story of the romance between a spirited governess and her employer, the mysterious Mr. Rochester. Readers responded wholeheartedly to Jane's life story, from her lonely childhood to her final triumphal union with her "master."

Tragically, Branwell, Emily, and Anne all died of tuberculosis within nine months of one another between 1848 and 1849. Charlotte was left alone with her father. She spent the next years writing *Shirley* (1849) and *Villette*

(1851). By now, the literary world of England knew the identity of "Currer Bell," and Charlotte went to London as the guest of her publisher to meet other writers and critics.

Charlotte had declined three offers of marriage in her life before she accepted her father's assistant, Arthur Bell Nicholls, in 1854. She was very happy in her brief marriage but died of sickness due to pregnancy when she was only thirty-nine.

Charlotte and Emily Brontë bequeathed us books of great power and beauty. We shall never know what they might have created had they lived longer.

Ruth Ashby

Maria Mitchell

(1818–1889)

"[Astronomical] observations . . . are peculiarly adapted to women. . . .
The eye that directs a needle in the delicate meshes of embroidery
will equally well bisect a star with the spider web of the micrometer."
—Remarks to students at Vassar, 1878

"How much science needs women," astronomer Maria Mitchell used to say. Science definitely needed her. At a time when a woman's day was divided between sewing and cooking, Mitchell became the first woman astronomer in America and the first woman to be admitted to the American Academy of Arts and Sciences.

In the whaling community of Nantucket, Massachusetts, where Maria Mitchell grew up, life revolved around the ocean and the stars that enabled sailors to navigate its waters. She learned about navigation from her father, who taught her how to adjust seaman's chronometers (extremely accurate timepieces). She also learned astronomy through her father's love of the sky. In 1831, she helped her father set up the telescope in readiness for an eclipse of the sun. While her father observed the eclipse, Maria "gave the count," that is, counted the seconds by the clock so that the exact time of the eclipse could be recorded. This measurement also enabled her father to calculate the longitude of Nantucket.

Mitchell's education came from working as the librarian of the Nantucket library. There she could listen in on lectures covering all the scientific interests of the day. At night, she continued sky watching from the rooftop of her family's home. On October 1, 1847, she saw

Maria Mitchell and her students at Vassar College, c. 1878.

something she had never seen before. Just above the star Polaris, there was a faint light where there had previously been a blank. Maria Mitchell had discovered a new comet.

From that moment, Mitchell's life changed. For her discovery, she was awarded a gold medal by the king of Denmark and became world famous. In 1848, she was the first woman to be elected to the American Academy of Arts and Sciences, and in 1850, she became the first woman member of the American Association for the Advancement of Science. She was employed to work on the *American Ephemeris and Nautical Almanac*, which helped seamen find their way on the open sea by predicting the movement of the stars one or more years in advance.

In 1865, Mitchell joined the faculty of the newly formed Vassar College as professor of astronomy and director of the college observatory. She was an unconventional teacher, refusing to give grades or report student absences. She was also a strong influence on her students, some of whom followed her into the sciences. Maria taught at Vassar for twenty-three years, until a year before her death in 1889.

Ruth Ashby

Clara Schumann

(1819–1896)

"The practice of art is, after all, a great part of my inner self. To me, it is the very air I breathe."
—Letter to Robert Schumann, 1852

Pianist, teacher, composer, and devoted wife, Clara Schumann had a great influence on nineteenth-century classical music. Throughout her life, she tried to balance career and family and often made the decisions traditionally reserved for the husband in nineteenth-century society.

Clara Wieck was born on September 13, 1819, in Leipzig, Germany. Her father, Friedrich, was a well known music teacher who oversaw every aspect of his family's life. A tyrant, he made life so unbearable at home that his wife obtained a divorce when Clara was five. Nineteenth-century German law stipulated that the children belonged to the husband, so Clara and her two younger brothers were forced to remain with their father.

Friedrich Wieck gave his five-year-old daughter piano lessons. It is fortunate that Clara truly enjoyed playing the piano because her life would have been miserable otherwise. She had no close friends. There was almost no conversation in the Wieck home, and Clara could barely distinguish spoken words. She was actually considered to be deaf until she was eight. On the other hand, she became a musical prodigy who could read musical notes before she could read words.

Her piano playing advanced quickly, and Clara gave her first public recital when she was nine years old. By the time she was eleven, she had composed four pieces of music.

One of her father's students was Robert Schumann, a gifted pianist whom she met when she was twelve and Robert was twenty-one. They became close over the next four years. When Clara was sixteen, she and Robert declared their love for each other.

Clara's father was furious about the relationship and refused even to acknowledge Robert. Despite Wieck's attempts to keep them apart, the lovers managed to communicate through letters and secret meetings. They were secretly engaged when Clara was eighteen. Robert took Wieck to court, and finally the marriage took place on September 12, 1840. Clara had earned her dowry by playing a concert tour.

In spite of their passionate love for each other, Robert did not encourage Clara to perform. He wanted her to stay at home and be a wife and mother. At first, Clara did as he wished. Instead of performing, she had eight children, (four were to survive) and edited the music he composed—and composed some pieces of her own which were published under Robert's name. Yet, she was torn. Eventually, she hired nurses to take care of the children and began to tour again. In 1852, she gave fifteen concerts. At first, Robert traveled with her, but he became angry and jealous of her growing fame. His pride led him to drink, and he became depressed.

Eventually, it became necessary for Clara to take over the breadwinning role in the family. Robert's emotional instability led to several nervous breakdowns. In 1853, he was put into an institution after a suicide attempt and diagnosed as manic-depressive. Clara visited him often and was with him when he died on July 29, 1856.

After Robert's death, Clara Schumann saw to it that her husband's name and work would be remembered. A memorial to Robert Schumann was erected in Bonn. Clara also published an edition of Robert's piano music, complete with his notes on how each piece should be played.

Clara needed to continue supporting her children, and so she began to give lessons and to perform again. She embarked on lengthy concert tours, becoming one of the first pianists to do so regularly. Her friendships with well known composers—Mendelssohn, Wagner, and, especially, Brahms—flourished, and her intelligence and knowledge of composition influenced their work.

When in the late 1870s illness began to interfere with Clara's ability to play, she settled in Frankfurt, Germany. There she became one of the most valued teachers at the conservatory. After suffering two strokes, she died on May 20, 1896, surrounded by her loving family and a few devoted friends.

Judy Gitenstein

Queen Victoria

(1819–1901)

"I will be good."
—1830

When she was eleven, Victoria found out that someday she would be queen of Great Britain. "I will be good," she is said to have declared, and she meant it. Throughout her sixty-four-year reign, the longest in English history, Queen Victoria showed herself to be a very complex woman: stubborn, loving, temperamental, imperious, and kind. Yet, always she tried to be the best she could be. Her conscientiousness allowed the British monarchy to survive in an age of revolutions, and her sense of duty came to characterize the age in which she lived: the Victorian Age.

A youthful Queen Victoria ascends the throne in 1838. Painting by Thomas Sully.

Alexandrina Victoria was born at Kensington Palace in London, the only child of Edward, duke of Kent, fourth son of King George III, and Victoria, princess of Saxe-Coburg. As a child, she was isolated from the court by her mother and her mother's advisor, who hoped to have sole influence over her. Victoria's greatest ally was her governess, Baroness Lehzen. After the death of William IV, third son of George III, Victoria succeeded to the throne in 1838. She promptly declared her independence and banished her mother to the other end of Buckingham Palace.

The eighteen-year-old queen was initially very popular with her subjects. Fair-haired and graceful, she had a silvery voice and small hands, of which she was always proud. Her cousin, Prince Albert of Saxe-

Coburg-Gotha, wrote of her at this time, "Victoria is said to be incredibly stubborn and her extreme obstinacy to be constantly at war with her good nature."

Victoria was introduced to the intricacies of British government by the experienced prime minister Lord Melbourne. Her fondness for him led her to take sides in party politics. Her popularity suffered as a result until Prince Albert convinced her to remain more neutral.

Victoria fell head-over-heels in love with Albert when he came to visit in 1839 and, as protocol demanded, quickly proposed to him. They had a very successful partnership. As pregnancy followed pregnancy (she gave birth to nine children in all), Victoria came to share her political duties equally with her husband. They were alike in their devotion to family and built homes in Osborne on the Isle of Wight and Balmoral, Scotland, to which they annually retreated. Above all, Albert encouraged Victoria to be as hardworking and conscientious as he was.

The high point of Victoria and Albert's reign was the Great Exhibition of 1851. Conceived and organized by Prince Albert, the exhibition brought together the wonders of modern art and science under the glass dome of the Crystal Palace. The exhibition was an overwhelming success, and Victoria felt justly proud of her husband's accomplishments.

Albert's untimely death in 1861 devastated the queen. She mourned his loss for the next forty years. She also retreated from public life, and for a while, her popularity plummeted.

Yet, she always carried out her political duties, trying to exert as much influence as possible on policy at home and diplomacy abroad. Her favorite prime minister, Benjamin Disraeli, became a good friend and helped ease the loneliness of her position. They were both committed to upholding and expanding the British Empire around the world, especially in Asia and northern Africa. Disraeli created the title "Empress of India" for Victoria in 1876.

The queen was rarely in sympathy with the social reforms of the day. She disliked change, and as she had little contact with poverty or hardship in her own country, she usually didn't recognize why reforms were necessary. Yet, to individuals in need, she could be compassionate and generous.

By the time her reign was celebrated in the Golden Jubilee of 1887 and the Diamond Jubilee of 1897, Queen Victoria had become a legend. She lived to see her children and grandchildren on the thrones of Europe; when she died at age eighty-one, she had thirty-seven great-grandchildren. Those who witnessed her funeral in 1901—the purple hangings with white satin bows lining the London streets—realized they were seeing the end of an era.

Ruth Ashby

Susan B. Anthony

(1820–1906)

"There never will be complete equality until women themselves help to make laws and elect lawmakers."
—"The Status of Women, Past, Present and Future," May 1897

The most famous of American suffragists, Susan B. Anthony fought for women's voting rights for fifty-five years. She became so identified with her cause that when the Nineteenth Amendment to the United States Constitution was finally ratified, guaranteeing women the right to vote, it was known as the Anthony Amendment.

No person should be discriminated against because of their sex or race. Susan Anthony learned this Quaker concept from her parents and took it very much to heart. As a young woman, she worked in the antislavery movement, a cause she actively pursued until the Fourteenth Amendment was passed in 1863, banning slavery in the United States.

At that time, however, it was considered improper for a woman to speak her thoughts in public. Women could not vote and had no voice in government or public affairs. Anthony realized that the issue of women's rights was similar to that of slavery: one human being should not have fewer legal rights than another. When Susan B. Anthony met Elizabeth Cady Stanton in 1851, the course of history was profoundly changed. Together they forged the movement for women's legal equality in the United States.

In 1869, Anthony and Cady Stanton cofounded the National Woman Suffrage Association, which became the National American Woman Suffrage Association in 1890. The organization's primary goal was to secure the vote

Elizabeth Cady Stanton and Susan B. Anthony, still partners in old age.

for women through an amendment to the Constitution. Once women had a voice in public affairs, they reasoned, women would be able to change the many laws that treated them as inferiors to men.

Although she had always been a shy person, Susan Anthony soon became a prominent, effective speaker for women's rights. She spent weeks on end traveling by train, by stagecoach, and in buckboards to small towns and cities throughout the country to lecture and organize. Sometimes she faced hostile audiences who interrupted her talks, threw rotten fruit, and tried to

Susan B. Anthony dollar, minted 1979.

shout her down. And sometimes she found audiences of women and men who agreed wholeheartedly with her ideas about women's equality.

In 1872, Anthony was arrested in Rochester, New York, for daring to cast a vote at the polls. She went to trial and was found guilty but refused to pay the hundred-dollar fine, declaring, "Resistance to tyranny is obedience to God."

After a half century of constant campaigning, hundreds of state petition campaigns, referendum elections, and constant lobbying of Congress, Anthony still had not seen women achieve voting rights. At a large convention of the National American Woman Suffrage Association in 1906, Susan B. Anthony gave her final speech. She ended it with this challenge: "The fight must not cease; you must see that it does not stop. . . . Failure is impossible." She died just one month later, and memorial services were held for Susan B. Anthony all across the country. It was another fourteen years before the Anthony Amendment was finally ratified, on August 26, 1920.

Bonnie Eisenberg and Mary Ruthsdotter

Florence Nightingale

(1820–1910)

"A woman who takes a sentimental view of Nursing (which she calls 'ministering' as if she were an angel) is of course worse than useless. . . ."
—Advice to nursing students, c. 1873

It was Florence Nightingale's triumph that by the end of the nineteenth century she had transformed the despised occupation of nursing into a legitimate profession for women.

Born in Florence, Italy, Florence Nightingale was the second daughter of Fanny Smith and William Edward Nightingale, wealthy, liberal members of the English upper class. Growing up in London, Derbyshire, and Hampshire, Florence was expected to lead a life devoted solely to family and the pleasures of society. Yet, even as a child, she felt different from other people. "I craved for some regular occupation, for something worth doing instead of frittering time away on useless trifles," she remembered later. Then, on February 7, 1837, when she was seventeen years old, she believed she heard God's voice, calling her to his service.

Florence Nightingale, the Lady with the Lamp, tends to the wounded at Scutari hospital.

It was another eight years before Florence realized where her mission lay. When she announced she wanted to be a nurse, her mother was horror-struck. She refused to let her beautiful and accomplished daughter be degraded by such menial work.

Determined to pursue her calling, Florence began to study public health on her own. While maintaining a full social schedule, she became one of the day's experts on public health and hospitals. She even turned down a marriage proposal from a man she loved because she felt ordinary domestic life would interfere with her goal.

Another five years passed before Nightingale was able to overcome parental opposition and enter the Institute of Protestant Deaconesses at Kaiserswerth, Germany, for the only formal training she would ever receive. She was thirty years old.

In 1853, Nightingale became superintendent of the Hospital for Invalid Gentlewomen in London. She was so successful that when the Crimean War began in 1854, the government asked her to go out with a party of nurses. Within three days, Nightingale and thirty-eight nurses had set off for Turkey.

Conditions at the Scutari hospital were horrendous. Sick and wounded men lay on straw pallets on the bare, filthy ground. There were no blankets, no clean clothes, no bandages, no kitchens, no operating tables, and too few doctors. Even so, medical officers did not want to accept Nightingale's help. They were finally forced to only because she had the authority to purchase supplies. She took charge of the sanitation and personally attended the wounded men. Every night, she would make the rounds of the wards, offering comfort and counsel; grateful soldiers called her the Lady with the Lamp.

In 1856, Nightingale returned to England a national heroine. But she was not interested in fame. She had one overriding purpose: to reform the health administration of the British army. Though her own health declined and she became an invalid for the next fifty years, Nightingale steadfastly carried on the work of reform from her couch. As the world's foremost authority on public health, she was consulted on hospitals and sanitation in England, India, Europe, and America.

In 1860, she established the first school for nurses: the Nightingale Training School at St. Thomas's Hospital, London. Her book *Notes on Nursing* (1859), written for the ordinary woman in charge of nursing her family, became a best-seller.

When she died at age ninety, Florence Nightingale was already a legend. In November 1907, King Edward VII made her the first woman ever to receive one of Britain's highest honors, the Order of Merit.

Ruth Ashby

Elizabeth Blackwell

(1821–1910)

"The application of scientific knowledge to women's necessities in actual life can only be done by women who possess at once the scientific learning of the physician, and as women a thorough acquaintance with women's requirements—that is, by women physicians."
—Elizabeth and Emily Blackwell,
Medicine As a Profession for Women, 1860

Elizabeth Blackwell did not grow up wanting to be a doctor. In fact, when she was young, she was ashamed of illness and disgusted by the human body. Yet, when a dying friend said that her worst sufferings could have been avoided had she been treated by a woman doctor, Blackwell knew she had found her vocation. In the nineteenth century, many women were ashamed to expose themselves to a male doctor. And a man did not know a woman's body as well as a woman did—how could he? The world called out for female physicians, and Blackwell was determined to become the first.

Elizabeth Blackwell was born near Bristol, England, the third of nine surviving children of Samuel and Hannah Lane Blackwell. Her father was a religious man of deeply held reformist beliefs, and he brought his children up in a liberal and enlightened atmosphere. So Elizabeth received the same education as her brothers, which was unusual at that time.

When she was eleven, her father's sugar refinery burned down, and the whole Blackwell family moved to America. Samuel Blackwell's business did not prosper, and when he died in 1838, he left his family nearly penniless. For a while, Elizabeth tried teaching, but she never really liked it. She was searching for some other way to earn a living when a friend urged her to become a physician. Blackwell later wrote, "The idea of winning a doctor's degree gradually assumed the aspect of a great moral struggle, and the moral fight possessed immense attraction for me."

Blackwell applied to the most prominent medical schools in the country and was promptly turned down by all of them. She was finally accepted by an obscure medical college in Geneva, New York, whose students voted her in as a prank.

At first ostracized by town and college alike, Blackwell persevered. On January 23, 1849, she became the first woman to receive a medical degree. She continued her studies at La Maternité in Paris, where she worked as a nurse-midwife. While there, she contracted an eye infection and lost sight in one eye.

Back in New York in 1851, Blackwell had difficulty attracting patients. She opened a dispensary for poor women in hopes of expanding her practice. To alleviate her loneliness, she adopted a seven-year-old orphan, Kitty Barry, who became her companion for the rest of her life. In 1857, the dispensary was expanded to become the New York Infirmary for Women and Children. Eventually, with the help of her sister Dr. Emily Blackwell—who had received her medical degree at Western Reserve University in 1854—Elizabeth Blackwell realized a long-cherished dream when, in 1868, she established the Woman's Medical College in conjunction with the infirmary.

Elizabeth Blackwell spent the last forty years of her life in England, where she helped found the National Health Society, whose motto was: "Prevention is better than cure." Throughout her professional life, she emphasized the importance of good sanitation and personal hygiene in maintaining good health. She died at age eighty-nine and is buried beneath a plain Celtic cross in the village of Kilmun, Scotland.

Ruth Ashby

Clara Barton

(1821–1912)

"It is wise statesmanship which suggests that in time of peace we must prepare for war."
—*The Red Cross*, 1898

By the time Clara Barton was five, she could gallop on a colt, holding only its mane, through the fields near her home in Oxford, Massachusetts. Hearing her father's stories about his experiences in the French and Indian War, Clara longed to become a soldier herself.

Clara's two brothers and two sisters, who were much older, protected her so much that she sometimes felt she had six parents, not two. Clara loved the attention, though, and she spent her days learning to read from her sisters and learning math from her brothers.

When Clara was eleven, she nursed one of her brothers through an illness that lasted two years. Somewhat lonely and shy as a child, she discovered she was good at taking care of others. Clara did well in school, especially with Latin, chemistry, and philosophy. When she graduated at eighteen, she became a teacher and quickly earned the respect of her pupils. Clara then moved to New Jersey, where she opened the first public school in the state. But when a male principal was appointed above her, she left in protest.

Barton moved to Washington, D.C., where she worked in the United States Patent Office. She was one of the first women appointed to a civil service post. Although her male coworkers resented her and treated her unfairly, she finished out her appointment.

Barton was still living in Washington when the Civil War broke out in 1861. When she learned that there weren't adequate medical supplies for the wounded soldiers, she convinced the War Department to let her gather supplies from the community and distribute them in army camps and on the battlefields. In a letter home, she wrote, "I wrung the blood from the bottom of my clothing before I could step, for the weight about my feet." Barton worked tirelessly, giving first aid, preparing food, and distributing supplies. She earned the respect of army doctors and commanding officers and deserved her nickname, Angel of the Battlefield.

In 1865, with the encouragement of President Lincoln, Barton set up an office to help find missing soldiers. She also traveled and lectured about her war experiences. Her shyness long forgotten, she held her audiences spellbound with her vivid and lively speeches.

Exhausted from her speaking tour, Barton went to Europe in 1869 to recuperate. It was in Switzerland that she learned about a newly formed organization called the International Committee of the Red Cross. The Red Cross was officially recognized by the Geneva Convention, an international agreement designed to ensure the protection of soldiers and civilians during wartime.

Upon returning to America, Barton began an aggressive campaign to organize an American Red Cross society and to push the United States to ratify the Geneva Convention. She took her appeal directly to the State

Department and the White House and published pamphlets and newspaper articles to educate the public about the Red Cross. Barton won her battle single-handedly—Congress finally voted to ratify the convention.

Clara Barton founded the American Association of the Red Cross on May 12, 1881, and served as its president until 1904. In 1906, she organized the National First Aid Association. She was active until her death at age ninety-one in her hometown of Oxford. Today, the International Red Cross helps people cope with a variety of crises during peacetime and in war, both in America and in other countries around the world.

Judy Gitenstein

Antoinette Brown Blackwell

(1825–1921)

*"Evolution has given and is still giving to woman an increasing
complexity of development which cannot find a legitimate field
for the exercise of all its powers within the household. There is
a broader, not a higher, life outside, which she is impelled to
enter, taking some share also in its responsibilities."*
—*The Sexes Throughout Nature*, 1875

Antoinette Brown Blackwell was one of the first women in America to obtain a college education. After studying theology at Oberlin College, she went on to become the first ordained woman minister in America. Active and resolute, she led a long life of intellectual productivity and social concern.

Born in Henrietta, New York, Antoinette (Nettie) Brown was the seventh of the ten children of Joseph and Abby Morse Brown. Eager to learn, Nettie followed her older brothers and sisters to school when she was only three and later attended the newly founded county high school. Growing up in a devout, liberal household, she always took a special interest in religion. At the age of nine, she publicly declared her faith and was accepted as a member of the Congregational Church.

Nettie had her family's full support when she attended Oberlin College in 1846. Oberlin, the first coeducational college in America, had just opened its doors to women. There Nettie befriended feminist and abolitionist Lucy Stone.

Nettie's family objected strongly, however, when she decided to pursue a theological degree with hopes of entering the ministry. Like the members of the Oberlin faculty, the Brown family took

Antoinette Brown Blackwell

seriously St. Paul's warning, "Let your women keep silence in the churches." (Nettie was later to argue that St. Paul's original words had been poorly translated from the Greek and that this was an injuction against women gossiping, not preaching in church.) Ultimately, Oberlin allowed her to take the theological course but not to receive the degree. However, on September 15, 1853, Antoinette Brown was ordained as minister of the First Congregational Church in Butler and Savannah, New York.

After just one year, she lost her faith in the traditional Calvinist doctrine of the Congregational Church, left the ministry, and became a Unitarian. In 1856, she married Samuel Charles Blackwell, brother of Lucy Stone's husband, Henry Blackwell, and physician Elizabeth Blackwell. Nettie and Samuel were happily married for forty-five years and had seven children, of whom five girls survived infancy.

For the first two decades of her marriage, Antoinette Blackwell was busy raising a family. She continued to study on her own, however, especially the new evolutionary and social theories of Charles Darwin and Herbert Spencer. In 1875, she published *The Sexes Throughout Nature,* in which she attempted to disprove Darwin and Spencer's "scientific" claim that women were physically and mentally inferior to men. Other books included *The*

Physical Basis of Immortality (1876), *The Philosophy of Individuality* (1893), and *The Social Side of Mind and Action* (1915).

Antoinette Blackwell continued her work in the ministry, serving as pastor emeritus at the All Souls Unitarian Church in Elizabeth, New Jersey, from 1908 to her death. In 1920, she voted in the first election after the passage of the Nineteenth Amendment, which gave women the right to vote. She died a year later at the age of ninety-six.

Ruth Ashby

Mary Harris "Mother" Jones

(1830–1930)

"The militant, not the meek, shall inherit the earth. Not today,
perhaps, and not tomorrow, but over the rim of the years
my old eyes see the coming of another day."
—*The Autobiography of Mother Jones,* 1925

At one hundred years of age, her white hair and grandmotherly appearance made "Mother" Jones look like a gentle old woman, but the legendary labor organizer was still very outspoken about her role in the world. "Get it right," she once told a reporter. "I'm not a humanitarian. I'm a hell-raiser!"

Mary Harris Jones was thirty-six, an Irish immigrant living in Memphis, Tennessee, when yellow fever struck the valley. Her husband and their four young children all died in that horrible epidemic. Brokenhearted but not broken, she moved to Chicago and began life over as a dressmaker. Four years later, the great Chicago fire reduced her home and shop to ashes. Again she had to start over.

As she earned her living sewing in the homes of wealthy Chicago families, Mary Harris Jones rankled at the luxuries they had while so many working-class people went hungry. She began to attend meetings of the Knights of Labor, the country's first mass labor organization. For the next fifty-nine years, Jones worked as a labor organizer. She became known as Mother Jones to her "boys"—the coal miners and railroad workers ruthlessly exploited by big-business interests.

Mother Jones had no permanent home. She traveled constantly from one industrial area to the next, often sleeping on the floor of a worker's shack with her purse for a pillow. Her passionate speeches quickly brought her audiences to their feet, ready to take whatever action was necessary and to stick with it through thick and thin.

Although she was not always successful, the marches and confrontations she organized brought wide publicity and public sympathy for the causes she championed. In Pennsylvania, where child labor was common and safety regulations were virtually unheard of, she organized a group of young children who worked

Mother Jones

in the textile mills in a march to gain support for their strike. The band of factory children marched 145 miles, stopping at small towns along the way, speaking to people and raising money for the strike. They went all the way to President Theodore Roosevelt's home in New York. They wanted to tell him, firsthand, what it was like in the mills, but he refused to talk with them. Another time, in Colorado, Mother Jones led a battalion of miners' wives armed with mops and brooms who successfully drove off the workers who had been hired to replace their striking husbands.

Although she frequently faced hostile sheriffs and was repeatedly jailed or run out of town, Mother Jones kept coming back to help the poor organize for social justice. Because of her work, the press called her the most dangerous woman in America. When she died at age one hundred, Mother Jones was planning another campaign.

Bonnie Eisenberg and Mary Ruthsdotter

Lakshmi Bai

(c. 1830–1858)

"Mera Jhansi Nahin Denge!" *("I will never give up my Jhansi!")*
—Reply to the British, 1854

Lakshmi Bai, the Rani of Jhansi, uttered these words when her small kingdom in India was threatened by the British. In resisting the British, Lakshmi Bai became an early heroine in India's struggle to free itself from British rule.

Lakshmi Bai was born into a wealthy, high-caste family in a small northern India principality called Jhansi. As a child, she was taught to read, write, and debate. She grew up with adoptive brothers, learning how to ride horses and use weapons.

Lakshmi Bai, the Rani of Jhansi. Watercolor from Kalighat, India.

When she was about fourteen years old, Lakshmi Bai married Gangadhar Rao, the maharaja (Hindu prince) of Jhansi. Gangadhar Rao, between forty and fifty years of age at the time of their marriage, was a sophisticated gentleman, though some historical documents note that he was short-tempered and capricious. After her active childhood, Rani Lakshmi Bai, *rani* being the shortened form of *maharani,* or wife of a maharaja, found the life of a queen too confining. She asked her husband to allow her to ride again, but he ignored her requests. Legend says that Lakshmi Bai gathered maidservants and taught them horsemanship, jumping, and how to use swords. More likely, however, she began drilling her military units after her husband's death.

Gangadhar Rao died when Lakshmi Bai was just eighteen. Since their only son had died at age three months, Gangadhar Rao had adopted one of his young relatives to be his heir. The British rejected this adopted heir, however, and moved to take over Jhansi. Lakshmi Bai responded by stating: "The people of Jhansi under rule of the late rajah, and of the rani [herself], were in as good a condition as those under the British rule." Lakshmi Bai also pointed out to the British that since the maharaja's death she had successfully conducted the affairs of state in Jhansi.

The British ignored Lakshmi Bai's arguments, insisting that Jhansi had been misgoverned and that she owed enormous debts incurred by her husband. Lakshmi Bai was ready to join the spreading Great Rebellion, which the British called the Sepoy Mutiny. When the British set out to reconquer all the rebel states, including Jhansi, Lakshmi Bai recruited a large army. She devoted special attention to her army's training and strengthened the defenses of her principle city, Jhansi.

In 1858, the city of Jhansi underwent a terrible siege by the British. During the siege, the women, organized by the rani, carried ammunition, stood watch, and brought food and water to the soldiers. Jhansi finally fell. Lakshmi Bai managed to slip away under the cover of darkness. Riding hard, she outdistanced her pursuers. Later she and her troops seized the nearby fortress of Gwalior, one of the stongest in India. After conquering Gwalior, Lakshmi Bai fell in battle. Some say she was shot in the chest or back; legend says that she was fighting with the reins of her horse in her mouth and swords in each hand when she was killed. With her death, Jhansi was captured by the British.

Lakshmi Bai's exploits captured the hearts and imagination of people all over India. The Rani of Jhansi has been called India's Joan of Arc because she sacrificed her life for the cause of India's freedom. One popular Indian ballad written after her death evokes her fighting spirit:

> How valiantly like a man fought she,
> The Rani of Jhansi
> On every parapet a gun she set
> Raining fire of hell,
> How well like a man fought the Rani of Jhansi;
> How valiantly and well!

Lyn Reese

Emily Dickinson

(1830–1886)

"If I read a book and it makes my whole body so cold no fire
ever can warm me, I know that is poetry. If I feel physically
as if the top of my head were taken off, I know that is poetry.
These are the only way I know it. Is there any other way."
—Conversation with Thomas Wentworth Higginson, 1870

Emily Dickinson has been called a mystic, a madwoman, a "little house-keeping person," and a genius. Though she is acclaimed as one of the greatest American poets, her life remains mysterious more than a hundred years after her death.

The outward events of Dickinson's life are clear. She was born in Amherst, Massachusetts, the second child of Edward and Emily Dickinson. Her father was a successful lawyer, one-term congressman, and treasurer of Amherst College, which his father had founded. The Dickinson family were always close. Emily's brother, Austin, married her best friend, Susan Gilbert, and moved into a house next door. Her younger sister, Lavinia, never married and, like Emily, remained at home, keeping house and taking care of her family.

For a girl of the nineteenth century, Emily had an excellent education. She attended the local Amherst Academy and then Mount Holyoke Female Seminary (later College). It is not known why she left the seminary after just one year. She seems to have had plenty of friends and a normal social life.

Yet, after her adolescence, Emily progressively withdrew from society, seeing very few people and seldom leaving her home. She visited Washington, D.C., and Philadelphia in her twenties and later went to Boston for some eye exams. But by the late 1850s, she rarely ventured beyond the grounds of her father's house, and visitors at the end of her life had to talk to her through the closed door of her room. Sometimes she would lower baskets of gingerbread from her bedroom window to children below.

No one really knows why Emily Dickinson chose a life of such seclusion. Certainly, she was aware of the specialness of her poetic calling. Devotion to poetry demanded time, space, and the freedom to create. She started writing poetry regularly when she was twenty and by the end of the decade was creating feverishly. Between 1858 and 1864, Dickinson wrote about eight hundred poems. She collected them in small hand-sewn packets and showed only a selected few to friends and family.

The poems are original, startling, and inventive. Dickinson wrote about nature, love, death, God, and poetry in short, pithy verse derived from hymn and ballad form. She freely experimented with rhythm, rhyme, and punctuation, replacing ordinary commas and periods with the expressive dash.

Some of Dickinson's poems and letters are addressed to a "Master" whom she loved and lost. Certainly, she had various male friends and mentors with whom she corresponded. Yet, today, it is difficult to say whether she was ever in love or with whom.

In 1862, Dickinson wrote a letter to Thomas Wentworth Higginson, a man of letters, to ask whether her poems were "alive." Higginson gave her encouragement but only partially understood her originality. Only seven of Dickinson's poems were published during her lifetime.

> ## This Is My Letter to the World
>
> Emily Dickinson's poems—1,775 in all—are untitled and usually known by their first lines.
>
> This is my letter to the World
> That never wrote to Me –
> The simple News that Nature told –
> With tender Majesty
>
> Her Message is committed
> To Hands I cannot see –
> For love of Her – Sweet – countrymen –
> Judge tenderly – of Me
>
> —Poem no. 441, c. 1862

Dickinson spent her last years at home nursing her parents. She died at age fifty-six in the same house in which she was born. After her death, her sister, Lavinia, found more than a thousand of her poems tied up in neat booklets in a bedroom chest. The first volume of her poetry was published in 1890.

Readers today are still awed by the passion, wit, and intelligence of these poems, written by a woman who led such a quiet life. We want to know more about her. Yet, she might have been referring to herself when she wrote:

> To pity those that know her not
> Is helped by the regret
> That those who know her, know her less
> The nearer her they get.
> —Poem no. 1400, c. 1877

Ruth Ashby

Louisa May Alcott

(1832–1888)

> *"I hate to think I've got to grow up, and be Miss March, and
> wear long gowns, and look as prim as a China aster!
> It's bad enough to be a girl, anyway, when I like boys'
> games and work and manners!"*
> —Jo March, *Little Women*, 1868

It's no wonder generations of readers have identified with the rebellious Jo, for when Louisa May Alcott wrote *Little Women*, she based the character on herself as a girl. Like Jo, the young Louisa was a lively, impulsive tomboy who had trouble curbing her temper and her tongue. Her experiences and those of her sisters became the basis for one of the best-loved children's classics of all time.

The second of four girls, Louisa May was born in Germantown, Pennsylvania, to Amos Bronson Alcott and Abigail May Alcott. Her father was a self-educated philosopher and teacher. His educational reforms were so controversial that he could never keep a teaching position for long. He did not earn a sufficient living, and the family was always poor and in need.

In the first twenty-eight years of Louisa's life, the Alcott family moved twenty-nine times. Louisa spent most of her youth in Boston and Concord,

Massachusetts. In 1843, her father brought his family to a farm called Fruitlands, where they tried an experiment in communal living. Fruitlands failed, and the family moved on. One of their homes had a barn, where Louisa and her sisters acted in plays she had written. By the time Louisa was in her late teens, she was working to earn money for her family.

First, Louisa tried teaching and domestic work, and then she turned to writing. Soon she became a successful writer of short stories for popular magazines and newspapers. Many of the stories were sensational thrillers, written under a pseudonym. She published her first adult novel, *Moods*, in 1864.

In 1862, after the Civil War had broken out, Alcott traveled to Washington, D.C., to become a nurse. She contracted typhus in the hospital and had to be sent home. For the rest of her life, Alcott suffered from ill health.

Alcott was thirty-five years old when she sat down to write *Little Women*, which was published in two volumes in 1868 and 1869. It became an

Louisa May Alcott, c. 1885

immediate best-seller, and she realized her old dream of paying off all her family's debts. Alcott followed this book with *An Old-Fashioned Girl* (1870), *Little Men* (1871), *Eight Cousins* (1875), *Rose in Bloom* (1876), and *Jo's Boys* (1886), among others. For the rest of her life, she was the chief breadwinner of her family.

Little Women made Alcott famous around the world. She enjoyed being lionized on her trip to Europe in 1870 but was only annoyed when admirers invaded her quiet home in Concord. As she grew older, she became an active feminist and was the first woman in Concord to register to vote when Massachusetts gave women limited suffrage in 1879.

Louisa May Alcott died at age fifty-six on the day of her father's funeral, ten years after her mother's death. She had taken care of her family, as she had vowed to do.

Ruth Ashby

Tz'u-hsi

(1835–1908)

Horrid stories abound about Tz'u-hsi, and many questions remain about her life. Her reign as empress of China was marked by shrewd plotting, a strong and dynamic rule, and murder.

Tz'u-hsi was born in Peking on November 29, 1835. Her father, a government clerk and provincial administrator, taught her how to read and write. At a young age, she was selected to enter the palace of Emperor Hsien Feng as a low-ranking concubine. Using her intelligence and literacy to her benefit, Tz'u-hsi was promoted quickly to the position of emperor's secretary. This move greatly elevated her status and provided her with the opportunity to learn about the administration of the state.

Tz'u-hsi eventually became a senior advisor to the emperor, and in 1856, her status increased even more when she bore him his first son. The emperor's chief wife, Tz'uan, had been unable to bear a male heir. When the emperor died in 1861, five-year-old T'ung-Chin became emperor, along with a ruling council of eight elders.

As T'ung-Chin's mother, Tz'u-hsi had approval over every decree. She pushed to establish laws to end the foot binding of women and to legalize marriage between Manchurians and Chinese. She and the ruling council worked to bring about the reform and Westernization of China; schools and language centers were established, and railways were constructed.

When T'ung-Chin died at the age of nineteen, Tz'u-hsi adopted her four-year-old nephew and named him heir. This maneuvering guaranteed that control of the empire remained in her hands. It did violate the laws of succession, but Tz'u-hsi skirted this issue by having the law changed.

Tz'u-hsi abused her power in even more serious ways. In the late 1880s, she appropriated funds earmarked for the navy to build her summer palace in northwest Peking. Because of her pilfering, no new ships were built. China, therefore, was not adequately prepared when the Japanese attacked Korea, which the Chinese controlled. The Chinese lost the Sino-Japanese War of 1894-95.

When Tz'u-hsi's nephew reached governing age and was crowned, he instituted the Hundred Days of Reform and laws to end the corruption in his aunt's administration. Tz'u-hsi rallied the opposition and organized a coup. She had the emperor seized and placed him in confinement, and she ordered his favorite concubine drowned in a well. Many of the emperor's reformers

Her Imperial Majesty the Empress Dowager of China, Tz'u-hsi. *Painting by Hubert Vos, 1905-6.*

were also killed, and China was once again under Tz'u-hsi's absolute rule.

She would be involved in another rebellion, but this one she would not win. The Boxer Rebellion, a peasant uprising to drive Western Christian missionaries and other foreigners from China, peaked in 1900. The revolters burned churches and the homes of foreigners, and Tz'u-hsi ordered that foreigners be killed. When foreign troops invaded Peking, however, the royal court fled. Tz'u-hsi was forced to accept heavy peace terms two years later, including reparations to foreign countries who had suffered losses in the rebellion.

Tz'u-hsi remained in control of the dynasty until her death in 1908. Before she died, she ordered her nephew to be poisoned, and she named three-year-old Pu Yi the new emperor. Although Tz'u-hsi was an opportunist who often abused her power, she did institute laws that improved the lives of Chinese women. Her iron rule also strengthened the dynasty, which was overthrown three years after her death.

S. Suzan Jane

Queen Liliuokalani

(1838–1917)

"Oh, honest Americans, as Christians hear me for my downtrodden people! Their form of government is as dear to them as yours is precious to you. Quite as warmly as you love your country, so they love theirs."
—Hawaii's Story by Hawaii's Queen, 1898

Queen Liliuokalani was the last reigning monarch of the Hawaiian Islands, forced to give up her throne when Hawaii became part of the United States.

Liliuokalani, called Lydia as child, was born in Hawaii into the family of a high chief, her parents being councilors to King Kamehameha III, who reigned from 1825 to 1854. Lydia attended the Royal School, run by American missionaries, and received the best education available. She enjoyed a lighthearted childhood, happily playing outdoors, riding horseback, singing, and participating in family song-writing competitions.

Lydia's brother Kalakaua, who had reigned as king in the late 1800s, had named her heir to the throne upon his death. During his reign, he had given governing power to a cabinet composed of Americans. This cabinet had succeeded in passing a constitution that gave voting rights to foreign residents but denied the vote to most Hawaiian natives. During the nineteenth century, many American missionaries and businesspeople settled in Hawaii, and as their population grew, they tried to weaken the monarchy and gain political power. When Liliuokalani became queen in 1891, she was determined to restore the power and authority of the crown. She saw it as her mission to preserve the islands for the native residents.

Although well liked and resolute in her task, the new queen had several factors working against her. In 1890, a new United States tariff, or tax, had revoked Hawaiian sugar's "free and favored entry" status and had a devastating impact on the sugar industry in Hawaii. By the time Liliuokalani became queen, the islands' economy had already been severely damaged. The legislature, composed mostly of Americans, resisted her attempts to organize a new native cabinet. When she tried to institute a new constitution, prominent American businessmen living in Hawaii called upon the United States government to intervene.

American troops occupied government buildings in Honolulu and deposed Liliuokalani, while American civilians set up a new government and applied to the United States for annexation of the islands. When Liliuokalani tried to regain control in 1895, she was placed under house arrest for eight months. In 1898, Hawaii was annexed to the United States by a joint congressional resolution.

Liliuokalani was released as a private citizen, and she continued to live in Honolulu. As a citizen, Liliuokalani pursued her interest in traditional Hawaiian music and culture. She

Queen Liliuokalani, the last reigning monarch of Hawaii.

became a composer noted for her harmonious blending of ancient Hawaiian and Western musical traditions. Her most famous piece is the romantic song "Aloha Oe" ("Farewell to Thee"). Liliuokalani died in 1917.

Today a popular symbol of Hawaii's character and spirit, Liliuokalani has become a cherished connection to the islands' past. In 1982, a bronze statue of her was placed on the state capitol grounds, and in the dedication brochure, she was described as "the Polynesian chieftess of olden times, in whom centuries of tradition had bred a belief in the sacred bond between a people and their land; the strong-willed, well-educated Victorian monarch who valiantly defended her inherited sovereignty and made it her overriding duty to safeguard and preserve Hawaiian independence."

Bonnie Eisenberg and Mary Ruthsdotter

Sarah Bernhardt

(1844–1923)

"I am the most lied-about woman in the world."
—*Memories of My Life,* 1907

"There are five kinds of actresses," author Mark Twain wrote. "Bad actresses, fair actresses, good actresses, great actresses—and then there is Sarah Bernhardt." Sarah Bernhardt mesmerized audiences around the world with her inspired performances during her sixty-one-year career, but she made her own life the most dramatic role of all.

Sarah was born Rosine Bernard, the oldest of three girls, in Paris. Her father and mother never married, which was considered scandalous in the nineteenth century. At age sixteen, Sarah enrolled in the Conservatoire, France's national school of drama, where she realized her passion for acting. After graduating, she was admitted to the Comédie-Française, the national theater of France, which presented the very best classical plays.

Bernhardt made her stage debut with the Comédie-Française in 1862. Her performances were barely noticed by critics, and her contract was canceled after she slapped a senior actress for insulting her sister. In 1866, Bernhardt signed on with the Odéon theater. Through six years of intensive work, she gradually established her reputation. Her strong, clear voice and charismatic stage presence earned her consistently good reviews from the critics and the adoration of French audiences. She soon developed a loyal following who dubbed her the Divine Sarah.

During the Franco-German War in 1870, Bernhardt organized a military hospital in the Odéon theater. After the war, in 1872, she returned to the

Comédie-Française, and although she played only a few title roles, they won her rave reviews.

In 1879, Bernhardt traveled to London with the Comédie-Française. Her success abroad caused her to develop an inflated ego and a temper that weren't appreciated in the Comédie-Française. Upon her return to France, Bernhardt formed her own traveling company in 1880, and she quickly became an international idol. She appeared regularly in England and traveled throughout Europe, the United States, Canada, Australia, and South America.

The Divine Sarah plays the dying Camille during her first American tour in 1880.

Bernhardt's brilliant career was filled with singular achievements. She was one of the first actresses to play male roles, including the title role in *Hamlet* at her own Théâtre Sarah Bernhardt in 1899. At the age of fifty-six, she amazed audiences when she played Napoleon's twenty-one-year-old son in Rostand's *L'Aiglon*. When she played the nineteen-year-old Joan of Arc, she was in fact sixty-four years old. Nothing seemed to stop her—not even a knee injury that caused her right leg to be amputated in 1915. She simply reworked her parts so that she could remain seated through most of her scenes.

Bernhardt's unconventional personal life was as dramatic as her professional life. She often rehearsed long into the night, and sometimes she would spontaneously throw a party after a grueling performance. She gave close friends pictures of herself in the coffin in which she slept, and she kept a menagerie of animals in her home, including a lion. When Bernhardt wasn't rehearsing or performing, she could sometimes be found sculpting or painting—she even studied corpses to learn accurate anatomy.

Sarah Bernhardt died while working on a film. It may have been an exaggeration when critics called her the eighth wonder of the world, but her indomitable spirit sustained her, and her accomplishments expanded the boundaries for women's theatrical roles.

Judy Gitenstein

Mary Cassatt

(1844–1926)

"A woman artist must be . . . capable of making the primary sacrifices."
—Interview, c. 1920

Mary Cassatt knew that women who wished to become artists often had to give up conventional family life. It was a sacrifice she was willing to make. While still in her teens, Cassatt set her mind on becoming a professional artist. By the end of her life, she had not only achieved her goal but had earned a reputation as one of the era's finest painters.

Mary was born in Allegheny, Pennsylvania, but she and her family lived in Europe from 1851 to 1855. During this time, they toured the great art galleries and museums, and the masterpieces Mary viewed inspired her to pursue an art career. By the time she was seventeen, she had become determined to attend art school, even though her father is said to have remarked that he would almost rather see her dead. He finally relented, however, and Cassatt enrolled in the Pennsylvania Academy of Fine Arts. When she began to realize that female students weren't taken seriously at the school, she returned to Paris to study.

Cassatt was disappointed in France too when she learned that women were not admitted to the most prestigious art schools. Instead, she studied with private teachers and learned to paint in the traditional style of the art establishment. Cassatt won her first public recognition when the conservative Paris Salon accepted one of her paintings for their 1868 exhibition. Over the next two years, she worked to develop her skills. When the Salon exhibited her canvases in 1872 and again the following year, she became famous throughout Europe.

As Cassatt developed her own personal style, her work became more daring and bold. She painted her subjects with bright colors, distinct brushstrokes, and lively lighting. Renowned painter Edgar Degas noticed her work and struck up

Portrait of the Artist, *by Mary Cassatt, 1878.*

a friendship with Cassatt that would last until her death. Degas encouraged her to use everyday people and things as subjects for her painting.

Cassatt soon broke with the Paris Salon and joined the group of experimental painters who were called Impressionists. Her American exhibit in 1876 included the first impressionistic paintings to be shown in the United States. She finished eleven new paintings for the Impressionists' 1879 show in Paris, and although the work exhausted her, the reviews were superlative. Cassatt repeated this triumph in the Impressionists' 1880 and 1881 shows.

Mothers and children, captured in everyday moments of their lives, eventually became the dominant theme of Cassatt's paintings and etchings. In

Berthe Morisot

Berthe Morisot (1841–1895) was another prominent Impressionist painter of the late nineteenth century. Born into a well-to-do French family, she started painting in childhood and began studying with Jean-Baptiste-Camille Corot in 1861. In 1868, Morisot met Édouard Manet and later married his brother, Eugène. With Monet, Degas, Cézanne, and others, she organized the first Impressionist exhibition in 1874. Throughout her career, Morisot painted with light colors and a loose brushstroke. Like Cassatt, Morisot became known for her luminous everyday scenes of women.

1892, she was invited to paint a twelve by fifty-eight foot mural for the Women's Building of the Chicago World's Columbian Exposition. Her fame increased as her work continued to take experimental turns.

Despite living most of her adult life in France, Cassatt called herself "definitely and frankly American." Although her work was not fully appreciated in the United States during her lifetime, she played an important role in introducing Impressionists as well as other European artists to her native country. Cassatt was forced to stop working in 1915 because of her failing eyesight, but she continued to entertain young artists. By the end of her life, she had earned a lasting place in art history and a firm reputation as one of America's great modern painters.

Bonnie Eisenberg and Mary Ruthsdotter

Sarah Winnemucca

(c. 1844–1891)

"The council-tent is our Congress, and anybody can speak who has anything to say, women and all. . . . If women could go into [your] Congress, I think justice would soon be done to the Indians."
—Life Among the Paiutes: Their Wrongs and Claims, 1883

Sarah Winnemucca stood as an eloquent defender of the rights of Native Americans at a time when the United States government was seizing Indian land and forcibly relocating Indian tribes.

Sarah Winnemucca, born Thoc-me-tony, or "Shell-flower," was the fourth of nine children of the Paiute chief, Winnemucca II. As a young girl, Shell-flower and her brothers and sisters moved from the Paiute homeland in western Nevada to live with her grandfather on a ranch in northern California. He wanted her to learn the white man's ways, so he sent her to live with a stagecoach agent's family, who gave her the name Sarah. She had a gift for languages, learning English, Spanish, and two Indian languages in addition to her native Paiute.

At her grandfather's request, Sarah and her sister Mary went to St. Mary's Convent school in San Jose, California, in 1860. At this time, most Indian children were sent to segregated schools, and Sarah and Mary were discharged from St. Mary's after only one month. Parents of other students, who were of Spanish descent, did not think their children should go to school with Indians.

Sarah Winnemucca in the "Indian Princess" costume she wore on her East Coast lecture tour, 1883.

As more settlers moved west, the Paiutes, like many other Indian tribes, were forced off their homelands. After Sarah and Mary returned home to western Nevada, they and their people were moved to Camp McDermott in northeast Nevada and later to the Malheur Reservation in Oregon. Once settled in Oregon, Sarah served as an interpreter and as a teacher at an Indian school. When war broke out between the Paiutes and their enemies, the Bannocks, in 1878, it was Sarah who persuaded her people to end the conflict peacefully.

Suzette and Susan La Flesche

Many Native American women of the late nineteenth century used their talents to promote the rights of their people. Among them were sisters Suzette (1854–1903) and Susan (1865–1915) La Flesche, born into the Omaha tribe in Nebraska. A professional speaker known as Bright Eyes, Suzette lectured about broken treaties, Indian hardships, and the theft of Indian lands. Her lectures helped influence the passage of the Dawes Severalty Act of 1887. This was the first time individual Native Americans were given title to their own land; the Act also ceded tribal territory to the United States.

Susan became the first Native American female physician. After graduating from the Women's Medical College of Pennsylvania, she returned to the Omaha reservation to treat her own people. She also worked to educate Indians about the disease of alcoholism and went to Washington, D.C., to lobby against the sale of liquor on reservations.

In 1879, the United States government relocated the Paiutes again, to the Yakima Reservation in Washington. Angered by the unceasing relocation and brutal treatment of her people by the agents on the reservations, Winnemucca began a campaign for her people's rights. In 1880, she went to Washington, D.C. to meet with Secretary of the Interior Carl Schurz and President Rutherford B. Hayes. Though she won a presidential order authorizing the Paiutes' return to Oregon, the move was never funded, and the Yakima Indian agent refused to free any Paiutes from the reservation.

Sarah returned to Vancouver, Washington, and to teaching Indian children. Then, from 1883 to 1884, she went on a grueling lecture tour, accompanied by her now husband, Lieutenant L. H. Hopkins. Donning her ceremonial Paiute "princess costume," she lectured up and down the East Coast, calling for Indian and white equality and criticizing the Indian Bureau's handling of her tribe. She was a powerful speaker. One spectator commented that she spoke with "such persuasion and conviction . . . that many people were moved to tears." She gave almost three hundred lectures in all and gathered thousands of signatures for a petition demanding that the Paiute be given the Malheur Reservation. Her 1883 autobiography, *Life Among the Paiutes,* sold well and paid for the tour.

In 1884, Congress passed a bill granting land to her tribe, but the secretary of the interior wouldn't execute it. Discouraged, Winnemucca returned to Nevada and opened a school for Paiute children. She taught for three years, until illness forced her to retire. She died of consumption at the age of forty-seven.

Sarah's dream of helping her people return to the Malheur Reservation in Oregon was never realized. But her perseverance, eloquence, and dedication to educating non-Indians about Indian life served as a model for later Native American movements.

Deborah Gore Ohrn

Carry Nation

(1846–1930)

"A woman is stripped of everything by them [saloons]. Her husband is torn from her; she is robbed of her sons, her home, her food, and her virtue. . . . Truly does the saloon make a woman bare of all things."
—Public statement, c. 1863

Carry Nation was one of the most colorful prohibitionist reformers of the early twentieth century. Guided by her visions and by the religious certainty that she was battling evil—alcohol being the evil she despised most—she took direct action against a habit she believed to be causing misery for large numbers of women and children.

Carry Moore was raised in an unusual family. Her mother suffered delusions and often fancied herself to be Queen Victoria of England. Her father humored his wife by pretending to be Prince Albert, which surely was confusing for young Carry. Carry had only a few years of schooling because when she was young, she was often ill and was plagued by visions and anxiety. When she reached adulthood, Carry married a man who had been a boarder with her family. He turned out to be an alcoholic and died from his addiction within a few years of their marriage. This experience profoundly influenced Carry's view of temperance.

Carry Nation wields her infamous hatchet.

When Carry married David Nation, a lawyer and newspaper editor, they moved first to Texas and then to Medicine Lodge, Kansas, in 1890. Nation devoted a great deal of energy to organizing clothing and food drives for the poor. She worked as a teacher and saw to it that no children were deprived of an education because they lacked proper school clothing.

On June 6, 1899, Nation had a vision that would direct the course of the rest of her life. She had been working with the Women's Christian Temperance Union to encourage the state of Kansas to enforce its anti-liquor laws, but with little success. In her vision, God instructed her to go to Kiowa, Kansas, and, brandishing a weapon in her hand, to close down a saloon. She followed her vision to the Dodson Saloon, and there—with hatchet and bricks in hand—she smashed tables, mirrors, windows, bottles, and glasses, forcing the drinking establishment to close.

Nation's actions made the news, and word of her attack spread quickly, earning her instant fame. She worked her way through other saloons in town and then moved on to other towns in the state. Although the period during which she wrecked bars was actually brief, she managed to close dozens of saloons. Carry Nation was six feet tall, very strong, and weighed close to two hundred pounds. On top of that, she had a way with words that could leave a saloon keeper shaking in his boots even if she didn't have her hatchet at her side—but she always did!

Carry Nation rages in the "War Between Rum and Religion."
The Freethought Ideal, *Ottawa, Kansas, March 1, 1901.*

In 1901, Nation embarked on an East Coast lecture tour, then took her message across the country. To support herself, she wrote her autobiography and sold miniature hatchets engraved with CARRY NATION—JOINT SMASHER. But she did have a loyal following of people who sent donations, which she used to pay court fines, finance prohibition magazines, and support a home for wives and mothers of alcoholic men. In 1910, she collapsed on a stage in Arkansas and died within six months.

Carry Nation is usually portrayed as a fanatical anti-alcohol terrorist who liked to smash saloons. Though certainly single-minded, she was also among the first of a long line of American women and men who have had the courage to take direct, though often unpopular, action against social evils.

Bonnie Eisenberg and Mary Ruthsdotter

Louisa Lawson

(1848–1920)

"Women are not angels but human creatures, and they need human recognition. They cannot do without this Earth and the men who are upon it, therefore they need the same kind of justice as men do."
—*The Dawn*, No. 5, September 1891

Louisa Lawson's philosophy was shaped by her experience as a wife and mother of five in the Australian outback and, later, as a woman raising her children alone in Sydney. A nineteenth-century suffragist writer, poet, editor, and publisher, Lawson knew that true equality would come only when women were permitted to work as equals with men. She made a lasting contribution to the women's suffrage movement in Australia.

She was born in Guntawang, New South Wales, in 1848. At the age of eighteen, she married Peter Larson, a Norwegian sailor and gold digger. Life as the wife of a gold digger in nineteenth-century Australia was difficult. The family moved often, and Lawson gave birth to some of her children in a flimsy tent.

In 1876, family concerns drew Lawson into politics when she began campaigning for a local school but found that she was not permitted to at-

Votes Around the World

Australia was only the second country in the world to grant women the vote, after New Zealand in 1893. Next were Finland in 1906, Norway in 1913, and Iceland in 1915. The Soviet Union gave women the right to vote in 1917, the year of the Bolshevik Revolution. Canada also granted women voting rights in 1917 in all provinces except Quebec, where women didn't have the right to vote until 1940. Then followed Austria and Poland in 1918, Great Britain in 1919, and the United States in 1920.

Other countries lagged behind the United States: women in France, Guatemala, and Japan didn't win the vote until 1945. China granted the right in 1947, Iran in 1963, and Syria in 1971.

Kuwait and Saudi Arabia are two countries that have yet to grant the right to vote to women.

Information from the Division for the Advancement of Women, UN

tend meetings because she was a woman. She separated from her husband at the age of thirty-three and started a life on her own, moving to Sydney with her children.

She supported herself by working as a seamstress and in her spare time founded a women's discussion group, the Dawn Club, in 1888. The Dawn Club's interests were defined as "health, temperance, suffrage, social purity, education, dress reform, and physiological matters." Lawson also published, edited, and wrote *The Dawn,* Australia's first feminist newspaper, from 1888 to 1905. She insisted that it be produced entirely by women, despite the opposition of the typographical unions.

Lawson's life shaped her writings and her views on the role of women. She believed that freedom for wives and mothers benefited the family as a whole. In an editorial in *The Dawn* in 1896, she wrote, "A woman's life should not be bounded by domesticity, not as a means of showing her dislike for that sphere, but for the highest good of those within it. The true mother gathers the riches of intellect, education, and ethics that she may administer them to those at home." Lawson proved her point when she arranged for her son Henry to publish his first book in 1894. He went on to become one of Australia's best-known fiction writers.

Lawson went bankrupt and was forced to close *The Dawn* in 1905. But she lived to see the victorious conclusion of the central battle of her life, when women gained the right to vote in Australia in 1902.

Elisabeth Keating

Olive Schreiner

(1855–1920)

"We are born cursed from the time our mothers bring us into the world till the shrouds are put on us. . . . They begin to shape our cursed end . . . when we are tiny things in shoes and socks. We sit with our little feet drawn up under us in the window, and look out at the boys in their happy play. We want to go. Then a loving hand is laid on us: 'Little one, you cannot go' they say: 'Your little face will burn and your nice white dress be spoiled.' "
—*The Story of an African Farm,* 1883

Olive Schreiner felt deeply the injustices done to women in a male-dominated society. A born rebel, she became one of the foremost feminists of her day, influencing contemporary thought through her novels, short allegories, and nonfiction.

Olive Schreiner

Olive was born in the Cape Colony, South Africa, the sixth of twelve children of a German missionary, Gottleb Schreiner, and his English wife, Rebecca. Growing up in an intensely religious home, Olive was a bright, imaginative child with an inquisitive mind. When her baby sister Ellie died, she rejected organized religion and at age ten became a "free thinker." In conservative Cape society, such independence immediately labeled her an outsider.

Olive had little formal education, but she read voraciously on her own, especially the works of progressive thinkers like Herbert Spencer, Charles Darwin, and John Stuart Mill. When she was twelve, her father lost his employment and could no longer support his children. Olive was passed from family member to family member until she was old enough to be employed as a governess. Sometime in her late teens, she developed the chest condition—probably asthma—that plagued her for the rest of her life.

Schreiner began to write seriously in the years between 1873 and 1881, when she was trying to earn a living teaching. She had already completed two novels when she left Africa for England at age twenty-six. *The Story of an African Farm* was published in London and made its author something of a celebrity. Its account of a young girl's rejection of religion and conventional female roles was partly autobiographical. The book gained Schreiner entry into progressive intellectual circles, and she embarked on a quasi-love affair with psychologist Havelock Ellis that turned into a lifelong friendship.

Returning to Africa in 1889, she married lawyer and farmer Samuel Cronwright. They had one child, a girl who died just after birth. When the Boer War broke out in 1899, Olive and Samuel were placed under house arrest for championing the Boer cause against the English. After the war, Schreiner became a fervent supporter of the rights of black Africans.

In 1911, Schreiner published *Woman and Labour,* the massive work on woman and society that she had been writing on and off for decades. The book's demand that women be allowed to work, that they no longer be "sex parasites" dependent on the labor of men, greatly influenced feminist thought in the early twentieth century.

In the last years of her life, Schreiner joined the English peace movement in protest against World War I. She died at age sixty-five and is buried with her husband, child, and favorite dog on the summit of a mountain overlooking the South African veld.

Ruth Ashby

Fannie Farmer

(1857–1915)

"Progress in civilization has been accompanied by progress in cookery."
—*The Boston Cooking-School Cookbook,* 1896

Cooks today expect to find clear directions and specific measurements for recipes every time they open a cookbook. Until Fannie Farmer published *The Boston Cooking-School Cookbook* in 1896, however, such explicit recipes were unavailable. Fannie Farmer single-handedly transformed the preparation of nutritious and tasty meals from a mysterious art to a precise scientific process.

The daughter of a printer, Fannie Farmer grew up in a poor family in Medford, Massachusetts. When she was sixteen, she suffered a stroke that left her left leg paralyzed and ended her plans to attend college. Instead, she began working as a mother's helper and discovered that she had a fondness and talent for cooking. Fannie later turned this interest into a lucrative career.

The first step she took toward that goal was to enroll in the Boston Cooking School. When Farmer completed the two-year course, she was asked to stay on as assistant director of the school. By 1894, she had become the director and was developing new standards for food preparation.

Two other nineteenth-century women, Catharine Beecher and Ellen Swallow Richards, had established the field of home economics by promoting the use of scientific methods in the American home. Farmer followed their lead in the realm of cooking. Until that time, measurements for recipes usually were written in vague terms, such as "Mix together lard the size of a hen's egg with a fistful of flour." Farmer introduced standardized measurements to take the mystery out of successful cooking.

In 1896, Farmer published the *Boston Cooking-School Cookbook,* a collection of easy recipes for classic and everyday dishes combined with information about nutrition, etiquette, formal entertaining, proper home management, and the use of kitchen equipment. Although the publisher doubted the book would sell, it became an instant hit in homes across the country. Today, the still best-selling cookbook is known as *The Fannie Farmer Cookbook.*

With the success of her book, Farmer resigned from the Boston Cooking School to open Miss Farmer's School of Cookery. She taught mostly housewives through popular weekly demonstration lectures, and she gave classes for professional chefs in the evenings.

One of Farmer's continuing interests was proper nutrition. She wrote in *The Boston Cooking-School Cookbook*: "I certainly feel that the time is not far distant when a knowledge of the principles of diet will be an essential part of one's education." Farmer began to devise special diets for those recovering from illness, and she gave short courses to hospital nurses and dietitians. She taught for one year at Harvard Medical School and published *Food and Cookery for the Sick and Convalescent*, the book she considered to be her most important work.

From 1905 to 1915, Farmer and her sister wrote a regular column for the magazine *Woman's Home Companion*. In her later years, she lectured widely to women's groups, even after two strokes had confined her to a wheelchair. Her death did not diminish the popularity of her cookbook, and her name remains synonymous with good home cooking.

Bonnie Eisenberg and Mary Ruthsdotter

Charlotte Perkins Gilman

(1860–1935)

"So utterly has the status of women been accepted as a sexual one that it has remained for the women's movement of the nineteenth century to devote much contention to the claim that women are persons! That women are persons as well as females,—an unheard of proposition!"
—*Women and Economics*, 1898

The leading feminist theorist in America at the turn of the twentieth century, Gilman devoted her life to changing the role of women in American culture. Whether writing about history, psychiatry,

Charlotte Perkins Gilman, 1915

work, marriage, or child rearing, she strove to jolt her readers into new awareness and move society in a new direction.

Charlotte Anna Perkins was born in Hartford, Connecticut, to Mary Fitch and Frederick Beecher Perkins, the grandson of the well known theologian Lyman Beecher. Frederick Beecher deserted his wife when their third child was born, leaving his family in poverty. In the first eighteen years of her life, Charlotte moved nineteen times. Her mother deliberately withheld affection from her daughter, making Charlotte's childhood especially lonely.

In 1884, Charlotte married Walter Stetson, a handsome aspiring artist. When their daughter, Katherine, was born a year later, Charlotte suffered from severe postpartum depression. She sought the advice of a noted neurologist, who prescribed a "rest cure": enforced inactivity with no physical or mental stimulation of any kind. The cure nearly drove Charlotte mad. To save her sanity, she abandoned the treatment and left her husband. Charlotte wrote about her experience in her most famous short story, "The Yellow Wallpaper" (1892). A few years later, Walter married Charlotte's best friend, and Katherine was sent to live with them. The three adults remained friends, but Charlotte was attacked by the press for "abandoning" her child.

For the next five years, Charlotte traveled around the country, writing and lecturing on women in society. Her own quest to create a fulfilling life had encouraged her to rethink many tired assumptions and attitudes about women. It was now that she wrote her most famous book, *Women and Economics* (1898), a study of women's social and economic dependence. The book brought her recognition both at home and abroad. Her other books include *Concerning Children* (1900), *Human Work* (1904), and *Herland* (1915), a novel about an all-female utopia. She was a prolific author, writing every line of her own magazine, *The Forerunner,* from 1909 to 1916. For most of her working life, she was enormously popular as a writer and lecturer.

In 1900, Charlotte married her first cousin George Houghton Gilman, with whom she had a long and happy life. Two years before her husband died in 1934, Charlotte discovered she had inoperable breast cancer. She chose to meet her end in the same spirit of independence that had characterized her life. Charlotte moved in with her daughter, completed her autobiography, and wrote a farewell note to her family: ". . . it is the simplest of human rights to choose a quick and easy death in place of a slow and horrible one. . . . I have preferred chloroform to cancer." On August 17, 1935, Charlotte Perkins Gilman used chloroform she had saved up to end her own life.

Ruth Ashby

Jane Addams

(1860–1935)

*"A city is in many respects . . . enlarged housekeeping. . . . May we
not say that city housekeeping has failed partly because women, the
traditional housekeepers, have not been consulted
as to its multiform activities?"*
—*Newer Ideals of Peace,* 1907

Jane Addams felt that women had a special mission to improve the conditions of everyday life—whether in the home, the city, or the world. The most admired American woman of her time, she was a pioneer social reformer who promoted social work in the United States.

Jane was born in Cedarville, Illinois, the eighth of nine children of Sara Weber Addams and John Addams, a prosperous timber merchant and banker. Her mother died when she was only two, and Jane was raised by

Jane Addams reads to children at Hull House, early 1930s.

her stepmother and older sister. Her father encouraged his intelligent daughter to work hard and excel.

A member of the first generation of college women, Addams attended the Rockford (Illinois) Female Seminary from 1877 to 1881. After graduation, she found herself restless and unfocused. She enrolled in medical school but was unable to continue due to a spinal illness.

On a second trip to Europe in 1888, Addams caught a glimpse of her life's work. While in London, she visited Toynbee Hall, a "settlement house" where educated young men lived in a poor neighborhood and sponsored lectures, classes, and other activities for the neighborhood residents.

In 1889, Addams and her friend Ellen Gates Starr decided to start a settlement house modeled after Toynbee Hall. They moved into an old mansion in one of Chicago's slums and named the mansion "Hull House" after the Chicago businessman who donated the land. It became America's best-known settlement house, offering academic and job-oriented classes as well as cultural, recreational, and daycare programs for the culturally diverse immigrants who lived in the neighborhood. Within four years, some two thousand people a week were coming to Hull House.

With three other women, Julia Lathrop, Florence Kelley, and Dr. Alice Hamilton, Addams also made Hull House a center for social reform. These women and some of the residents worked to improve the condition of the neighborhood and to change city and state laws on housing, public welfare, women's rights, and child labor.

Addams worked for women's rights on a national level too, becoming a vice president of the National American Woman Suffrage Association in 1911. She even got into politics, in 1912 serving as a delegate to the first national convention of the Progressive Party, which supported female suffrage.

Much more controversial was Addams's stand as a pacifist. When World War I (1914–1918) broke out, she joined an international group of women on a peace mission to Europe. On her return, she was labeled unpatriotic when she announced that soldiers had to be given intoxicants to lead a bayonet charge. After the war, her pacifism became associated in the public mind with Communism, and she was denounced as the "most dangerous woman in America." She was even expelled from the Daughters of the American Revolution.

Her international reputation thrived, however, and in 1931, she became the first woman to win the Nobel Peace Prize. Addams turned her prize money over to the Women's International League for Peace and Freedom, of which she was president, and to Hull House, to help the unemployed.

On May 21, 1935, she died of cancer in Chicago. Columnist Walter Lippman wrote in her obituary: "She had compassion without condescension. She had pity without retreat into vulgarity. She had infinite sympathy for common things without forgetfulness of those that are uncommon. That, I think, is why those who have known her say she was not only good, but great."

Deborah Gore Ohrn

Ida B. Wells

(1862–1931)

"The awful death-roll that Judge Lynch is calling every week is appalling, not only because of the lives it takes, the cruelty and outrage to the victims, but because of the prejudice it fosters."
—*Southern Horrors*, 1892

In 1892, the year that Ida B. Wells wrote a pamphlet exposing the terrors of mob violence, 235 black people were lynched in America—hanged, shot, stabbed, and burned. Journalist Wells devoted a lifetime to investigating lynching and promoting antilynching laws.

Ida B. Wells

When Ida Bell Wells was born in Holly Springs, Mississippi, she and her parents were slaves. Her father, James Wells, was a skilled carpenter, and after emancipation he owned his own shop. Eager to learn, Ida went to nearby Rust College, a freedmen's school. Then, when she was sixteen, her parents died in a yellow fever epidemic and Ida had to teach to support her five brothers and sisters.

For the first eighteen years after the Civil War, most Southern states had civil rights laws. But in 1883, the Supreme Court ruled that the federal Civil Rights Act of 1875 was unconstitutional. Now blacks could be refused entrance to hotels, restaurants, and theaters and forced into third-class or cattle cars on trains. After Wells was thrown out of a first-class train car, she wrote an article for a black newspaper about standing up for her rights. That article was the beginning of her career in journalism. Soon she was writing for the best black papers in the country.

Wells started her antilynching crusade after an old friend was shot and killed by a white mob in Memphis, Tennessee. In her newspaper, *Free Speech,* she proclaimed that black men were not lynched because they raped white women, as the white press asserted. They were lynched as part of an ongoing effort to intimidate the black community. White citizens were furious, and Wells's printing press in Memphis was destroyed. Undaunted, she moved to New York and continued her battle there. In 1893 and 1894, she carried her campaign to England, where the public was outraged by her revelations of mob brutality in America.

In 1895, Wells married Ferdinand Barnett, a Chicago lawyer and editor. The couple settled down in Chicago. While raising their four children, Wells-Barnett continued her civil rights work. She became the first president of the Negro Fellowship League in 1900 and a cofounder of the National Association for the Advancement of Colored People (NAACP) in 1909. While living in Chicago, she was chair of the Chicago Equal Rights League.

Wells-Barnett remained active and militant until the end of her life. After World War I, she was often the first black person on the scene of lynchings and race riots, collecting eyewitness accounts from observers. Her reports were influential and often helped prevent further injustice. Just before her death at age sixty-eight, she wrote *Crusade for Justice: The Autobiography of Ida B. Wells.*

Ruth Ashby

Beatrix Potter

(1866–1943)

"My dear Noel,
I don't know what to write to you, so I shall tell you a story about
four little rabbits whose names were Flopsy, Mopsy,
Cottontail and Peter."
—Letter to Noel Moore, September 4, 1893

Anyone reading Beatrix Potter's illustrated letter to young Noel Moore will recognize the story to come: *The Tale of Peter Rabbit.* A favorite since its initial publication in 1901, the book launched

Beatrix Potter on her writing career and made her one of the best-loved children's book authors of all time.

Helen Beatrix Potter was born in London to Rupert Potter, a wealthy lawyer and amateur photographer, and his wife, Helen. Like other children of the upper-middle class, Beatrix and her younger brother, Bertram, were raised by governesses and spent most of their time in the nursery on the third floor of their London town house. There, isolated and somewhat lonely, the children amused themselves by raising a series of animals—mice, lizards, a rabbit, a bat, and several frogs. Beatrix shared the family interest in art and finished her first sketchbook when she was just eight years old, often using her pets as models. She and Bertram even boiled a dead fox so that she could correctly draw the fox's skeleton.

Every summer, the Potters took a long vacation in Scotland or the Lake District in England. There Beatrix developed a love of nature that would remain with her the rest of her life. From age fourteen to age thirty, she kept a secret, coded journal in which she wrote her most private thoughts. In later years, even she found it hard to decipher. She continued her art, becoming an expert wildlife illustrator, and sold some of her drawings to a greeting-card company.

When Beatrix was seventeen, Bertram was sent away to boarding school, and she acquired a new companion, Miss Annie Carter. They became very close and remained friends after Annie was married. It was for her son Noel that Potter invented the character of Peter Rabbit in 1893.

Eight years later, she turned her illustrated letter into a book, *The Tale of Peter Rabbit.* At age thirty-five, Beatrix Potter was suddenly a best-selling author. Within a few years, she had made a Peter Rabbit doll and helped in the design of wallpaper and a board game. Peter Rabbit became the world's first licensed character.

Potter enjoyed her success. In a letter to her publisher, she wrote, "It is pleasant to feel I could earn my own living." More books soon followed: *The Tale of Benjamin Bunny, Mrs. Tiggy-Winkle,* and some twenty others. Potter's little nursery books quickly became a hit in England and were marketed around the world.

Though she was now in her late thirties, Potter continued to live with and take care of her parents, even after she became engaged to her publish-

My rabbit Peter is so lazy, he lies before the fire in a box, with a little rug. His claws grew too long, quite uncomfortable, so I tried to cut them with scissors. but they were so hard that I had to use the big gardens scissors. He sat quite still and allowed me to do his little front paws but when I cut the other hind foot claws he was tickled, + kicked, very naughty. If he were a wild rabbit digging holes they would be worn down + would not need cutting.

Here are some rabbits throwing snow balls.

Beatrix Potter writes about her own rabbit, Peter, in an illustrated letter to Noel Moore, February 4, 1895.

er's son, Norman Warne, in 1905. Tragically, he died a month after the engagement.

In 1913, the forty-seven-year-old author married her lawyer, William Heelis, over her parents' objections. With the royalties from her books, she bought Hill Top Farm, an eighteenth-century cottage in the Lake District where her family vacationed. There she turned her energies to farming, sheep breeding, and rural life. Potter often received letters from children around the world who wrote to say they loved her books.

When she died at home at the age of seventy-seven, she left her farm and some four thousand acres of land to England's National Trust. But Beatrix Potter is remembered best for her enduring tales and drawings of a bunny in a little blue jacket.

Deborah Gore Ohrn

The
Global Community
1890 to the Present

The Global Community

1890 to the Present

"Away with your man-visions! Women propose to reject them all, and begin to dream dreams for themselves."
—Susan B. Anthony, 1871

Susan B. Anthony and the other suffragist pioneers of the nineteenth century did not live to see most of their dreams fulfilled. Yet the energy of their commitment propelled the next generation of feminists forward. (The word *feminism* itself was first coined in France in 1882.) The new century would see nearly universal female suffrage and the gradual acquisition of women's rights the world over.

A lone suffragist stands up for her right to vote.

In order to achieve their ends, feminists often had to challenge some very fundamental cultural traditions. Most societies accept established practices as "natural," or ordained by God. Thus it could be considered natural for a woman in North American Algonquian society to be a tribal sachem and in Chinese society for her to be a household slave. Feminists, always a small minority in any population, were often punished when they questioned the status quo. Yet much of the credit for the changed status of women today goes to a small band of radicals who dared to say the unsayable and do the undoable. Slowly, country by country, culture by culture, ideas about women's rights that had been considered outrageous in 1820 became acceptable or even fashionable by 1890—or 1920—or 1970.

Young and old, women rally to win the power to vote, c. 1909.

In most Western countries, getting the vote took an exhausting seventy years or more. In the United States, the National American Woman Suffrage Association campaigned doggedly, state by state, until finally they thought they had enough support for a constitutional amendment. When the amendment failed to materialize, the more impatient Women's Party began picketing Woodrow Wilson's White House. In Britain, suffragettes (as they were called) were even more militant. Women took to the streets in large numbers, marching on Parliament and chaining themselves to the fences of public buildings. One desperate woman threw herself under the hooves of the royal horse at the Derby Day race. In retaliation, the government arrested demonstrators by the hundreds and force-fed them when they organized hunger strikes. Still, in both America and Great Britain, women did not win the vote until after World War I. The war, which mobilized millions of women to work in factories or offices while their men were in battle, convinced many that the women who had sacrificed so much for their country deserved a voice in how it was run. In more conservative Catholic countries like France and Italy, the vote had to wait until after World War II.

By the end of the nineteenth century, women's rights movements had gained momentum in much of the rest of the world as well. Non-Western feminists used many of the same arguments as their Western counterparts,

A 1909 cartoon satirizes what would happen if American women could vote.

by whom they were greatly influenced. Yet they spoke from their own cultural traditions. In Japan, for instance, after the overthrow of the feudal samurai state in 1868, men and women alike engaged in an ongoing debate about how to modernize their country. Eloquent and beautiful Kishida Toshiko lectured widely in the 1880s on behalf of women: "In ancient times there were various evil teachings and customs in our country. . . . Of these, the most reprehensible was the practice of 'respecting men and despising women.'" She and others argued for equal access to education, for women's property and civil rights, for equality in marriage, and for the abolition of concubinage and prostitution.

But by 1890, the Japanese government had had enough. Like the Europeans after the French Revolution, they passed a law denying women access to any kind of political action and in 1898 initiated a civil code that again imprisoned women within the tyrannical Confucian family. Ultimately, the times were against the forces of conservatism, however. Japanese feminists struggled on, though most of their goals were not met until after World War II.

In China, the daring Qiu Jin, inspired by the Japanese example, dressed in men's clothing and led an uprising against the imperial government. Other Chinese reformers established girls' schools and anti-foot binding societies. In Egypt, Huda Shaarawi founded the Egyptian Feminist Union in 1923. Argentine feminists held the First International Feminist Congress (attended also by Peru, Chile, Uruguay, Italy, and the United States) in 1910 to discuss women's education, legal position, and suffrage, and the problem of child abandonment. Brazilian women founded a flurry of feminist journals in the 1880s and 1890s advocating education, self-fulfillment, and even suffrage. Their efforts paid off when in 1932 Brazil became the third country in the Western Hemisphere—after the United States and Ecuador—to grant women the vote.

Women's rights seesawed in the first half of the twentieth century, rising and falling with each successive war or revolution. In Russia after the Revolution of 1917, the Bolsheviks declared the absolute equality of the sexes in the new Communist order. As head of the Soviet Woman's Organization, the socialist visionary Alexandra Kollontai optimistically tried to establish communal social services for women that would free them from their ancient bondage in the family. But she lost her main support when Lenin died in 1924 and traditional patriarchal values reasserted themselves with the rise of Stalin in the 1930s. Again, women became solely responsible for child care and housekeeping even when they worked at full-time jobs for the state.

Though German women had won constitutional equality after World War I, when the Nazis came to power in 1933, they were expelled from government jobs and lost their political power. The ideal German mother, Hitler declared, devoted herself wholly to *"Kinder, Kirche, und Küche,"* "children, church, and kitchen." Italian dictator Benito Mussolini was even blunter: "In our state women will count for nothing."

The militaristic, ultrapatriarchal regimes of Germany, Italy, and Japan plunged the world into a war of unprecedented devastation. World War II (1939–1945) saw the death and displacement of tens of millions of people around the globe. In the fifteen years that followed the peace, while nations and individuals tried to heal and rebuild, women's rights were put on the back burner and women returned to the home. Then the silence was broken. In 1963, an American writer and housewife named Betty Friedan published *The Feminine Mystique*, a book about the "problem that has no name":

> It was a strange stirring, a sense of dissatisfaction, a yearning that women suffered in the middle of the twentieth century in the United States. Each suburban wife struggled with it alone. As she made the beds, shopped for groceries, matched slipcover material, ate peanut butter sandwiches with her children, chauffeured Cub Scouts and Brownies, lay beside her husband at night—she was afraid to ask even of herself the silent question—"Is this all?"

The vote, it seemed, had not brought the equality it promised. Women

From left to right: Gloria Steinem, Dick Gregory, Betty Friedan, Rep. Barbara Mikulski, and former Rep. Margaret Heckler march in a 1978 Equal Rights Amendment rally in Washington, D.C.

still had neither the privileges nor the responsibilities of men in the public sphere: not in politics, business, religion, the economy, the military, or the arts. Even in the worldwide antiwar and anti-establishment movements of the 1960s, women were at best subordinate and at worst treated as sex objects. One American civil rights worker spoke for hundreds of other male activists when he sneered, "The only position for women in SNCC [Student Non-violent Coordinating Committee] is prone." Like female abolitionists in the 1840s, women radicals of the 1960s discovered that to free others they must first free themselves. They needed a liberation movement of their own.

The women's rights agenda from the 1970s till now has been dedicated to equality of the sexes in the workplace and in the home. One of the key issues has been reproductive rights. Until the 1970s, easy access to contraception was impeded by religious disapproval, medical indifference, and public concern about sexual immorality. Early proponents of birth control, like Margaret Sanger in the United States, were often arrested for distributing materials deemed obscene. By the 1950s, contraceptive information was generally available to middle- and upper-class women, but contraceptives themselves were not always obtainable. Many women resorted to abortions, which, because they were illegal, were terribly unsafe. It has been estimated that before the *Roe* v. *Wade* Supreme Court decision on abortion in 1973, at least one million American women a year had illegal abortions—and some ten to fifteen thousand died. It's not surprising, given the grim statistics, that the right to a legal abortion was one of the first battles women fought. Today, the wide selection of contraceptive devices available has made it easier for many women in the world to prevent unwanted pregnancy.

The global woman's rights movement has reaped enormous benefits. More women have more say in politics, in business, in religion, and in the home than ever before. In the last forty years, women have been elected heads of governments in Bangladesh, Pakistan, India, Ireland, Great Britain, Norway, Argentina, the Philippines, and Israel, among others. They sit on the boards of our corporations, run our universities, broadcast our news, write our fiction, teach our young, heal our sick, and defend our streets and our countries. In wealthy, industrialized nations and often even in developing nations, most women live better than ever before—in terms not just of material comfort but of status and opportunity as well.

The picture is not all rosy. Overall, women are still underrepresented in the institutions that govern our countries, our customs, and our faiths. A few statistics tell the story: Only one politician in ten is a woman, and the

Latin American women rally in the International Convention in Bolivia. The sign in the foreground asks, "When are we going to live better?"

percentage in developing nations is far lower. Women still do 60 percent of the world's work for 10 percent of the pay. There is still a 25 percent gap in literacy between men and women in the developing world. And so on.

Ancient evils still haunt developing nations. In twenty-eight African countries, genital mutilation is still practiced on about two million girls a year. In China, female infanticide and the abortion of female fetuses is on the increase because the government has decreed that each family may have just one child—and most couples want that one child to be a boy. (Ironically, now that there are fewer women of marriageable age, Chinese women have actually risen in prestige!) In India, the annual number of dowry deaths— the burning of brides by their husbands because they have not brought sufficient wealth to the marriage—is up, despite official efforts to ban the dowry altogether. And approximately one million children, mostly girls, in Southeast Asia, who have been kidnapped or sold by their parents to pay debts, are prostitutes in the international sex-trade industry.

There's no reason for industrialized countries to feel complacent, either. They are hardly exempt from sex-related crimes, as testified to by the rising number of rape, murder, sexual harassment, and domestic violence cases in the United States.

Still, something has changed. The voice of one woman crying in the patriarchal wilderness—of Christine de Pizan or Mary Wollstonecraft or Sor Juana or Qiu Jin—has grown a hundred thousand, a hundred million strong. After five thousand years, the iron grip of patriarchy is finally weakening. At the 1994 International Conference on Population and Development, the delegates from some 150 nations agreed on a document endorsing "gender equality, equity, and the empowerment of women." The final "plan of action," widely hailed as unprecedented, acknowledges that runaway human population growth can be stabilized only by giving women more control over their own lives. Control not by husband, not by father, not by priest or mullah or minister, not by brutal dictator or paternalistic parliament but by women themselves.

We are nearing the year 2000. This would be a fine time for human beings, female and male, to enter into a new contract with each other. We know that the aggression and urge to reproduce that enabled us to conquer the earth cannot help on a planet with too many people, too much violence, and a fragile and damaged ecosystem. Those of you reading this book will live in a different world than the women portrayed here, but your lives will likewise be full of challenge. Most of us cannot hope to equal the achievements of the women in this book, but we can emulate their spirit. We too can dream our own dreams, as Susan B. Anthony said, and we can act on them.

And so, onward to the new millennium.

Ruth Ashby

Marie Curie

(1867–1934)

"I was taught that the way of progress is neither swift nor easy."
—From *Pierre Curie*, 1923

The first world-famous woman scientist, Marie Curie dedicated her life to the study of radioactivity. For her outstanding achievements, she became the first woman in history to win two Nobel Prizes, one in physics and one in chemistry.

Marie grew up in Warsaw, Poland, when the country was under Russian control. Although she had graduated from high school with honors, she wasn't allowed into the university because she was Polish. This rule forced the determined Marie to take classes secretly. She became fascinated by science and decided that her future career would involve chemistry—an unusual goal for a woman of her time.

After working as a governess for several years and saving money, Marie traveled to France to attend the Sorbonne, a part of the University of Paris. Following three years of intensive study, she became the first woman ever to receive a master's degree in physics. She soon graduated with a second master's degree in mathematics.

While at the Sorbonne, Marie met another dedicated scientist, Pierre Curie, whom she married in 1895. The Curies lived an aus-

Marie Curie in her Paris laboratory, 1921.

tere life and were completely focused on their scientific research. Marie continued to work full-time even after their two daughters, Irène and Eve, were born.

Marie began her doctoral studies in 1897, and the following year, she discovered polonium and radium, two elements with radioactive properties similar to those of uranium. Her research during this time focused on X rays, or rays emitted by certain elements that can pass through opaque materials. She called this property radioactivity.

Marie was awarded her Ph.D. in 1903, the same year she and Pierre and their colleague Henri Becquerel received the Nobel Prize in physics for their work on radioactivity. Marie's professional success was soon dampened by personal loss. In 1906, Pierre died. Marie was awarded his professorship, becoming the first woman teacher at the Sorbonne.

Despite the loss of her husband and research partner, Marie was determined to continue their work. She succeeded in isolating radium as a pure metal and in devising a technique of measuring the X rays it emits in order to determine its level of radioactivity. In 1911, her work was honored with another Nobel Prize, this one in chemistry.

During World War I, Marie and her daughter Irène developed the use of x-radiography (X rays) and studied other medical applications of radiation. Although the radioactive substances she discovered are now used to treat some forms of cancer, radiation was responsible for Marie's own death from leukemia. Without knowing it, she had slowly poisoned herself by constantly handling highly radioactive materials without protecting her body.

Irène and her husband, Frédéric Joliot-Curie, went on to win the Nobel Prize in physics for their research in artificial radioactivity. Marie Curie herself left a legacy of groundbreaking research that influenced progress in science and medicine and earned her world renown.

Bonnie Eisenberg and Mary Ruthsdotter

Sophia Hayden

(1868–1953)

Sophia Hayden was the first woman to graduate from MIT's architecture program. Yet her first commission, an exposition building to symbolize nineteenth-century women's advancement, would also be her last. For Hayden, her gender proved to be an insurmountable obstacle to professional recognition.

Hayden was born in Santiago, Chile, to a New England father and South American mother. At the age of six, she was sent to Boston to live with her paternal grandparents. She developed a passion for architecture during high school, and in 1886, she was admitted to MIT. There she won the respect of her professors as a brilliant and dedicated student.

However, after graduating with honors in 1890, Hayden could not find work as an architect. In the late nineteenth century, the field was dominated by men who were not open-minded enough to hire a woman to join an architectural firm. Instead, Hayden took a job teaching drawing at a high school in Boston. Then, in 1891, Hayden saw her chance. An announcement called for women architects to enter a competition to design the Women's Building at the World's Columbian Exhibition in Chicago. The twenty-two-year-old Hayden won the competition with an Italian Renaissance design.

Over the next two years, Hayden faced many difficulties. She was paid only fifteen hundred dollars, while male architects for the exposition were paid three to ten times that amount. She also had to satisfy the many demands of the board, including their stipulation that materials designed by women be incorporated into the decoration, whether or not they were suitable. But Hayden persevered. Hers was the first exposition building to be started and the first to be completed. The secretary to the president of the board later remarked, "It was generally known about the Construction Department that no one could change, by any amount of persuasion, one of her plans when she was convinced of its beauty or originality. She was always quiet but generally carried her point."

At the opening of the exposition, Hayden received an award "for delicacy of style, artistic taste, and geniality and elegance of the interior hall." Yet the professional recognition she had hoped for did not come. Critics of her building invariably focused on the fact that she was a woman: the structure was described by one as "dainty but tasteful," while another said that its "graceful timidity or gentleness, combined however with evident technical knowledge, at once differentiates it from its colossal neighbors and reveals the sex of its author."

Frustrated by such biased treatment, Hayden retired from architecture. Immediately, rumors circulated that she had had a nervous breakdown. The editors of *American Architect and Building News* wrote that reports of her mental collapse provided "a much more telling argument against the wisdom of women entering this especial profession than anything else could."

Eight years later, Hayden married an artist, William Blackstone Bennett, and lived quietly in Massachusetts for the rest of her life. Her brief career left no legacy, since the Women's Building was pulled down when the exposition closed. Yet she paved the way for future generations. At the time of her death, there were 308 registered women architects in the United States. Today, there are over 10,000.

Elisabeth Keating

Maya Lin

Today, there are more women architects than ever before. One of the most prominent is Ohio-born Maya Lin (1959-   ), who designed the Vietnam Veterans Memorial in Washington, D.C. When she was just an undergraduate architecture major at Yale University, Lin won a national competition for the memorial. Her design called for "two long, low black granite walls" built partly into the ground and listing the nearly fifty-eight thousand dead and missing from the Vietnam War. Though its innovative design was at first controversial, since its dedication in 1982, the memorial has been acclaimed by veterans' groups and art critics alike.

Lin has since designed other public buildings and memorials throughout the United States, among them the Civil Rights Memorial in Montgomery, Alabama, and New York City's Museum of African Art.

Alexandra David-Neel

(1868–1969)

"Adventure is my only reason for living."
—My Journey to Lhasa, 1927

Alexandra David-Neel went where no Western woman had gone before. Explorer, Buddhist scholar, and writer, she risked danger and death to explore extraordinary places in central Asia.

Alexandra David was born in Paris to middle-class French parents. Their marriage was an unhappy one and Alexandra often ran away, dreaming of adventure and travel. Embarking on a career as an opera singer, she quickly began to fulfill that dream, traveling with her troupe through Asia, North Africa, and Greece.

She fell in love with the places she visited in east Asia. Determined to explore the region, she retired from the world of opera in 1903 to travel as a journalist, writing magazine articles about the places she visited and the Eastern way of life.

The following year she married an engineer, Philippe-François Neel, who worked as a representative for the French government in Tunis. She later wrote that she found marriage and the roles of wife and mother threatening to her freedom and independence. She chose not to have children and from 1903 to 1911 diligently pursued her writing career while studying in London and Paris, rarely seeing her husband. In a letter to Philippe, she admitted, "I am a savage. . . . I love only my tent, my horses, and the desert."

In 1911, David-Neel persuaded her husband to pay for her long-desired trip to the Far East. She packed her bags and went alone to India, where she studied and practiced Buddhism. She became fascinated with Tibet, a nearly inaccessible country situated on a plateau between China and India. The first European woman to interview the Dalai Lama, the spiritual ruler of Tibet who was then briefly exiled in India, David-Neel earned a reputation as a dedicated Buddhist scholar. To learn more about Tibetan spiritual life, she spent two years living alone in an isolated mountaintop cave, where she prayed, meditated, and studied Buddhist teachings.

Her next goal was to visit the sacred city of Lhasa, long a forbidden place to non-Tibetan peoples. At one of the many Buddhist monasteries she visited, she was given a young man named Yongden as a traveling companion. Together, they set off on a perilous, year-long journey. They traveled mostly on foot, crossing the vast, blazing Gobi Desert and the rugged Himalayan Mountains, where the snow was often waist-high. Before entering Tibet, David-Neel disguised herself as a peasant woman, dying her hair and darkening her face. Yongden became her Buddist-monk son. Thanks to David-Neel's expert knowledge of Tibetan culture and language, her true identity remained hidden.

On January 1, 1924, Alexandra David-Neel entered the forbidden city of Lhasa. She was fifty-five years old and had been away from home for fourteen years. She stayed in Lhasa for several months before heading back to India and then to Europe and her husband. In 1927, she recorded her many amazing experiences in *My Journey to Lhasa*.

David-Neel remained in Europe for ten years before she returned to Tibet in the mid-1930s. She traveled with Yongden, now her adopted son and the companion in all her travels. When the Japanese invaded Tibet in 1944, Yongden and the seventy-six-year-old explorer fled on foot with other refugees. David-Neel spent the rest of her life in France, where she wrote dozens of books about central Asia and Tibetan Buddhism. She died in 1969, nearly 101 years old.

Deborah Gore Ohrn

Emma Goldman

(1869–1940)

*"Anarchy stands for the liberation of the human mind from the
domination of religion; the liberation of the human body
from the domination of property; liberation from the shackles
and restraints of government."*
—*Anarchism and Other Essays*, 1911

To law-enforcement officials, reformer Emma Goldman was once known as the "most dangerous woman in America." Yet her defense of anarchism was ultimately an advocacy not of violence but of freedom—to live, to work, to love. Passionately eloquent and committed, she was the most controversial of American feminists and social reformers in the first half of the twentieth century.

Emma was born in the Jewish quarter of Kovno, Russia (now Lithuania), to Taube Bienowitch Goldman and Abraham Goldman. From the start, as she later wrote, she was "largely in revolt." Her childhood was an unhappy one, marred by the turmoil of her parents' marriage. Her mother, who had two daughters from a previous marriage, thought Emma was an added burden. Her father, a lower-middle-class shopkeeper with a violent temper, took his business frustrations out on his family, especially on Emma. Emma was also in constant trouble at school. Once, she was even denied a passing mark on a high school examination because a teacher refused to sign a certificate of good character.

Emma Goldman

In 1881, the Goldmans moved to St. Petersburg, where Emma went to school for six months before taking a job in a cousin's glove factory. After work, she enjoyed joining university students for intellectual debates on the social, political, and labor issues of the day.

Four years later, rather than submit to a marriage arranged by her father, Goldman immigrated to America with her half sister Helena. They settled in Rochester, New York, where both found work at a clothing factory. Goldman was appalled at the conditions she and other Eastern European immigrants endured: low pay, exhausting fifteen-hour workdays, crowded tenements. Goldman blamed economic capitalism—in which private individuals control the means of production in order to make a profit—for this exploitation of workers.

After a failed marriage to another young émigré, Goldman moved to New York City, where she joined the anarchist movement, which opposed all forms of government and authority. Violence was often a part of anarchist actions, and Goldman helped her longtime companion, Alexander Berkman, plot to kill the steel magnate Henry Clay Frick. The plan failed, and Berkman went to prison for fourteen years, while Goldman was never charged. She did, however, later serve one year at the prison on Blackwell's Island in New York for telling crowds of unemployed people that "it was their sacred right" to take bread if they were starving.

During her imprisonment, Goldman came to reject violence as a means of change. After her release, she went to Europe to study nursing and took up midwifery to support herself when she returned to the States. Nevertheless, in 1901, when President William McKinley was shot by an anarchist, the authorities accused her of inciting the assassin. She did not know the young man, and the police could never prove any link between them. Still, Goldman could not help defending him.

Goldman began traveling across the United States giving speeches on anarchism, free speech, and birth control, some of which she published. She also wrote a book called *Anarchism and Other Essays* and edited the radical magazine *Mother Earth* with Berkman when he got out of prison.

Goldman's causes were not popular ones, and she had many critics. They nicknamed her "Red Emma" for what they felt was her advocacy of communism—even though she was not a member of the Communist party. In 1919, Berkman, Goldman, and 247 other Americans were deported to Russia for having opposed the military draft. Deeply disillusioned with the totalitarian rule she found there, Goldman spent only two years in Russia and then moved to Sweden, where she continued writing books.

Goldman was allowed to return to the United States only once, in 1934, for a lecture tour during which she promised not to talk politics. She spent the rest of her life in Europe and Canada, lecturing and writing against war and repression. Her autobiography, *Living My Life*, was published in 1931. In February 1940, a stroke ended her life.

Despite imprisonment and exile, Emma Goldman never abandoned her dream of a perfectable society. She once said, "Everyone is an anarchist who loves liberty and hates oppression. But not everyone wants liberty for the other fellow. That is my task."

Deborah Gore Ohrn

Rosa Luxemburg

(1870–1919)

"See to it that you remain human. . . . Being human means joyfully throwing your whole life 'on the scales of destiny' when need be, but all the while rejoicing in every sunny day and every beautiful cloud."
—Letter to a friend, December 28, 1916

Rosa Luxemburg's story is the story of a life fully lived. A socialist, feminist, and pacifist, Luxemburg was one of the most important leaders of the European Socialist movement in the late nineteenth and early twentieth centuries.

She was born in Russian Poland in 1870 to Polish Jewish parents and grew up in Warsaw, the youngest of five children. Rosa was a brilliant student and was admitted to a prestigious school. Yet, from the start, she knew she was different from her classmates. A quota on the number of Jews who could be admitted to her school meant that, unlike most of the students, she had to take a competitive entrance examination to get in.

She also walked with a limp from the age of five because of poor medical treatment of a dislocated hip. Proud and independent, young Rosa threw herself into sports and into her studies. She said she would rather be thought of as "strong" than as crippled. Through these experiences, Rosa developed a sympathy with the oppressed that would shape her life. She also decided that whatever the obstacle, she could overcome it.

Rosa became interested in politics in high school and joined the outlawed Socialist Proletariat party at the age of sixteen. She believed that socialism, based on the principle that workers should unite to have a say in their wages and working conditions, would lead to a society in which each person could achieve his or her own full potential. She soon learned that she would

This West German stamp of Rosa Luxemburg, issued in 1974, stirred controversy from conservatives and liberals alike.

pay a price for her political beliefs. As a senior in high school, Rosa qualified for a gold medal in academic achievement, but the medal was withheld "on account of her rebellious attitude towards the authorities."

When the Russian authorities killed and imprisoned most of the leaders of the Proletariat party, Luxemburg fled to Zurich, Switzerland. At the age of nineteen she enrolled in the university and studied botany, mathematics, and politics. By the age of twenty-three, she was a leader in the international Socialist movement. In Paris, she and her lover, Leo Jorgisches, started their own Socialist newspaper, which she wrote and he published. She spent most of her life in Germany, where she founded the Spartacus party, which advocated a peaceful workers' revolution.

Luxemburg was independent-minded and believed that the truth could be discovered only through the free exchange of ideas. At a time when most Socialists rejoiced over the Bolshevik Revolution in Russia, she criticized the Bolsheviks for dissolving the Constituent Assembly and for restricting suffrage, writing, "freedom only for the supporters of the government, only for the members of one party, is no freedom at all. Freedom is always and exclusively freedom for the one who thinks differently."

Luxemburg was also a pacifist. Unlike the Russian Communists, she considered war, regardless of the results, to be a return to barbarism. She believed that workers from all nations must use peaceful means, like mass strikes, to achieve their ends. Her pacifist views were unpopular with the

German government as well. Its policy of militarism, nationalism, and imperialism would result in the outbreak of war throughout Europe in World War I. The government needed the support of German workers to win the war, and Luxemburg's charisma and wide following made her dangerous.

Luxemburg was imprisoned many times for her beliefs. From jail, she continued to write books, articles, and long letters to friends, and to pursue her love of nature by growing a small garden. No matter what the threat, she continued to believe, as she had from childhood, that through willpower and hard work, she could achieve her goals. In World War I, she was imprisoned for her opposition to the war. A few months after her release in 1919, she was beaten and killed by the German police, her body mercilessly thrown into a canal.

Elisabeth Keating

Maria Montessori

(1870–1952)

"If help and salvation are to come, they can only come from the children, for the children are the makers of men."
—*The Absorbent Mind*, published posthumously in 1967

Maria Montessori devoted a lifetime to the education of children. Her innovative, often controversial ideas helped revolutionize the teaching of the young in the twentieth century.

Maria was born in Chiaravalle, Italy, to Alessandro Montessori, an army officer, and Renilde Stoppani. Her strong-willed, articulate mother helped Maria pursue her dream of a higher education, which her more conservative father did not support. At age thirteen, Maria enrolled in a technical school for engineering but later changed her mind when she began to study biology at the University of Rome. She went on to the university's medical school, where she was prohibited from taking some courses with her fellow male students and even had to dissect her first cadaver by herself. But she was persistent, and in 1896, Maria Montessori became the first woman to graduate from the University of Rome's school of medicine.

Montessori specialized in pediatrics and after graduation joined the staff of the university's psychiatric unit. Soon, she was appointed as director of a school for mentally retarded children. Using specially devised teaching materials, she taught the children for two years and discovered that they could do as well on state exams as regular students. As she later wrote, "I became convinced that similar methods applied to normal students would develop or set free their personality in a marvelous and surprising way."

Maria Montessori with one of her pupils.

In 1907, Montessori began teaching three- to seven-year-olds in a *casa dei bambini* ("house of children") in a poor district of Rome. Using the school to test her theories about learning, she developed a child-centered approach quite different from that of the traditional teacher-directed classroom. Her goal was to develop the whole personalities of children by exposing them to a classroom environment suitable to their age and level of development. She discovered that if children were not force-fed information, they learned naturally and spontaneously, actually preferring work to play. In a Montessori classroom, teachers guided students in self-paced, self-directed learning projects without rewards or punishments, encouraging them to learn by using their senses of touch, sight, sound, and smell.

That same year, Montessori opened the first official Montessori School in Rome. She embarked on a lecture tour, writing, speaking, and giving teacher-training courses. By 1935, hundreds of Montessori schools had opened throughout Europe and the United States. Montessori met with much opposition from teacher organizations in America, however, and after

1918, enthusiasm for her ideas waned, not to be revived until the 1950s. In 1929, Montessori created the Association Montessori International.

During the 1930s and 1940s, fascist regimes closed all the Montessori schools in Italy and Germany, and Montessori spent World War II in India, where educators were very receptive to her ideas. By the time of her death at age eighty-one, she had witnessed the renewal of the Montessori movement worldwide.

The changes Maria Montessori wrought in early childhood education can be seen today in such concepts as the open classroom, hands-on learning, reading readiness programs, and individualized learning. Above all, she established the revolutionary idea that education starts with the child.

Deborah Gore Ohrn

Alexandra Kollontai

(1872–1952)

"No more domestic 'servitude' for women! No more inequality within the family."
—"Communism and the Family," 1918

Born the daughter of a wealthy Russian general during the reign of Czar Alexander II, Alexandra Kollontai grew up with everything a child could want. She was painfully aware, however, that she had luxuries peasant children did not, and she was disturbed by the conditions in which her family's servants lived. As she grew up, she began to reject everything associated with the upper class, except for her two great loves: reading and traveling.

At age sixteen, Kollontai traveled through Europe on a "grand tour" and discovered the writings of Communist and Socialist theorists. Their ideas became especially important to her after 1893, when she married and had a son. On a trip with her husband, Kollontai visited factories and witnessed the appalling conditions of the proletariat (working class). As her sympathy for their plight grew, she sought out groups working to overthrow the government controlled by the czar. She left her family to study economics in Zurich, then returned to St. Petersburg in 1898 to work as a revolutionary.

Kollontai devoted herself to revolutionary activities full-time in 1905, focusing on organizing women workers. She believed not only in women's right to work for wages but also in their right to sexual freedom and control over their own fertility. She felt that in order for women to be equal with men they needed economic independence from them. Kollontai viewed

Alexandra Kollontai

motherhood as a social function—mothers provided the state with future generations of workers. Therefore, she argued, child care and domestic work should be a social responsibility funded by the state. She envisioned communal kitchens, nurseries, and laundries so that women would be freed from domestic burdens to work for wages outside of the home.

As a result of the Russian Revolution in 1917, the Communist party, led by Lenin, came to power. Lenin appointed Kollontai the only woman member of the Central Committee of the party. She organized the first Congress of Worker and Peasant Women in 1919, and as the first director of the Women's Section of the Central Committee, she tried to draw women into the political arena. Kollontai's ideas were reflected in the sweeping Family Code legislation of the new state. The Family Code abolished the distinction between legitimate and illegitimate children; gave parents equal authority over their children; gave husband and wife control over their own earnings; made divorce with equal division of property obtainable; assumed women's right to work; and established free maternity hospital care.

The reforms in communal living and child care that Kollontai envisioned were, however, lost in the civil strife that enveloped Russia throughout the 1920s. Kollontai became disillusioned by the party's push for rapid industrialization at the expense of social programs. Her outspokenness about sexual freedom cost her the support of many in the Communist party, and Kollontai was replaced by a person with more conservative views.

From 1923 to 1945, Kollontai served as the Russian minister to Norway, Mexico, and Sweden, and she continued to promote and write about women's right to work, their sexual freedom, and fertility issues up until her death in 1952. Kollontai's greatest achievement was establishing the concept of women's economic independence and autonomy in the largest country in post–World War I Europe.

Lyn Reese

Qiu Jin

(1875–1907)

> *"Comrades, I say to you,*
> *Spare no effort, stuggle unceasingly,*
> *That at last peace may come to our people.*
> *And jewelled dresses and deformed feet*
> *Will be abandoned.*
> *And one day, all under heaven*
> *Will see beautiful free women,*
> *Blooming like fields of flowers,*
> *And bearing brilliant and noble human beings."*
> —Excerpt from "To the Tune 'The River is Red' "

When Qiu Jin wrote this poem, her Chinese women contemporaries remained tied to the traditional Chinese family system, still subservient to father, or husband, or son. Poet and revolutionary Qiu Jin was one of the first to challenge the old ways and work for more social freedom and equality with men.

Qiu Jin was born into a respectable and moderately wealthy family, and her parents insisted that she receive a good education. She enjoyed riding horseback and using swords, and she liked to read romantic novels with dashing heroes. Qiu Jin married at the age of twenty-one. Although she lived in Beijing and associated with interesting, well-educated people, she felt burdened by her marriage to a man who had more conventional views than she did. In Beijing, Qiu Jin became concerned about the Western and Japanese troops that had come to occupy China, and she believed that the Manchu government was wrong to allow foreigners to control the country's destiny.

Foot Binding

The Chinese custom of foot binding dates back to the tenth century. At first, it was a mark of upper-class status, but later, the custom spread throughout much of the population. Before her fifth birthday, a little girl's feet would be broken and her toes bent under her soles. To keep them from growing, the feet would remain tightly bound under layers of bandages for the rest of her life. The painfully crippled feet that resulted, no more than three and a half inches long, became an object of erotic devotion. For a thousand years, foot binding helped keep Chinese women subordinate and restricted within the home.

In 1903, Qiu Jin left her husband and went to Japan to study. There she became recognized for her daring personality. She often dressed in men's clothing, carried a sword, and drank wine. A diligent student, she became an advocate for education and equal rights for women. In an effort to provide role models for other women, she wrote articles celebrating historical Chinese women.

Qiu Jin returned to China in 1906 and began to publish a monthly women's magazine. She recommended that women train in the skills needed to support themselves in various professions and encouraged them to stand up to the oppression of their families and the government.

Qiu Jin believed that women could only achieve equal rights if the old, corrupt Manchu government was abolished and replaced with a modern, Western-type state. She was the first Chinese woman to become a revolutionary and advocate of violence as a way of overthrowing the government.

Qiu Jin joined forces with her cousin Hsu Hsi-lin, who had also engaged in revolutionary activities out of concern for China's future. The two cousins helped unite numerous secret revolutionary societies to work against the Manchu government, and they organized military units. Qiu Jin became principal of a school for girls, which served as a front for her revolutionary activities.

On July 6, 1907, Hsu Hsi-lin was caught before the uprising he and Qiu Jin had planned could occur. Under interrogation, he admitted his revolutionary views and was executed. On July 12, government troops arrived at Qiu Jin's school, and she was captured. Although she refused to admit her complicity in the plot, documents seized by the troops clearly implicated her in revolutionary activity, and she was beheaded.

Qiu Jin was instantly acknowledged as a martyr and heroine. Some saw her as a courageous woman who died rebelling against the enemies of China; others admired her as a symbol of female independence.

Lyn Reese

Mary McLeod Bethune

(1875–1955)

"The true worth of a race must be measured by the
character of its womanhood."
—Address, "A Century of Progress of Negro Women,"
Chicago Women's Federation, June 3, 1933

Educator, writer, lecturer, organizer—Mary McLeod Bethune was a pioneer in all her endeavors. For more than fifty years she championed democratic and humanitarian causes, and she made a vital contribution to the education of African-American children.

Born on July 10, 1875, Mary was the second-to-last of seventeen children. Her parents had been slaves, but they now owned a small plot of land on which they had built the family's cabin. As a young girl, Mary wanted more than anything to learn how to read, but there were no schools open to black children. When Mary turned eleven, however, her dream came true. A Presbyterian mission school opened five miles from her home in Mayesville, South Carolina, and the young black teacher from the North was seeking pupils. Mary was accepted immediately. She learned quickly and then passed on her knowledge to younger students and her siblings.

After graduating from the Moody Bible Institute in Chicago in 1895, Mary started a Sunday school in Augusta, Georgia. In 1899, she moved to Florida with her husband, Albertus Bethune, and their infant son, Albert. Mary had heard that a new railroad was being built, and she knew that there were no schools for African-Americans in the area. In 1904, with only $1.50 in savings, she opened the Daytona Normal and Industrial Institute for Negro Girls. The private school operated in a rundown four-room cottage that Bethune rented, and supplies included boxes used as desks, splintered pencils, elderberry ink, and any useful items the town dump had to offer. The students—five girls aged eight to twelve—paid fifty cents per week tuition. The school's motto was "Enter to learn, depart to serve."

Bethune had a strong faith—and good business sense. Her speaking abilities enabled her to raise money from many sources, including philanthropist John D. Rockefeller and James Gamble, who owned the Ivory soap company. In less than two years, Bethune had rebuilt the school and bought the land it sat on. The school's enrollment soared to 250 students. In 1923, the school merged with the all-male Cookman Institute and later was renamed Bethune-Cookman College. The college, which awarded its first bachelor of science degrees in elementary education in 1943, continues to prosper today.

In addition to her contribution to African-American education, Bethune promoted civil rights at the national level. In 1935, she cofounded the National Council of Negro Women, which helped expand public housing and Social Security and welfare programs, and fought against discrimination. The following year, she became national advisor on minority affairs to President Franklin D. Roosevelt. She was already a close friend of the first lady, Eleanor Roosevelt, who shared her humanitarian views.

As national advisor, Bethune promoted Roosevelt's New Deal to the black population and encouraged African-Americans to join the military. Roosevelt, in turn, supported the NCNW and the National Youth Administration, an organization providing job training for young people. Bethune also organized the "Black Cabinet," a group of professionals and advisors who tried to ensure that black issues were addressed in Washington. In 1945, she was sent to San Francisco to help found the United Nations.

Bethune died of a heart attack at her home in Daytona Beach, Florida, on May 18, 1955, and was buried at Bethune-Cookman College. In her will, she left a message for all children, and especially for African-American children: "Believe in yourself, learn, and never stop wanting to build a better world."

Judy Gitenstein

Huda Shaarawi

(1879–1947)

*"Women reflected on how they might elevate their status and worth
in the eyes of men. They decided that the path lay in participating
with men in public affairs. . . . Their leap forward was greeted
with ridicule and blame, but that did not weaken their will.
Their resolve led to a struggle that would have ended in war,
if men had not come to acknowledge the rights of women."*
—Harem Years: The Memoirs of an Egyptian Feminist,
published posthumously in 1987

In 1923, Huda Shaarawi committed an almost unthinkable act: stepping
from a train into a crowded Cairo station after returning home from a
women's conference in Europe, she removed her veil. This was the first
time any veiled woman in the Middle East had defied tradition so publicly.
At first, there was shocked silence. Then the women who had come to greet
her broke into applause. Some tore off their veils too. For Huda, this signaled
the final break with her old life as a protected woman within a harem and
the beginning of her new life as the leader of a women's movement.

The daughter of a wealthy administrator, Huda grew up in Cairo, Egypt.
When she was a child, she was jealous of the advantages given her brother
because he was a male. When she was thirteen, Huda learned of her arranged
marriage as a second wife to a much older cousin. She "wept long and hard"
and at first refused to obey. Finally, she was told, "Do you wish to disgrace
the name of your father and destroy your poor mother who might not survive
the shock of your refusal?" Huda reluctantly agreed to the marriage.

The marriage did not go smoothly, and Shaarawi lived apart from her husband
for seven years. During these years she met women who wanted to change their
status. In Egypt at this time, it was considered proper for women to stay mainly
in the private world of the home, or harem. In public, women wore the *hegab*,
the traditional veil that covers a woman's hair and often much of her face. Many
women who wanted to break this tradition traveled to Europe every year

and found role models in women who sought changes in their own countries.

When Shaawari was twenty-one, she reconciled with her husband and had two children. She was, however, a different person from the thirteen-year-old girl her husband had married. Shaawari began organizing lectures for women, which brought women outside their homes and into public halls for the first time. She invited speakers who talked about the condition of women and even convinced royal princesses to help her establish the first women's welfare society, which raised money to help impoverished women.

Veiling

Veiling is the concealment of women behind a thin, transparent fabric worn over all or part of the face, head, and shoulders. The practice of veiling began in the ancient Near East and was meant to identify "respectable" women when they ventured from the home. Veiling is traditionally both a sign of status and a means of restricting women from contact with men outside the immediate family circle.

In the Koran, Muhammad bid women to "draw their veils over their bosoms" and told his own wives to stay secluded in the private area of their homes. After his death, his words were interpreted to mean that women should hide their whole face and that all women (except those in the lower classes) should remain secluded. In the twentieth century, women and men throughout the Islamic world have questioned and modified the age-old customs of veiling and seclusion. Today, the debate continues between religious conservatives, who say that veiling is a way of asserting Islamic identity, and liberals, who argue that it is an outward sign of women's subordination in Islamic cultures.

After World War I, Egypt's struggle to free itself from British rule escalated. Many woman joined the effort, ignoring the harem way of life for the first time to take part in public political action. In 1919, Shaarawi helped organize the largest women's anti-British demonstration. When British soldiers tried to stop a women's march, Shaarawi was ready to defy them until she realized that that would endanger the women's lives. Instead, she had the women stand still, in silent protest, for three hours in the hot sun, before they dispersed.

When Shaarawi's husband died in 1922, she made the decision to stop wearing her veil in public. In 1923, she helped found the Egyptian Feminist Union and was elected president, a position she held for twenty-four years. The union campaigned successfully for reforms such as raising the minimum marriage age for girls to sixteen, increasing educational opportunities, and improving women's health care.

Shaarawi led delegations of Egyptian women to international conferences and organized meetings for Arab feminists from other countries. She founded the All-Arab Federation of Women in 1944. Her act of public unveiling and her work for women's independence served as an example for many others throughout the Middle East. She had became a symbol of the fight for women's rights everywhere.

Lyn Reese

Margaret Sanger

(1879–1966)

"Every child a wanted child."
—Slogan

Margaret Higgins Sanger, the founder of the American birth control movement, was born in Corning, New York, to Michael Higgins and Anne Purcell Higgins. Her father was a fiery stonemason who would rather talk politics than work, and the family had continual financial problems. Her mother, Anne, was pregnant eighteen times in thirty years and gave birth to eleven living children. She died at age fifty, worn out and ill from tuberculosis. The poignant example of her mother's life gave Margaret an urgent interest in women and the issue of birth control.

Margaret attended Claverack College in New York from 1896 to 1899 but had to leave because of lack of money. After her mother died, she enrolled in nursing school. While there, she met and married William Sanger, an architect, with whom she had three children. In 1910, they moved to New York City, where Margaret found a job as a visiting nurse and midwife on the impoverished Lower East Side. She was appalled to see the poverty, disease, and death rate among the women, who, despite these conditions, continued bearing children.

In 1910, birth control devices like diaphragms and douches were available to women who could afford them. But they were illegal, and the Comstock

Law of 1873 had made distributing any contraceptive information through the mail illegal as well. Most doctors supported the Comstock Law, so poor and uneducated women had nowhere to turn. Their primary method of contraception was abortion. In her autobiography, Sanger told the story of a poor mother of three who died after a self-induced abortion and how the death impelled Sanger to fight for women's right to contraception: "I would tell the world what was going on in the lives of these poor women. No matter what it should cost, I would be heard."

As a first step, Sanger wrote a series of articles called "What Every Girl Should Know" for a Socialist newspaper. The articles provided women with information about reproduction, and one was declared obscene under the Comstock Law. Sanger decided to overturn the law. In 1914, she founded a newspaper called *Woman Rebel* that dealt with sex education and deliberately sent it to subscribers through the United States mail. Sanger was arrested but left the

Margaret Sanger testifies for birth control before a House committee in Washington, D.C., May 19, 1932.

Birth Control and American Law

Even as Margaret Sanger opened birth control clinics nation-wide, contraception remained illegal in many states. It wasn't until 1965 that the United States Supreme Court, in *Griswold v. Connecticut*, declared contraception to be a constitutional right of married couples. In 1972, the court declared that it was the right of unmarried people as well.

In 1973, the Supreme Court decriminalized abortion, stating in *Roe* v. *Wade* that "the right of privacy . . . founded in the Fourteenth Amendment's concept of personal liberty . . . is broad enough to encompass a woman's decision whether or not to terminate her pregnancy." Today, state regulations and funding for abortions vary widely. Yet, despite repeated lobbying and protests by antichoice groups, the Supreme Court has repeatedly reaffirmed the basic right to abortion expressed in the *Roe v. Wade* decision.

country on the eve of her trial. She used the following year in Europe to research what people in other countries were doing about family planning. When she returned to the States, her case was dismissed. She was disappointed, because the Comstock Law remained unchallenged—but she was free.

Undeterred, Sanger and her sister Ethel Byrne opened America's first birth control clinic in Brooklyn, New York, in 1916. They were arrested for keeping a "public nuisance," spent thirty days in jail, and appealed the court's decision.

The publicity from the trial helped Sanger's cause. The New York State law was thereafter changed to allow doctors to give women contraceptive advice for "the cure and prevention of disease"—which could be caused by pregnancy.

Sanger's single-minded crusade took a toll on her family life. As she traveled around the country and the world on speaking assignments, she left her children behind and was devastated when her five-year-old daughter died of pneumonia in 1915. Margaret and William divorced in 1920, and two years later, she married J. Noah Slee, a wealthy businessman who supported her work.

The rest of Sanger's life was devoted to legalizing birth control. In 1921, she organized the American Birth Control League, later known as the Planned Parenthood Federation of America, and in 1927, she planned the first world population conference, in Geneva. For years she fought a series of court battles against the federal post office and male medical establishments to legalize birth control clinics. In addition, she supported changes in state laws to allow the distribution of family planning information by medical professionals.

Her victories were many. By 1932, more than eighty birth control clinics operated in the United States. In 1936, the Comstock Law was reinterpreted to allow the mailing of contraception, and in 1937, the American Medical Association recommended that contraception be taught in medical school and that birth control methods be researched.

Sanger retired from the leadership of Planned Parenthood in 1938 and moved to Arizona. She came out of retirement to serve as the first president of the International Planned Parenthood Federation in 1952 and traveled around the world giving speeches advocating birth control. Just six years after the first birth control pills for women were marketed in 1960, Margaret Sanger died of heart failure in an Arizona nursing home.

For more than fifty years, Margaret Sanger battled state and federal governments, the medical profession, religious leaders, and the force of public opinion to secure for women the right to control their own bodies. We owe her a profound debt.

Deborah Gore Ohrn

Helen Keller

(1880–1968)

"Everything has its wonders, even darkness and silence, and I learn,
whatever state I may be in, therein to be content."
—*The Story of My Life,* 1903

Helen Keller was not born blind. But when she was a year and a half old, she fell gravely ill, probably with scarlet fever, and lost both her sight and her hearing. For the next five years, she lived in a world of her own, lost in darkness and silence.

Helen was the daughter of Captain Arthur and Kate Adams Keller of Tuscumbia, Alabama. They suspected that their wild little girl was intelligent but had no way to communicate with her. In 1887, they hired a teacher from the Perkins School for the Blind in Boston, Anne (Annie) Sullivan. Annie tried to teach Helen the finger alphabet. At first, the finger games meant nothing to her. But a month after Annie's arrival, Helen suddenly understood that each pattern formed a word. She could "speak"—and "hear."

Helen Keller with her teacher and friend, Annie Sullivan.

Helen made rapid progress. Soon, she had learned to read using the Braille alphabet, and even to talk out loud, though never clearly. News of her amazing accomplishments appeared in newspapers throughout the world. Her first autobiographical story was published when she was just fourteen. She went on to attend regular schools. At the Cambridge School for Young Ladies, she proved herself to be a gifted and eager student. She even studied French and Greek along with the usual subjects of literature, mathematics, geography, and history.

Keller went on to Radcliffe College, where she attended classes with the other girls, then rushed back to her room to transcribe into Braille as much as she could remember of the lectures Anne Sullivan had finger-spelled for her. With her phenomenal memory, she was an excellent student and graduated in 1904.

Keller's first book, *The Story of My Life* (1903), became a worldwide best-seller, translated into fifty languages. Its popularity made Helen Keller a celebrity. With Annie, she embarked on a public lecture tour of the United States and Europe. But eventually she became bored with talking about herself and began to write about other topics. She became an avid supporter of women's suffrage and the international peace movement before World War I. She corresponded with people all over the world.

As she grew older, Keller began to focus her attention on advising and fund-raising for the American Foundation for the Blind. She wrote a number of books and traveled throughout the world to support education and more humane treatment of people with disabilities. In 1964, she was honored with the Presidential Medal of Freedom for her life of advocacy.

Helen Keller was a pioneer and an important role model for success despite multiple disabilities. Today, many children with disabilities receive the special care and education they need to live meaningful lives thanks, in part, to Helen Keller.

Bonnie Eisenberg and Mary Ruthsdotter

Anna Pavlova

(1881–1931)

"I want to dance for everybody in the world."
—Motto

She nearly had her wish. During her thirty-year career, Pavlova traveled nearly five hundred thousand miles around the globe, dancing before millions of people. She introduced the ballet to countries where it had never been seen before. In her lifetime, she was the greatest ballerina in the world.

Anna Pavlova was born in St. Petersburg, Russia, during the reign of Czar Alexander II. Her father died when she was only two, and she and her mother were left nearly impoverished. Born prematurely, Anna was not expected to live past infancy. Yet, despite a sickly childhood, she survived, frail but ultimately healthy.

When Anna was eight, her mother took her to a performance of the ballet *Sleeping Beauty* at the Maryinsky Theatre. Anna was enraptured and announced that she wanted to take ballet lessons. "At eight years old," she wrote later, "I had found the one, the unchanging ambition of my life." Her mother objected, but Anna was insistent. Two years later, in 1892, she entered the Imperial School of Ballet.

Anna's graceful, ethereal dancing soon caught the eye of her teachers, and she began to dance in school performances. At sixteen, she joined the Imperial Ballet and immediately began to take on more demanding roles. In 1906,

Anna Pavlova posing during a Belgian engagement in 1927.

she was promoted to prima ballerina, the highest honor she could receive.

Like other leading dancers of the Imperial Ballet, Pavlova went on tour when not appearing on stage in Russia. Her dancing caused a sensation in Europe, the United States, and Canada. The best-known dance of her career was Saint-Saën's two-minute "Dying Swan," choreographed for her by Michel Fokine.

For Pavlova, ballet—the music and the dance—was a kind of religion. She wanted to share it with the world. In 1911, she formed her own company, and for the next twenty years, she never stopped traveling. Pavlova took her troupe to the United States, Canada, Europe, South America, Central America and the Caribbean Islands, China, Japan, India, the Philippines, Borneo, Egypt, South Africa, Australia, and New Zealand. She made her base at Ivy House, her home in London, where she trained her pupils and the members of her company. On the grounds, she kept a pond for her pet swans, which had become her mascots.

Pavlova's magnetism and her absolute devotion to her art earned her the admiration of all who worked with her or saw her dance. She was married to her manager, Victor Dandré, but she never had any children. She felt that art and family life were incompatible. Instead, she expressed her love for children by teaching her young pupils and by setting up a home for Russian orphans in Paris.

Ballet was Pavlova's whole life. Even when she found traveling exhausting, she could not bear to retire. At age fifty, Pavlova succumbed to pneumonia as she was about to set off on another world tour.

Ruth Ashby

Virginia Woolf

(1882–1941)

*"A woman must have money and a room of her own if she
is to write fiction."*
—A Room of One's Own, 1929

Virginia Woolf wrote some of the most splendid fiction in the English language. Yet she was always aware that a woman's creativity depended not just on talent and hard work but also on the physical, financial, and psychological freedom necessary for her gifts to flourish. Her novels as well as her feminist essays made her a spokeswoman for women artists everywhere.

Adeline Virginia Stephen was born in London to Sir Leslie Stephen, a notable editor and critic, and Julia Stephen. Virginia, as she came to be called, grew up in a large household, with four half brothers and sisters from her parents' first marriages and three from their own. The Stephens moved in well-to-do literary circles and entertained many prominent writers and scholars. Summers were spent at a house by the sea in Cornwall.

Like most upper-middle-class Victorian girls, Virginia was denied a formal education. Yet she had access to her father's excellent library, and in this highly literate household, the young Virginia received a very good education indeed. She also started to keep a diary.

When Virginia was thirteen, her beautiful and loving mother died, and in her grief, Virginia had the first of her mental breakdowns. When she was fifteen, her half sister Stella also died. Dark days followed as Virginia and her older sister Vanessa tried to keep house and take care of their aging father.

Virginia Woolf, 1903

It was 1904 when Leslie Stephen died and Virginia, Vanessa, and their brothers Thoby and Adrian immediately moved to a house in the Blooms-bury section of London. Virginia was freed from the obligations of middle-class society to live the kind of intellectual life she wanted. Her brothers' friends visited from Cambridge University—and the Bloomsbury Group was born. In addition to the Stephens sisters, the group included artist Duncan Grant, art critic Clive Bell, whom Vanessa married, writer Lytton Stra-chey, and economist John Maynard Keynes. Together, they helped forge the twentieth-century mod-ernist movement in art and literature.

In 1912, Virginia mar-ried Leonard Woolf, a polit-ical writer and journalist. They never had children, though for a while Virginia wanted them. Her recur-ring manic-depressive bouts convinced Leonard that it would be wiser for her to remain childless. Nonetheless, the Woolfs had a loving marriage, and Leonard was proud and supportive of his brilliant wife. In 1917, the Woolfs founded the Hogarth Press to publish the works of modern writers.

Anonymous Was a Woman

In *A Room of One's Own*, Woolf pondered the fate of creative women through the centuries:

When one . . . reads of a witch being ducked, of a woman possessed by devils, of a wise woman selling herbs, or even of a very remarkable man who had a mother, then I think we are on the track of a lost nov-elist, a suppressed poet, of some mute and inglorious Jane Austen, some Emily Brontë who dashed her brains out on the moor or mopped and mowed about the high-ways crazed with the torture that her gift had put her to. Indeed, I would venture to guess that Anon, who wrote so many poems without signing them, was often a woman.

Virginia worked obsessively on her first novel, *The Voyage Out*, for more than six years before it was published in 1915. It was followed by *Night and Day* (1919), *Mrs. Dalloway* (1925), *To the Lighthouse* (1927), *Orlando* (1928), and *The Waves* (1931), among others. Moving away from the lengthy Victorian novel with its well constructed plot, Virginia Woolf's novels are shorter, more personal, and more oblique. They focus on small, illuminated moments: a dinner party, an afternoon by the sea, intermissions in a village pageant. And they are told not by an omniscient narrator but through the medium of a character's inner consciousness.

Virginia Woolf also wrote feminist essays and books, most notably *A*

Room of One's Own and *Three Guineas* (1938). The former explores women's creativity and relates it to their self-image and position in society. The latter is a plea against war, which Virginia associates with patriarchal culture.

Three Guineas did not, of course, prevent World War II, and in 1941, after the war began, the Woolfs moved to a rented house in Sussex. Despite her successful career and growing fame, Virginia had never overcome her battle with mental illness. Throughout her life, the completion of a novel triggered depression. As the Germans bombed London and invasion seemed likely, Virginia finished her last book, *Between the Acts*, and wrote three letters—one to Vanessa and two to Leonard—describing her despair. Then she filled her pockets with stones, waded into the nearby River Ouse, and drowned.

Virginia Woolf left a legacy of excellence. Many consider her to be the finest woman writer of the twentieth century.

Deborah Gore Ohrn

Rose Schneiderman

(1884–1972)

"I would be a traitor to these poor burned bodies . . . if I came here to talk good fellowship. . . . The life of men and women is so cheap and property is so sacred. . . . It is up to the working people to save themselves."
—Speech after the Triangle Shirtwaist Company fire, March 25, 1911

For many immigrants at the end of the nineteenth century, America seemed like the promised land. But once there, they were faced with low-paying jobs and often desperately poor living conditions. Many American and immigrant women became active in labor reform. Rose Schneiderman was one who rose to leadership in the movement.

Rose and her family left Poland for New York City when she was eight years old. Her father died when she was ten, and she was able to attend school only a few more years before having to work to supplement her mother's wages. Rose got a job as a cashier in a department store, where she worked as many as seventy hours a week for the meager salary of two dollars. Long hours and low pay were common, and the workers' only recourse was to turn to the labor or trade unions that began in the 1830s. Unions sought better wages and decent working conditions, but at the time, most unions admitted only men.

Schneiderman became a cap maker in 1898, and in 1903, she helped organize a local chapter of the Hat, Cap, and Millinery Workers for Women. The local chapter grew quickly, and Schneiderman was elected to the union's executive board in 1904. The following year, she joined the Women's Trade Union League (WTUL), which created women's unions, promoted laws to protect women laborers, and educated women in the workforce. Schneiderman served as the New York branch vice president and then became a full-time organizer in 1907.

Schneiderman rapidly became an articulate spokesperson for women's rights in the workplace. She organized strikes of women garment workers that led to the formation of the International Ladies Garment Workers Union (ILGWU). The 1911 shirtwaist workers' strike, commonly known as the Uprising of the Twenty Thousand, was probably her most famous protest. Schneiderman organized the strike after nearly 150 workers at the Triangle Shirtwaist Company died in a tragic fire because they were locked inside the building.

Schneiderman became the WTUL president in 1918 and held the position until 1949. She focused the union's efforts on the education of women workers as well as on the passage of laws to protect them, including the legislation of a minimum wage and an eight-hour workday. In 1919, she took her skills as a labor reformer abroad, helping to establish the International Congress of Working Women.

Schneiderman ran as the Farm Labor candidate for the United States Senate in New York in 1920, and although she lost, she attracted national attention. In 1921, she created the Bryn Mawr Summer School for Women Workers to facilitate the education of women laborers. She was also appointed to President Roosevelt's "Brain Trust," a group of close advisors.

Schneiderman died in New York City in 1972. In addition to devoting her life to improving the lot of working people, she had galvanized a united force— a "sisterhood"—of women workers. Other leaders may have demanded higher wages, but Rose Schneiderman demanded—and won—respect for women.

Judy Gitenstein

Gabrielle "Coco" Chanel

(1883–1971)

"Fashion is not something that exists in dresses only. . . . Fashion is in the sky, in the street, fashion has to do with ideas, the way we live, what is happening."
—Oft-repeated maxim

Gabrielle "Coco" Chanel ruled Parisian fashion for almost six decades, inspiring women to cast aside corseted, uncomfortable clothing for more simple, classic designs. She made the name Chanel synonymous with elegant fashion that never goes out of style.

Gabrielle was born in a town near Issoire in south-central France. Her mother died when she was six. When they were abandoned by their father, Gabrielle and her two sisters were sent to different places to live. Gabrielle spent many years in an orphanage and at seventeen was sent to a convent in Moulins, in central France.

Two years later, she and an aunt became assistants in a shop that made infants' clothing and bridal wear for the wealthy who lived in the castles nearby. The shop also made women's everyday clothing, and Gabrielle became known for the quality of her alterations. When she moved to her own apartment,

Chanel models one of her own designs, 1937.

customers began seeking her out there to have their clothes altered. By age twenty-one, she had a loyal following.

Chanel's fashion debut came in 1913, when she opened a small boutique in Deauville, a resort for the rich. The store featured her own sweater and skirt designs as well as accessories. The following year, she opened a boutique in Paris. Within five years, she had built a business that appealed to both the rich and the not-so-rich who appreciated her simple, comfortable designs. Her use of jersey was inspired by the black convent smocks she had worn as a girl. Women were thrilled to abandon the corseted styles in favor of Chanel's dresses, and her designs revolutionized the fashion industry.

Today, a Chanel suit still carries her signature design tailored for the working woman.

Coco Chanel turned fashion into big business. She is best known for making high fashion available to working women. Her clothing—knit suits, jersey dresses, and inexpensive costume jewelry—was comfortable and easy to wear. Her designs were affordable to many women, and the daytime styles could easily cross over into evening wear if necessary.

When World War II broke out in 1939, Chanel closed her dress shop. Materials and fabrics were difficult to obtain since most were being allocated to the war cause, and she felt that women were unlikely to spend money on clothing during the war. During this time, Chanel concentrated on selling her wildly successful perfume, Chanel No. 5, introduced in 1922. The perfume was so named because a fortune-teller had once told her that five was her lucky number!

Chanel's dresses made a comeback in 1954, when she was seventy-one years old. Her public, which expected some new designs, was at first disappointed. But she showed the world that style and good fashion are timeless. She reintroduced her highly copied suit: a collarless, braid-trimmed jacket with a slim skirt. In fact, her black dress with white collar and cuffs, quilted leather handbag, and long strings of pearls are as fashionable today as they were when she first designed them.

Coco Chanel died on January 10, 1971, in her apartment at the Ritz Hotel in Paris. She was a brilliant businesswoman who, at the height of her career, employed more than three thousand people in her fashion house, textile business, perfume laboratories, and costume jewelry workshop. Even today, it is easy to spot a "Chanel" on the street or in the fashion pages. Twenty-five years after her death, Chanel is still the most famous name in the fashion world.

Judy Gitenstein

Eleanor Roosevelt

(1884–1962)

"Where, after all, do universal rights begin? In small places, close to home . . . in the world of the individual person . . . where every man, woman, and child seeks equal justice, equal opportunity, equal dignity without discrimination. Unless these rights have meaning there they have little meaning anywhere. Without concerned citizens' action to uphold them close to home, we shall look in vain for progress in the larger world."
—Speech at the United Nations, 1958

Eleanor Roosevelt devoted her life to the cause of human rights. Humanitarian, social reformer, and advocate for peace, she was one of the greatest women of the twentieth century—"the first lady of the world."

Anna Eleanor Roosevelt was born in New York City into an affluent but troubled family. Her beautiful mother, Anna Hall Roosevelt, often ignored her plain, quiet daughter, whom she nicknamed "Granny." Eleanor's adored father, Elliot Roosevelt, was an irresponsible alcoholic. By the time Eleanor was ten, both her parents and her younger brother had died, leaving her and her older brother to be raised by stern Grandmother Hall.

The shy child did not come into her own until age fifteen, when she enrolled at Allenswood, a girls' finishing school in England run by the unconventional, energetic Marie Souvestre. Under Mademoiselle Souvestre's guidance, she blossomed. She later remembered her three years at Allenswood as the happiest years of her life. When Eleanor came back to New York, she put the school's social ideals into action, working as a volunteer at a settlement house and joining the National Consumers League to help secure health and safety for workers.

Eleanor Roosevelt looks over the Universal Declaration of Human Rights, November 1949.

On March 17, 1905, Eleanor married her distant cousin Franklin Delano Roosevelt. At the wedding, the bride was given away by her uncle Theodore Roosevelt, then president of the United States. The young couple settled down in New York City in a home chosen by her mother-in-law, who dominated the household. During the next eleven years, Eleanor had six children, one of whom died in infancy.

Franklin Roosevelt's entry into politics in 1910 brought his wife out of the house and into the political arena. During World War I, when FDR was assistant secretary of the Navy, Eleanor organized political gatherings, worked as a volunteer in soldiers' canteens, and visited naval hospitals. When the family returned to New York, she became involved in women's causes and joined the League of Women Voters and the Women's Trade Union League.

Franklin was paralyzed by polio in 1921, and Eleanor became his legs and ears. Soon she was traveling all over New York for the Democratic State Committee and leading a delegation to the Democratic National Convention. During Franklin's tenure as governor of New York, she stood in for him on state inspections, touring institutions such as prisons and mental hospitals.

Eleanor had feared that her husband's election to the presidency in 1932 would end her political and reformist activities. Instead, she became the most active first lady in United States history. She reached out to ordinary citizens with her radio broadcasts and daily newspaper column, "My Day."

During the 1930s and 1940s, Eleanor Roosevelt became an outspoken advocate for the disadvantaged and oppressed in American society, whether they were women, blacks, Jewish refugees, tenant farmers, or textile workers. Her advocacy was not always successful, but at least groups previously ignored now had a voice at the White House. On behalf of African-Americans, Eleanor argued for the end of discrimination in the armed services and advocated a federal antilynching bill.

Despite their good working relationship, Eleanor and Franklin Roosevelt did not share the emotional intimacy of marriage after 1918, when Eleanor discovered her husband's affair with his secretary, Lucy Mercer. Instead, Eleanor developed many other close friendships.

After Franklin Roosevelt died in 1945, Eleanor's role in world affairs expanded. At the urging of President Truman, she became a delegate to the United Nations in 1946. As chair of the United Nations Commission on Human Rights, she was largely responsible for the 1949 adoption by the United Nations of the Universal Declaration of Human Rights. Eleanor Roosevelt continued to work for social justice and international cooperation until she died of tuberculosis in 1962. Her last official position was as chair of President Kennedy's Commission on the Status of Women in 1961.

During her lifetime, Eleanor met with criticism from many who disagreed with her liberal ideals. She also earned the love and admiration of people from all walks of life who felt that she represented the best hope of American democracy. As her biographer, Archibald MacLeish, wrote when she died: "She dies the object of the world's attention and is buried not only with the ceremonies reserved for the great but with something the greatest rarely achieve—the real grief of millions of human beings."

Ruth Ashby

Georgia O'Keeffe

(1887–1986)

*"I decided I was a very stupid fool not to at least paint as I wanted
to and say what I wanted to when I painted, as that seemed to be
the only thing I could do that didn't concern anybody but myself."*
—Exhibition catalog, January 1923

Georgia O'Keeffe was nearly thirty years old when she found her
own vision. The drawings and paintings she produced from 1916
until her death established her as one of the finest artists of the
twentieth century.

Georgia was born on a farm in Sun Prairie, Wisconsin, to Ida Totto
O'Keeffe and Francis O'Keeffe. As a child, she was a talented musician,
but by the age of ten, she knew she wanted to be a painter. When she was
fourteen, the family moved to Williamsburg, Virginia, where Georgia attended convent school and high school. She left to study at the Art Institute
of Chicago from 1905 to 1906 and then continued her studies at the Art
Students League in New York.

At this time, the prevailing styles in American art were still the realistic
and somewhat impressionistic styles of the nineteenth century. O'Keeffe
knew she had nothing to contribute to these schools, so she spent a few
years working as a commercial artist in Chicago, designing embroidery and
lace, and then went to Texas to teach art. Most important, she studied
with art educator Arthur Dow at Columbia University's Teacher's College.
He encouraged her to think of color and shape as abstract ways of communi-
cating her own ideas.

By 1916, O'Keeffe had the confidence to express her own originality.
Still teaching in Texas, she mailed some of her charcoal drawings to a friend
in New York, who in turn showed them to the famous photographer and
modern-art gallery owner Alfred Stieglitz. He was patron and mentor to
many modern American artists, among them John Marin, Arthur G. Dove,
and Marsden Hartley. He immediately recognized O'Keeffe's talent and
without her knowledge organized her first exhibition at his Gallery 291. In

Georgia O'Keeffe and her painting Jack in the Pulpit *at a 1943 exhibition at Chicago's Art Institute.*

1918, O'Keeffe quit teaching and moved to New York City to paint and be with Stieglitz. They married in 1924.

O'Keeffe's paintings are realistic and abstract at the same time, monumental images of flowers or mountains or skyscrapers that seem timeless because they are so simplified. Her close-ups of flowers are very beautiful, yet many people found them disturbing because of their sensual explicitness.

In 1929, O'Keeffe traveled to New Mexico and was inspired by the desert landscape. She returned to New York with a big barrel full of bones and animal skulls as subjects for her still lifes. Her desire to paint aspects of the New Mexican landscape brought her to a turning point in her life. She decided to live six months of every year at her rented ranch in New Mexico, away from her husband, who refused to leave the northeast.

After Stieglitz's death in 1946, O'Keeffe moved permanently to Abiquiu, New Mexico. By the time she died in 1986 at the age of ninety-nine, she was recognized as the greatest American woman artist of the century.

Till the end, Georgia O'Keeffe was passionate about her art. Everyday routine tasks exasperated her, so eager was she to return to the painting for which she lived: "Always you are hurrying through these things with a certain amount of aggravation so that you can get at the painting again because that is the high spot—in a way it is what you do all the other things for. Why it is that way I do not know.... The painting is like a thread that runs through all the reasons for all the other things that make one's life."

Deborah Gore Ohrn

Gabriela Mistral

(1889–1957)

For one hundred days each year, a dry, cold wind blows down from the Alps, swiftly chilling the plains of southern France. It is called the mistral, and it is the name that Gabriela Mistral chose for herself when she began to write poems. Her first name, Gabriela, she took from the Archangel Gabriel.

Mistral, born Lucila Godoy Alcayaga, grew up in the village of Montegrande, Chile. Her mother was devoted to taking care of her and her older sister, Emelina, despite her father's desertion when Gabriela was only three. But for Gabriela, the hardship of poverty gave way to the pleasure of living in the crisp valleys of the Chilean countryside, surrounded by the towering Andean mountains. At the age of nine, Gabriela did go to school. Although she only attended for three years, it was long enough to discover her love of poetry, and she started to write her own poems. Emelina, who was a teacher, later taught her sister at home, and she inspired Gabriela to become a teacher as well.

Working as an assistant teacher at the age of sixteen, Mistral moved to La Cantera in 1906 to take another job. It was there that she fell in love with a young railway worker. Although they eventually ended the relationship, she was deeply affected by his death two years later, when he committed suicide. The only item found on him was a postcard from Mistral. Mistral turned her grief into poetry. For several years, she kept *The Sonnets of Death* from being published because they were so personal.

Mistral never married, but as the years passed, her love of teaching grew. In 1912, she gained a diploma that allowed her to teach secondary school, and she was assigned to a school in Los Andes, near Santiago. The proximity of the city of Santiago opened up many writing opportunities: Mistral published her poetry in a wide selection of periodicals and established herself in Chilean literary circles.

When Mistral finally published three of the poems from *Sonnets of Death* in 1914, she won the national prize for poetry, *Juegos Florales*. Yet, as her popularity increased, she became more disenchanted with the literary set, finding them shallow. She did have loyal friends, though. One was

Gabriela Mistral, winner of the 1945 Nobel Peace Prize for literature.

Chile's minister of justice and education, Pedro Aguirre Cerda, who appointed Mistral director of a secondary school for girls in 1918. The school was located in rural Punta Arenas, whose rough terrain was the inspiration for Mistral's series of poems entitled *Patagonian Landscapes*.

When Mistral became the director of the new Sixth School for Girls in Santiago, she met the Mexican minister of education. In 1922, she accepted his invitation to join him in starting educational programs for the poor in his country. In Mexico, Mistral introduced mobile libraries to rural areas and edited a book of poetry and prose called *Readings for Women*. One of her goals was to make fine literature available to everyone, not just the elite. During this time, *Desolación*, the first volume of her collected poems, was published, and it became a huge success. She also published *Ternura*, a collection of children's poems.

Everything Is Round

Stars are circles of children
Looking at the earth as they play . . .
Wheat stalks are bodies of children
swaying and swaying as they play . . .

Rivers are circles of children
running off to the sea as they play
Waves are circlets of little girls
embracing this world . . . as they play . . .

As Mistral's repertoire grew, so did her popularity—she was becoming an international literary star. Almost instantly, her life changed from that of a private poet to that of a public figure: she was asked to attend conferences and make speeches, and at various times, she represented Chile at the League of Nations, at the United Nations, and at the Chilean consulates in Madrid, Lisbon, Rio de Janeiro, Nice, and Los Angeles.

Because of her role as an international writer and humanitarian, Mistral traveled extensively. She eventually settled in the United States and taught at Middlebury and Barnard colleges. In 1945, Gabriela Mistral won the Nobel Prize in Literature, the only Latin American woman poet ever to do so. When she accepted the award, she accepted it on behalf of Latin America and the "poets of my race."

Lyn Reese

Ichikawa Fusae

(1893–1981)

Ichikawa Fusae was a feminist and politician who led the women's suffrage movement in Japan for much of the twentieth century. Campaigning for social equality, she was elected five times to the House of Councillors.

Ichikawa was born into a farm family in Japan during a time when women had few rights and low social status. As she witnessed her father's abuse of her mother, she became determined to improve the quality of women's lives when she grew up. Ichikawa completed her teacher training and taught elementary school. Then she became the first woman reporter for a liberal newspaper and was assigned to report on factory conditions for working women. While she had been aware of the subservience of Japanese women in the home, her experiences as a reporter opened her eyes to the abuses occurring in the workplace as well.

In 1919, Ichikawa helped found the New Women's Association, an organization that advocated equal opportunities for men and women. One of the group's major achievements was to convince the government to revoke the law that forbade women to attend political meetings. Beginning in 1921, Ichikawa spent two and a half years in the United States, where she studied the women's movement and became involved

Ichikawa Fusae shares her victory with her supporters in the 1974 elections.

with the National Women's party, which sought equal rights for women at the governmental level.

Inspired and motivated to push for women's rights in her own country, Ichikawa returned to Japan in 1924. She founded the Women's Suffrage League, which campaigned for voting rights, published a magazine called *Women's Suffrage*, and was involved in consumer activism.

The Women's Suffrage League began to disband in 1940 as World War II raged. Ichikawa, however, saw the war as an opportunity to promote her cause even more effectively. Since men were away fighting, women had to take their places working full-time in the factories. Their wages, hours, and working conditions, though, were far from equal to those of men. Ichikawa continued to push the government to recognize the discrepancies between women's and men's work opportunities.

Ichikawa's fight for women's rights paid off in December 1945, when women over the age of twenty were given the right to vote, and women over the age of twenty-five could become candidates in national elections. In 1952, Ichikawa ran for public office, and although she did not belong to a major political party and lacked financial backing, she solicited mass support and was elected to the House of Councillors. Except for the years from 1971 to 1974, she served in the house until her death.

During her tenure as a house councillor, Ichikawa continued to focus on improving women's lives. She devoted much time to working with the League of Women Voters as well as with the Women's Suffrage Hall, a research institute aimed at increasing women's political awareness. She also campaigned against corrupt elections and money politics.

Ichikawa died at age eighty-eight in 1981. Her hope of changing women's status in Japanese society, and of instilling in women a sense of pride and involvement, was realized during her lifetime. Her work on behalf of equal rights and suffrage transformed the lives of generations of Japanese women.

S. Suzan Jane

Bessie Smith

(1894–1937)

"There ain't nothin' I can do, or nothin' I can say, that folks don't criticize me. But I'm goin' to do just as I want to anyway."
—"T'ain't Nobody's Biz-ness If I Do," 1923

Raised in poverty in Chattanooga, Tennessee, Bessie Smith *lived* the blues. As a child, she would sing on street corners, accompanied on the guitar by her brother Andrew. She made her professional debut at the age of nine at the Ivory Theater in Chattanooga.

Around 1910, the well-known blues singer Gertrude "Ma" Rainey took Smith on the southern circuit of segragated black theaters and tent shows. The traveling variety shows featured comedians, jugglers, wrestlers, singers, and dancers. Smith went on to sing with other shows, including the Florida Cotton Pickers and her own group, the Liberty Belles. After her performances, the theaters would sometimes give special shows for white audiences. No matter which crowds she sang to, Smith mesmerized them with her voice.

With the popularity of "St. Louis Blues," "Down-Hearted Blues," and "Gimme a Pigfoot," Smith landed a recording contract with Columbia Records. The four songs released in 1923 became instant hits. Smith recorded many songs for Co-

Empress of the Blues, Bessie Smith

Billie Holiday

Blues singer Billie Holiday (1913-1959) used her often tragic life as an inspiration for her music. Born to teenage parents in a black section of Baltimore, Billie had an impoverished and difficult childhood. She came to New York in her teens and began to sing at Harlem jazz clubs. One night, she was discovered by John Hammond, a record producer who was haunted by her melancholy voice. Soon, she was performing and recording with big band leaders like Benny Goodman and Count Basie. Nicknamed Lady Day, Holiday became a legendary performer, always appearing in a white gown with her trademark white gardenia in her hair. She made her smooth, sad voice do things other people's voices couldn't. Some said that she even sang *between* notes.

By the end of her life, Billie Holiday was plagued by depression and by the drug habit she had acquired on the road. Drugs finally killed her on July 17, 1959.

lumbia over the years, and her success helped save the company from bankruptcy. Although she made two thousand dollars a week at the height of her career, this amount was only a fraction of her true earnings, since it was common practice for artists in the "race record" divisions, as they were called, to be denied royalties.

Bessie Smith was recording at a time when it was difficult for African-Americans to break into the commercial world. Smith's success was tied to the rise and fall of Columbia's race records, which prospered in the 1920s and suffered in the 1930s during the Depression. Smith's popularity peaked between 1923 and 1930. During that time, she sang with the best musicians of the day and wrote many of her own songs, often on the themes of poverty and love and other emotions. Wearing satin gowns and headdresses, long strands of pearls, and feather boas, the vocalist became known as the Empress of the Blues.

Smith's songs all dealt with things familiar to her, including the temptation of alcohol. Her drinking caused unpredictable behavior—she was generous one moment and argumentative the next. Alcoholism, coupled with the Depression, caused her career to decline. People were less willing to spend money on entertainment, and with the advent of radio, they no longer had to buy records. Smith's songs, however, were not played on the radio because of their harsh lyrics.

At her last recording session in 1933, Smith sang a song called "Down in the Dumps." Sadly, the title suggested what was happening to her career. Smith was just making a comeback in 1937 with a hip, sophisticated jazz sound when she died from injuries sustained in a car accident in Mississippi.

Smith's family could not afford to buy a headstone, and her grave remained unmarked in a cemetery outside of Philadelphia for more than thirty years. In 1970, singer Janis Joplin and other musicians and fans purchased a stone for Bessie Smith's grave. It is engraved with the following words: "The greatest blues singer in the world will never stop singing."

Judy Gitenstein

Martha Graham

(1894–1991)

"I did not choose to be a dancer. I was chosen."
—"How I Became a Dancer," 1965

One of the founders of modern dance, Martha Graham was fiercely dedicated to her art. She regarded dance as a high calling to which she had been "elected" and which she served with reverence. Her unique technique, dramatic choreography, brilliant staging, and use of original scores all contributed to her revolutionary influence on twentieth-century dance.

Martha Graham was born into an upper-middle-class household in Allegheny, Pennsylvania. The first daughter of Dr. George and Jane Graham, Martha was serious, responsible, and self-assured. When she was fourteen, the family moved to Santa Barbara, California, where one day she saw a poster announcing the appearance of Ruth St. Denis in her exotic dance-drama *Egypta*. Martha insisted her parents take her. By the time the mesmerizing performance was over, Martha's mind was made up: she was going to become a dancer.

In 1916, Graham enrolled at the Denishawn School in Los Angeles, where she studied with Ruth St. Denis and her husband, Ted Shawn. Graham first made a name for herself in Shawn's primitive dance *Yochitl*. She appeared with Denishawn for seven years before leaving to dance with the Greenwich Village Follies and teach at the Eastman School of Music in New York.

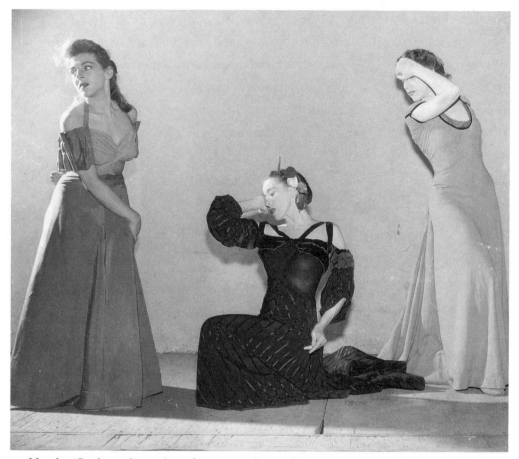

Martha Graham (center) and two members of her company in Deaths and Entrances, *a piece based on the lives of the Brontë sisters, 1944.*

In 1926, Graham broke away to become an independent dancer and eventually form her own company. Together with other pioneers in modern dance, she wanted to create a twentieth-century dance that was distinctly American. Her dances of the late twenties and early thirties—*Heretic, Revolt, Four Insincerities, Immigrant*—were powerful works of protest. Later, she moved on to more specifically American themes in such works as *Frontier, Appalachian Spring,* and *Letter to the World,* inspired by the life and work of Emily Dickinson.

Only the absolute dedication of her dancers and the generous assistance of patrons enabled Graham to pursue her vision. Her constant collaborator was composer Louis Horst, who wrote many of the original scores for her dances.

Graham dance technique, centered in the torso of the body, uses the contraction of the diaphragm to reveal inner tension. For audiences who were used to the graceful movements of classical ballet, Graham's dance seemed harsh, even ugly. "It's not my job to look beautiful," she once told a class of students. "It's my job to look interesting." Angular and powerful, Graham's dances expressed elemental emotion.

Graham's later dances were often based on Greek mythology. She also featured strong woman characters such as Clytemnestra, Hecuba, Mary Queen of Scots, Saint Joan, and the Brontës.

Graham herself danced until 1969, when she was seventy-five. After her retirement, she continued to direct the Martha Graham Dance Company and oversee the Martha Graham School of Contemporary Dance in New York City until her death at age ninety-six.

One of the great artists of the twentieth century, Martha Graham once said, "No artist is ahead of his time. He is his time; it is just that others are behind the time." Today, through the company and school she founded and the more than 180 works she choreographed, Martha Graham's legacy continues.

Ruth Ashby

Isadora Duncan

Free-spirited Isadora Duncan (1878-1927) was the foremost pioneer of modern dance in America. Born in San Francisco, Isadora started to dance as soon as she could walk and was teaching neighborhood children by the time she was six. By age twelve, she was performing for audiences in Chicago and New York. After persuading her family to move to Europe in 1899, she became an immediate hit in the drawing rooms of the elite. There, she performed her innovative barefoot dance, dressed in flowing tunics of neo-Grecian design.

Duncan's life was controversial and often tragic. All her life, she cared deeply for children, and one of her great dreams was to found a school to carry on her work. This dream was never fully realized, as all her schools eventually closed for lack of money. She herself was devastated when her two children died in a freak accident in 1913. Duncan's greatest contribution was to break away from the rigid rules of classical ballet and establish a dance of pure expression.

Marian Anderson

(1897–1993)

"As long as you keep a person down, some part of you has to be down there to hold him down, so it means you cannot soar as you otherwise might."
—Interview on CBS-TV, December 30, 1957

At the age of six, Marian Anderson was singing with her Sunday school choir. Listening to her sweet but powerful voice, everyone in the congregation knew that there was a musical genius in their midst.

Born into an African-American family in Philadelphia, Marian was the oldest of three children. When she was eight, her father bought the family a piano, but there was no money for lessons. Marian, deciding that nothing would stand in her way, taught herself how to play. Once she saw a violin in the window of a pawnshop, and she saved the pennies and nickels she earned washing steps and running errands to buy it.

By the time she turned thirteen, Marian was singing contralto in the adult choir at her church. When she decided to get formal voice training, one music school refused to take her because she was black. So, the choir raised the money to pay for private lessons instead. For her share, Marian performed at parties for five dollars, which at the time was a lot of money for a young girl to earn.

In 1925, Anderson placed first in a voice contest, winning the chance to sing with the New York Philharmonic. Although this was a promising start, she faced many obstacles because of racial prejudice. European audiences, however, were more accepting of classically trained opera performers of color, and Anderson traveled to Europe seeking new opportunities. In 1930, the Italian conductor Arturo Toscanini heard her sing and told her, "A voice like yours is heard once in a hundred years." Between 1925 and 1935, Anderson toured Europe three times, gaining a steady following and becoming ever more popular.

Returning to America with a growing reputation, Anderson hired Sol

Hurok, a powerful agent, as her manager. In 1935, she performed to rave reviews and a standing ovation at New York's Town Hall. From then on, she gave about seventy recitals each year. But even at the height of her success, racial segregation prevented her from performing with an opera company.

In 1939, Hurok tried to schedule a concert for Anderson at Constitution Hall, the national headquarters of the Daughters of the American Revolution. He was told that the hall was completely booked. The response implied that a black singer, no matter how beautiful her voice, was not welcome onstage or in the audience of the DAR's concert hall.

When the first lady, Eleanor Roosevelt, found out about the DAR's action, she canceled her membership. She then helped arrange for Anderson to sing at an outdoor concert at the Lincoln Memorial. Over seventy-five thousand people attended the concert, and millions more heard Anderson's rich voice over the radio.

Anderson's next major triumph came in 1955, when, at age fifty-seven, she made her debut as the first African-American member of the Metropolitan Opera Company. The audience gave her a standing ovation even before she started to sing.

Anderson used her talent and fame not only to further her opera career but also to work for equal rights for blacks. She performed at the inaugurations of President Eisenhower and President Kennedy and was awarded the Presidential Medal of Freedom, the highest honor a civilian can receive during peacetime. In 1958, she served as a United States delegate to the United Nations.

Marian Anderson died at age ninety-six in Portland, Oregon, after suffering a stroke. Her career had earned her international stardom, but she never forgot her roots. For years, she helped young African-American singers by sponsoring a scholarship to enable them to study. By being the first African-American to gain entry into the American opera world, she inspired future generations of performers to pursue their talents and achieve their goals.

Judy Gitenstein

Amelia Earhart

(1897–1937)

"In soloing—as in other activities—it is far easier to start
something than it is to finish it."
—*20 Hours: 40 Minutes—Our Flight in the* Friendship, 1928

At a time when it was still unusual to see an airplane pass overhead, Amelia Earhart was already flying fearlessly. During the decade of her fame, she set aviation records for distance, speed, and altitude, attracted enormous crowds wherever she went, and took every opportunity to promote women's equality.

While most young girls were restricted to more quiet activities, Amelia

Amelia Earhart

and her sister were encouraged to be as adventurous and physically active as they wished. As youngsters growing up in the American Midwest, they enjoyed horseback riding, playing rough games, and doing just about anything outdoors.

In 1919, while enrolled as a premedical student at Columbia University, Earhart took her first airplane ride in California. She knew immediately that flying was for her. Abandoning college, she signed up for lessons from pioneer woman pilot Neta Snook. Earhart made her first solo flight in 1921, and for her twenty-fifth birthday, she bought her first plane.

Since flying was relatively new, the 1920s were an era of air shows and flying stunts. Earhart soon became a fixture at airports and runways. Publicist George Putnam, who had managed Charles Lindbergh's historic flight across the Atlantic, was eager to stage a similar event. In 1928, he chose Amelia Earhart to be the first woman to cross the Atlantic by air. Although she was only a passenger on the risky flight, the tall, attractive, confident Earhart caught the attention of the public, who crowned her First Lady of the Air. Earhart married Putnam in 1931, and under his guidance, she earned a considerable amount through product endorsements and lecture tours, which she continued throughout her life.

The 2,026 miles Earhart flew solo across the Atlantic in 1932 was just the beginning of her unmatched record of aviation firsts. She soon added two transcontinental records and firsts for flying solo from Hawaii to California, from California to Mexico City, and from Mexico City to New Jersey.

On June 1, 1937, Earhart and a navigator set off from Miami, Florida, in a twin-engine Lockheed Electra. Their highly publicized goal was to make an unprecedented flight around the world. After they reached New Guinea, twenty-two thousand miles away, their next stop was a tiny speck of island in the South Pacific. "The whole width of the world has passed behind us," Earhart reported, "except this broad ocean. I shall be glad when we have the hazards of its navigation behind us." But they would not get beyond the seas, nor would they reach their destination. Radio communications became weaker and more garbled, but reports of low fuel were heard by the coastguard. The plane crashed, though it is unknown exactly where it landed. Despite an extensive search, the plane and crew were never found. The wreck of a plane discovered recently has not been conclusively identified as Earhart's.

Amelia Earhart's courageous pioneering—both as a woman and as an aviator—helped win the industry of aviation public confidence and acceptance. She blazed an exciting trail for future generations of adventurous women to follow.

Bonnie Eisenberg and Mary Ruthsdotter

Golda Meir

(1898–1978)

"One day, we will come back to the land from which we were
driven twice before. . . . We will live at peace with our
neighbors and peace with the entire world."
—Speech to the AFL-CIO, 1969

One of Golda Mabovitch's first memories was of her father, a carpenter, nailing boards over the front door of their Kiev home, hoping to keep out pogroms—moblike attacks on Jewish communities in Russia in the late 1800s and early 1900s. Many families wanted to emigrate, and the Mabovitch family was no exception. In 1906, Golda's father left Russia and settled in Milwaukee, Wisconsin, where she, her mother, and her two sisters joined him shortly thereafter.

Israeli prime minister Golda Meir speaking in Jerusalem, 1974.

Life in America was difficult for poor immigrant families. At eight years of age, Golda had to work every morning in her mother's grocery store, leaving her no choice but to arrive late at school. Later, her mother wanted her to give up high school, work in the store, and marry. But Golda was strong-willed and determined to continue her education. At age fourteen, she ran away to Denver to live with her older sister Sheyna and go to school.

In Denver, Golda continued high school. Zionists, Socialists, and anarchists visited her sister's home and aroused Golda's political interests. She became a Zionist—someone who believes in the right to a Jewish homeland—and joined the Labor Zionist party. The British designated Palestine as the Jewish national homeland in the Balfour Declaration of 1917. At that time, Golda took a full-time job with the Labor Zionist party, and she met and married Morris Meyerson.

The couple settled in Palestine, living and working on a kibbutz, a collective farm where members work in exchange for their homes and food and where everyone is considered equal. Golda enjoyed kibbutz life and became a representative of the Histadrut, a labor federation for Jewish workers in Palestine. In 1928, she rose to become secretary of the Women's Labor Council of Histadrut. As a public figure, she was responsible for raising money internationally for defense, food, and housing to help found the state of Israel. Her political rise was rapid and involved extensive travel, and although she regretted being away from her husband and two children, she believed she had to pursue her work in the name of Zionism.

During Hitler's rule in the mid-1930s, Jews emigrated from Germany and Austria to Palestine. When the British tried to limit the number of immigrants, Golda helped smuggle them in. At the end of World War II, the British turned the question of the Jewish homeland over to the United Nations, which voted for creating a Jewish state.

On May 14, 1948, Golda was one of twenty-five signers of Israel's Proclamation of Independence. Shortly thereafter, seven Arab countries declared war on Israel, but Israel emerged from the conflict victorious. In 1956, Israeli Prime Minister David Ben-Gurion named Golda minister of labor. He suggested that his cabinet begin to use their Hebrew names, so Golda Meyerson became Golda Meir, which means "to illuminate."

As Israel's first minister of labor, Meir orchestrated the building of thirty thousand houses and two hundred thousand low-income apartments. As a woman in a formerly all-male cabinet, she brought a new perspective to government. She could be quick with a comeback when she knew that her colleagues were wrong. Once, when the cabinet was discussing curfews for women because of an outbreak of attacks at night, Meir responded, "But it's the men who are attacking the women. If there's a curfew, let the men stay at home, not the women."

Meir became secretary general of the Mapai party and later of the Israel Labor party under Prime Minister Levi Eshkol. When Eshkol died in 1969, the party selected her to serve as prime minister until the next elections were held. As prime minister, Meir sought the support of the United States as well as armaments to build Israel's defense. The weight of the Arab-

Israeli conflict rested on her shoulders, and though she always sought peace for Israel, this was not always possible.

In 1973, Syrian and Egyptian forces launched a surprise attack against Israel on Yom Kippur, the holiest of Jewish holy days. Criticized for the country's lack of preparedness for the war—and for the large number of people in the Israeli Army who were killed—Meir had no choice but to turn the reins of government over to Yitzhak Rabin.

Golda Meir, at seventy-six, was not ready to retire, however. She continued to raise money, speak, and meet with world leaders in an effort to reach a peaceful agreement with the Arabs. When she wasn't traveling, she took care of her grandchildren in Jerusalem. She died at age eighty of liver infection and leukemia.

Judy Gitenstein

Zora Neale Hurston

(1901–1960)

"Mama exhorted her children at every opportunity to 'jump at the sun.' We might not land on the sun, but at least we would get off the ground."
—Dust Tracks on a Road, 1942

As a child, Zora Neale Hurston loved listening to folktales about characters like Brer Rabbit and High John the Conquer. Her early love of storytelling stayed with her, and when she grew up, she wrote hundred of articles, short stories, and plays celebrating African-American culture.

Born in 1901 to Reverend John Hurston and Lucy Ann Potts Hurston, Zora was the seventh of eight children. She grew up in Eatonville, Florida, where her father, a Baptist preacher, was the town's mayor. Her mother taught Sunday school and worked at home raising the children. Lucy Hurston always encouraged her children to strive for excellence and grab at opportunity. When Zora was thirteen, her mother died, and her world changed dramatically.

Zora didn't get along with her new stepmother. After living with different relatives for a number of years, she left home to work as a wardrobe assistant and maid for a traveling theater group. When the group arrived in Baltimore, Maryland, she quit and enrolled in the Morgan Academy, a mostly black high school. Zora graduated and entered Howard University in Washington, D.C., where she studied with important African-American teachers and published her first story.

In 1925, Zora moved to New York City, where she became friends with many African-American writers and artists of the Harlem Renaissance, the black arts movement of the 1920s. Hurston received a scholarship to attend Barnard College, where she studied anthropology, earning a bachelor's degree in 1928. As part of her graduate work at Columbia University, Hurston went to Florida and Alabama to interview

Zora Neale Hurston, c. 1940

African-Americans and record their stories and traditions. With financial help from a wealthy New York woman, Charlotte Mason, Hurston published her findings in a book called *Mules and Men* in 1931. This was the first book of African-American folklore compiled by an African-American.

After a failed love affair, Zora wrote *Their Eyes Were Watching God* in 1937. Like the main character in the book, Janie Stark, Zora was a strong-spirited woman who searched for her own identity and the fulfillment of her dreams. Hurston felt passionately about her work, and it became a priority in her life. She married twice, but her work always came first.

High John the Conquer

In 1944, Zora Neale Hurston adapted the story of High John the Conquer, a mythical black folk hero:

High John the Conquer came to be a man, and a mighty man at that. But he was not a natural man in the beginning. First off, he was a whisper, a will to hope, a wish to find something worthy of laughter and song. Then the whisper put on flesh. His footsteps sounded across the world in a low but musical rhythm as if the world he walked on was a singing-drum. The black folks had an irresistible impulse to laugh. High John the Conquer was a man in full, and had come to live and work on the plantations, and all the slave folks knew him in the flesh.

The sign of this man was a laugh, and his singing symbol was a drumbeat. . . . It was sure to be heard when and where the work was the hardest and the lot the most cruel. It helped the slaves endure.

They knew something better was coming. So they laughed in the face of things and sang, "I'm so glad! Trouble don't last always." And the white people who heard them were struck dumb that they could laugh.

In her autobiography, *Dust Tracks on a Road,* Hurston called her life "a series of wanderings." In 1936 and 1938, she received fellowships to pursue the work she loved, traveling throughout the southeastern United States and the Caribbean collecting black folklore. For the next ten years, Hurston wrote and published numerous books, articles, plays, and essays based on that research. By the 1950s, she wasn't making much money as a writer, so she moved to southern Florida and took a job as a maid. She still wrote in her free time.

After suffering a stroke in 1959, Hurston moved into a nursing home in Fort Pierce, Florida. Her independent and proud spirit wouldn't let her ask her family for help. She died on January 28, 1960, and was buried in a segregated cemetery in an unmarked grave. Thirteen years later, Alice Walker, the African-American poet and novelist, traveled to the site and placed a stone marker in the cemetery reading:

ZORA NEALE HURSTON
1901–1960
A GENIUS OF THE SOUTH
NOVELIST, FOLKLORIST, ANTHROPOLOGIST

Deborah Gore Ohrn

Margaret Mead

(1901–1978)

"Studying . . . peoples, who are living now as they have lived for centuries and who embody ways of thinking and feeling we do not know about, we [can] add immeasurably to our knowledge of who we ourselves are."
—Blackberry Winter, 1972

Even as a child, Margaret Mead was fascinated by people and their unique behavior. She questioned her grandmother endlessly about the tiniest details of her family's history; she "studied" everyone she knew and their relationships with one another. Without realizing it, the young Margaret was laying the groundwork for her life as an anthropologist.

Born into an academic family in Philadelphia, Margaret was the oldest of five children. She may have inherited her inquisitiveness from her mother, a sociologist, and her aptitude for study from her father, a professor of business. Margaret spent summers on her family's farm, climbing trees and exploring the land. Early on, she was schooled at home, and when she turned eleven, she went to a one-room school, which she attended for several years.

Mead's parents encouraged her to think independently. She later wrote in her autobiographical book *Blackberry Winter,* "I had no reason to doubt that brains were suitable for a woman. And as I had my father's kind of mind—

Margaret Mead holding a Manus baby in the Admiralty Islands in 1954.

which was also his mother's—I learned that the mind is not sex-typed." Mead received her bachelor's degree from Barnard College and her master's degree and doctorate in anthropology from Columbia University.

Fresh out of school, Mead set out in 1925 to study the people of Polynesia in the South Pacific. The book that resulted, *Coming of Age in Samoa* (1928), promoted the startling thesis that culture and environment, as much as biology, contributed to the differences between boys and girls. The book became wildly popular, especially with adolescents, in the United States and throughout the world.

Mead went on to win world fame through her studies of the cultures of Oceania, the South Sea Islands in the Pacific. Anthropology was a relatively new and wide-open field. Along with her colleagues Franz Boas and Ruth Benedict, Mead developed the techniques of observing, interviewing, photographing, and filming indigenous peoples that have since set the standards for conducting fieldwork.

Mead also achieved public recognition for her books *Growing Up in New Guinea* (1930), *Male and Female* (1949), and *A Rap on Race* (1969), which she wrote with African-American novelist James Baldwin.

Elsie Clews Parsons and Ruth Benedict

Like Margaret Mead, anthropologists Elsie Clews Parsons (1875-1941) and Ruth Benedict (1887-1948) championed the idea that every human culture is unique and valuable. Parsons began by studying the customs and rituals of her own culture. While teaching at Barnard College and Columbia University, she published a textbook, *The Family* (1906), in which she wrote that in order to be good wives and mothers, women had to have the same opportunities as men. *The Old-Fashioned Woman* (1913) discussed the perpetuation of learned sex roles. Later, Parsons wrote about the native peoples of the American Southwest, Mexico, Peru, and the Caribbean.

While Parsons was teaching at the New School for Social Research in New York City, she recommended that Ruth Benedict, a bright young student, pursue a doctorate in anthropology as well. Benedict went on to study and teach at Columbia and to do her fieldwork among the Pueblo and Apache peoples of New Mexico, the Serrano of California, and the Blackfoot of Montana. In 1935, she published her two-volume study of tribal legend and religion, *Zuni Mythology.* Her most famous book, *Patterns of Culture* (1934), contrasts three North American Indian cultures. During World War II, Benedict worked for the Office of War Information and wrote the highly successful *The Chrysanthemum and the Sword* (1946), an attempt to understand the culture of Japan.

Her third marriage, to Gregory Bateson, a British anthropologist whom she met in New Guinea in 1933, was her most successful because with Bateson she was better able to balance her career with marriage. The couple lived in New York City, where they raised their daughter, Mary Catherine.

Mead was often criticized by other anthropologists for not doing thorough research, for not knowing the languages of the people she studied, and for not living long enough among them. Her work may not have satisfied conservative scientists, but it was inspiring and entertaining for the millions of students and readers around the world whom she introduced to anthropology with her vivid and descriptive writing. Margaret Mead was a pioneer in a new field, and she has left a legacy for future generations of anthropologists.

Judy Gitenstein

Margaret Bourke-White

(1904–1971)

"Nothing attracts me like a closed door. I cannot let my camera rest until I have pried it open, and I want to be first."
—*Portrait of Myself,* 1963

Margaret Bourke-White would do just about anything to take a photograph. Camera in hand, she crept through gold mines, swayed from construction towers, snowshoed to logging camps, and hung from helicopters. It would all be worth it for the perfect shot.

Margaret Bourke-White was born to Joseph and Minnie Bourke-White in 1904 in New York City. Her father was an engineer and inventor who instilled a love of photography in his young daughter. An amateur shutterbug himself, Joseph taught his daughter to see the beauty in new industries and machines.

When the family moved to a small town in New Jersey, Margaret learned to love nature and wild animals. She decided to study snakes when she grew up. "I knew I had to travel," she wrote. "I pictured myself as a

Margaret Bourke-White behind the camera at the trial of Bruno Richard Hauptmann, the alleged Lindbergh kidnapper, 1935.

scientist . . . going to the jungle, bringing back specimens for natural history museums, and 'doing all the things that women never do.' "

Margaret's father died when she was in her first year at Columbia University. There, she studied with a famous photography professor, and even when she transferred to the University of Michigan to study herpetology, she found that her first love remained photography. When she received her bachelor's degree in 1927, she went to Cleveland, Ohio, and photographed the steel mills. Women were not allowed in the dirty and dangerous mills, but Bourke-White pleaded until permission was finally granted. When the photos were printed in several midwestern newspapers, they were so spectacular that magazine magnate Henry Luce summoned her to New York City to be his staff photographer.

Throughout the 1930s, she worked as photographer for *Fortune* and later *Life* magazines. Bourke-White's new photography studio was in the Chrysler Building in Manhattan, where she could crawl out over the street and take pictures of the city eight hundred feet below. She worked for an advertising agency half the year, photographing Goodyear tires or Buick cars. The other half, she worked on magazine photoessays about industry in the Soviet Union or dust storms during the Depression. Soon, Margaret Bourke-White's name was as famous as her photographs.

In 1935, Bourke-White and writer Erskine Caldwell collaborated on a book about Southern sharecroppers called *You Have Seen Their Faces*. It was a great success and introduced many people to the reality of American poverty. Bourke-White and Caldwell married a few years later, but their union dissolved when Bourke-White realized she had no time to devote to marriage.

During World War II, *Life* magazine sent her to Europe and Africa to take photographs. As an official Army Air Force photographer, Bourke-White photographed the bombing of Russia and the invasion of Italy. She even flew on a combat mission in Algeria. In 1945, she was with the American troops who liberated the Nazi death camps.

After the war, Bourke-White traveled worldwide for *Life*: to India, South Africa, and Korea. In 1946, she took one of her most famous photographs, a picture of the Indian leader Mahatma Gandhi at his spinning wheel.

In 1951, Bourke-White developed Parkinson's disease. She fought valiantly against the disease and wrote about her struggle in her autobiography, *Portrait of Myself*. In 1971, she died in Darien, Connecticut, at age sixty-seven.

For more than twenty-five years, Margaret Bourke-White gave people the world through pictures. She once said of photographers, "We are in a privileged and sometimes unhappy position. We see a great deal of the world. Our obligation is to pass it on to others." And so she did.

Deborah Gore Ohrn

Greta Garbo

(1905–1990)

"Being a movie star . . . means being looked at from every possible direction. You are never left in peace."
—c. 1925

Greta Garbo may have embodied the words *movie star* better than any other actress in the history of film. Her glamorous image on screen was so enthralling, it could make people almost forget the problems of the Great Depression, her fame so great that a letter addressed simply to "Greta Garbo, the most beautiful movie star in the world," could reach her in New York. Though she avoided publicity throughout her life, her aloofness made her even more fascinating. Instead of leaving her alone, her adoring public made her a legend.

The incomparable Greta Garbo

Greta Louisa Gustafsson was born in 1905 in Stockholm, Sweden. Her family was close and loving but poor, and Greta's early life was difficult. She and her older sister slept in the kitchen of their tiny apartment, while their older brother and parents slept in the living room. When the children's friends visited, they had to stay in the cramped kitchen, for their father, who worked at night, was usually asleep in the next room.

Greta grew quickly and became self-conscious about her height—she was the tallest girl in her elementary school class. When she was thirteen, her father got sick, and she was forced to drop out of school to get a job. She would always regret being unable to continue her education. While working as a salesclerk in a department store, Greta was filmed for a store ad and won a two-year scholarship to Stockholm's Royal Dramatic Theater Academy. "I was totally lacking in self-confidence and would often think that everything would go wrong the next day," she said.

Others had more faith in Greta's ability. At theater school, she was discovered by the director Mauritz Stiller, who took her under his wing and renamed her Garbo. Soon after, Louis B. Mayer of the Hollywood studio Metro-Goldwyn-Mayer offered Garbo a contract and the chance to come to America, on one condition. "In America, men don't like fat women," she was told. Determined to be hired by Mayer, Garbo lost weight, though it wasn't easy. Weight was a problem she would struggle with throughout her life.

At age twenty, Greta Garbo became an overnight success with her first Hollywood movie, *The Torrent*. Unlike that of many stars, her profile did not have a "good side" and a "bad side" but photographed well from every angle. Directors claimed that the camera loved her. While her costars needed more than one take to get their lines right, Garbo astounded everyone by doing her scenes perfectly the first time, without any rehearsal at all.

When sound was introduced in the late 1920s, it threatened to end the careers of many silent screen stars. But Garbo's voice was deep and rich, adding a new level to her expressive acting. Her first sound film, *Anna Christie*, was launched with the ad line "Garbo Talks!" It was an immediate hit. MGM took another chance when they cast Garbo in the 1939 comedy *Ninotchka*. Up to this point, all Garbo's roles had been serious. With posters that proclaimed "Garbo laughs!" *Ninotchka* too became a success.

The beginning of World War II in 1939 slowed Garbo's meteoric rise. The war cut off the large European market for American films and prevented Garbo from visiting her beloved Sweden. In 1941, at the height of her career, Greta Garbo surprised the world by announcing that she would retire. After making twenty-seven films in nineteen years, she had had enough. She returned to a simpler life, visiting close friends and family in Paris, Sweden, and the Swiss Alps. In 1951, she became an American citizen and settled in New York City in a large apartment overlooking the East River. She never made another movie, nor did she appear at the Academy of Motion Picture Arts and Sciences Awards to receive her one and only

Oscar, presented in 1955 for her lifetime achievement. Yet, up till her death at the age of eighty-four on April 15, 1990, she remained an adored and sought-after movie star.

While most movie stars crave publicity, Garbo never understood the adoration of her public. She felt that acting was just a job like any other, and she did not feel the need to give interviews that revealed intimate details about her private life. Garbo preferred to let her performances on screen speak for themselves. Besides, she said, newspaper and magazine writers got everything wrong, even her most famous statement: "I never said, 'I want to be alone.' I only said, 'I want to be *left* alone.' There is all the difference."

Judy Gitenstein

Frida Kahlo

(1907–1954)

"I never painted dreams. I paint my own reality."
—Interview, 1938

Frida Kahlo's paintings are so surreal they look as if they could be dreams. Yet they are actually autobiographical, a guide to Kahlo's emotional as well as physical life. The brilliant intensity of her work has made Kahlo Mexico's best-known woman painter.

Frida was born near Mexico City, the third daughter of Guillermo Kahlo, a German-Jewish photographer, and Matilde Calderon, his Mexican wife. Frida came down with polio when she was six years old. It took her almost a year to recover. Sadly, this was only the first of several painful disabilities that would dominate Frida's life. At age fifteen, Frida entered one of Mexico's finest schools, the National Preparatory School. There, she studied literature and art and met Diego Rivera, Mexico's most famous painter, when he was commissioned to paint a mural in the school's auditorium. She became infatuated with the overweight, talkative artist and swore she would later marry him.

That same year, her life was suddenly transformed by a horrible

Frida Kahlo's painting, Self-Portrait with Thorn Necklace and Hummingbird, *1940.*

accident. A bus hit the trolley car she was riding on, and a handrail tore into her abdomen. Her spine was broken in three places, and her right leg and foot were shattered. The accident left her semicrippled and in frequent pain throughout her life. During the months of her recuperation, she took up painting. The physical and mental trauma she endured would be a frequent subject of her work throughout her life.

During her courtship with Diego after she graduated from high school, Frida continued painting with new confidence. Frida thought Diego was the greatest painter in the world, and she relished his compliments of her work. Her early paintings reflect the flat, colorful style of Diego's murals.

Kahlo and Rivera's relationship survived stormy times. The couple married in 1929, divorced in 1939, and married again in 1940. Although they cared deeply for each other, they both had affairs. Kahlo wanted desperately to have a child, but instead she suffered three miscarriages. Through it all, the couple traveled widely and became well known. Although Diego's work was more often in the limelight, he encouraged his wife to form her own artistic identity.

Most of the paintings Kahlo created between 1926 and 1954 are self-portraits. They deal with her disabilities and physical pain, her stormy love for Diego, and her remorse at not being able to have children. She created her own complex visual symbols to convey her thoughts about life and death. Although her subject matter is often excrutiatingly personal, the primitive style and bright colors of her paintings make them mesmerizing and strangely attractive.

Kahlo began to exhibit her work internationally in the 1940s. Critics saw in her paintings Kahlo's genius and passion for life. She received many awards, took part in conferences and cultural organizations, and taught painting.

Toward the end of her life, her health took a turn for the worse. When her first major solo show opened in Mexico, she was quite ill and had to be carried into the exhibit on a stretcher. In 1953, part of her leg was amputated, and Kahlo spent months in the hospital. Though she was in constant pain, she continued to paint until she died on July 13, 1954, of a pulmonary embolism.

Her popularity continued to soar. The Frida Kahlo Museum, located at the house where she lived with Diego Rivera, opened in 1955. Thirty years later, her paintings were declared national treasures by the Mexican government—they cannot leave the country permanently.

Diego Rivera once said of Kahlo's work, "Frida is the unique example in the history of art of someone who tore open the breast and heart in order to speak the biological truth of what is felt within them. She is the only woman to express in her work an art of the feelings, functions, and the creative power of woman."

Deborah Gore Ohrn

Rachel Carson

(1907–1964)

*"For the first time in the history of the world, every human being is
now subject to contact with dangerous chemicals, from
the moment of conception until death."*
—Silent Spring, 1962

In 1958, marine biologist Rachel Carson received a letter containing an alarming question. A friend wrote to say that many birds had died after DDT was sprayed on crops to control insects. Could the commonly used pesticide be the cause? At the time, few people thought much about pollution. But the answer Rachel Carson found for her friend alarmed the nation and created a worldwide interest in a whole new field of science— ecology.

Rachel Carson, daughter of Robert and Maria Carson, was born and raised in Pennsylvania. She enjoyed nature, both in the woods and by the sea, and shared her mother's delight in the world around them. Rachel became a keen observer during their walks together, eager to investigate the mysteries she discovered.

Carson was an avid reader and planned to become a writer. During her second year at college, however, a biology class changed everything. She found the subject fascinating, and she already had many of the attributes scientific research required: patience, intelligence, and great powers of observation.

Now she was in a quandary. What did she really want to be—a scientist or a writer? "I thought I had to be one or the other; it never occurred to me, or apparently to anyone else, that I could combine the two careers." She graduated from the Pennsylvania College for Women in 1929 and earned her master's degree from Johns Hopkins University in 1932.

In 1936, Carson became an aquatic biologist with the United States Bureau of Fisheries. In this job, she was able to present scientific information in a way that was easily understandable. In 1947, Rachel was named publications editor-in-chief for the United States Fish and Wildlife Service.

One of the reports Carson wrote for the bureau led to her first book, *Under the Sea Wind* (1941). She wrote her second book, *The Sea Around Us* (1951), after three years of research. Her eloquent writing about the complicated ecology of the ocean made *The Sea Around Us* a best-seller. She followed this literary success with *The Edge of the Sea* in 1955. By this time, Rachel Carson had become well respected by both readers and scientists.

Sylvia Earle

Oceanographer Sylvia Earle (1935–   ) has led more than fifty deep-sea expeditions to study marine plants and animals in their own environment. Like Rachel Carson, she knew early in life that she wanted to be a scientist. When she became chief scientist of the National Oceanic and Atmospheric Administration (NOAA), she was an outspoken protector of marine life, pushing for restrictions on whaling, fishing, and dumping practices. Colleagues at NOAA nicknamed her Her Royal Deepness for her deep-sea dives, including a world-record-setting 1,250-foot descent to the bottom of the Pacific Ocean off Oahu, Hawaii. "It's lonely in space, but it's not lonely underwater," Earle insists. "Every spoonful of water is crammed with life."

Then her friend's letter arrived asking about the dying songbirds. Carson researched DDT and other pesticides and discovered that they caused irreversible damage to the environment and killed thousands of creatures in the air, on land, and in water. She wrote articles about her findings, but publishers, realizing the articles were highly controversial, would not print them. She finally made her work public by publishing *Silent Spring* in 1962. The pesticide companies did everything they could to discredit her findings, but her research was sound.

Within a year, *Silent Spring* had been published in many other languages, taking her warning about the potential for environmental damage to concerned people around the world. Carson died in 1964, but her pioneering work lives on and is now widely considered to have started the environmental protection movement.

Bonnie Eisenberg and Mary Ruthsdotter

Simone de Beauvoir

(1908–1986)

*"Thus humanity is male and man defines woman not in herself but
as relative to him; she is not regarded as an autonomous being."*
—The Second Sex, 1949

When Simone de Beauvoir wrote these words, she was France's foremost female intellectual. She had always tried to live her life as an independent woman and not merely as the companion to a more dominant male. Yet she was sensitive to the position of women worldwide as the subordinate, or "second," sex.

Simone de Beauvoir grew up in Paris, France, the oldest daughter of George and Françoise de Beauvoir. Her maternal grandfather went bankrupt when she was a baby and couldn't provide the marriage dowry her father had expected. So, although middle-class by birth and education, Simone and her sister, Helene, lived in poverty for most of their youth. Still, Simone remembered her childhood as being "very, very happy." She was a stubborn girl, given to violent rages when she didn't get her way. She also possessed an insatiable curiosity about everything in life and soon discovered that reading and writing were the greatest joys in the world. By the time she was eight, Simone could read novels in English as well as in French.

The young Simone was a brilliant student and received her degree in

Simone de Beauvoir

philosophy at the Sorbonne in 1929. There she met Jean-Paul Sartre, a fellow philosophy student—and they fell in love. Later, she would say that Sartre "corresponded exactly to the dream companion I had longed for since I was fifteen." De Beauvoir and Sartre agreed never to marry but to remain committed to each other while experiencing other relationships.

Theirs was a bold experiment, but de Beauvoir was determined to make it work. De Beauvoir and Sartre were separated briefly by World War II. During the war years, de Beauvoir wrote her first novel, *She Came To Stay*, which was quickly followed by four others.

After the war, Sartre and de Beauvoir became famous as the leading exponents of the philosophy of existentialism. This philosophy holds that individuals are born free and are responsible for what they do with their own lives. In *Memoirs of a Dutiful Daughter* (1958) and the other three volumes of her autobiography, de Beauvoir relates how she freely rejected her parents' conservative middle-class values to create a life devoted to literature.

De Beauvoir's most famous work, *The Second Sex* (1949), discusses woman's position in a world dominated by man. Its central thesis is that throughout history, man has regarded himself as the essential human and has relegated woman to the status of a relative being, the "Other." *The Second Sex* encourages both men and women to rise above their differences and "affirm their brotherhood." The most important feminist work of the first half of the twentieth century, *The Second Sex* has been translated into nineteen languages.

Simone de Beauvoir died at age seventy-eight and was buried on April 19, 1986, six years to the day after Jean-Paul Sartre's funeral. They are buried in the same grave in Montparnasse Cemetery, Paris.

Ruth Ashby

Mother Teresa

(1910–   )

*"I don't claim anything of the work. It is His work. I am like a
little pencil in His hand. . . . The pencil has only
to be allowed to be used."*
—Speech, Awakening Conference, Colorado, June 15, 1986

Mother Teresa received her call to do the work of God while riding on a train on September 10, 1946. "The message was clear," she later recalled. "I was to leave the convent and help the poor, while living among them." Since that day, Mother Teresa has transformed countless lives with her extraordinary humanitarian acts.

The woman who became known as Mother Teresa was born in what used to be Yugoslavia. Her Albanian parents named her Agnes Goxha Bojaxhiu. As a young girl, Agnes was deeply affected by the many stories she heard of Yugoslav Jesuit missionaries who had worked in India. By the age of twelve, Agnes knew that her future lay in missionary work.

After training in Dublin, Ireland, and then moving to Darjeeling, India, Mother Teresa began her mission as a teacher at St. Mary's High School. She later became principal and dedicated herself to the school for twenty years. Outside its walls, the slums were teeming with homeless street children, lepers, and those who had been tossed aside by India's caste (or class) system. Here, Mother Teresa found her life's work.

After she received her calling in 1946, Mother Teresa was finally given a mission in Calcutta which was aimed at helping people whose illnesses and/or social status had made them social outcasts.

With twelve sisters and a handful of neglected children gathered from the Calcutta slums, she began a school. Volunteers joined the sisters and soon the Missionaries of Charity became an official religious community with more than seven hundred sisters and a hundred brothers. The mission not only founded schools but also opened clinics for dying patients. "We want them to know there are people who really love them at least for the few hours that they have to live," stated Mother Teresa. She also established orphanages and homes for lepers and the crippled and retarded.

By the 1960s, Mother Teresa had become known as the Saint of Calcutta. She received many awards and honors, including the 1979 Nobel Peace Prize. But her goal, she has said, has not been to achieve recognition but "to give love, to meet the need that the person has at that moment."

Because of her vow of poverty, any money that Mother Teresa receives is used to establish missionary centers and to continue her work. In 1980, she suffered a heart attack, which required her to wear a pacemaker. After more than forty years of service to the world's poor, it was time for this seemingly tireless woman to slow down. She resigned as head of her religious order but still lives in the slums of Calcutta, serving as adviser to her followers and offering help wherever she can. Today, on seven continents and in eighty-seven countries, her mission "to service the poor purely for the love of God" continues.

S. Suzan Jane

Mildred "Babe" Didrikson

(1911–1956)

"Boy, don't you men wish you could hit a ball like that!"
—To an audience at an exhibition golf tournament, c. 1936

Her fans called her Babe because she reminded them of Babe Ruth. When Mildred was a young girl, her athletic skills dazzled her friends. Little did they realize, though, that Mildred Didrikson would win titles in basketball, track, and golf and be named Woman Athlete of the Year six times in a row by the Associated Press.

Raised in Port Arthur, Texas, Mildred Didrikson grew up playing sandlot baseball with the boys in her neighborhood. She led her high school basketball team to an impressive string of victories and was soon recruited to work at Employers Casualty Insurance Company and play for their semipro-fessional women's basketball team, the Golden Cyclones. Her first game was against the national titleholders, the Sun Oil Company team. Babe scored more points than the entire opposing team!

The versatile athlete, Mildred "Babe" Didrikson, in the early 1930s.

Track events were the next sport to catch Babe's interest. At her first meet, she entered four events and won them all. In 1932, at the Amateur Athletic Union Championships, Babe entered eight events, won five gold medals, tied one event, and finished second in another, thus single-handedly winning the team title. As she prepared for the 1932 Olympics in Los Angeles, her goal was "to beat everybody in sight."

Her high school coach said of her: "Babe was blessed with a body that was perfect. I can still remember how her muscles flowed when she walked." Didrikson described her talent like this: "All I know is that I can run and I can jump and I can toss things." At the Olympics, she did just that, winning a gold medal and setting a new world record in the javelin toss, winning a gold medal in the eighty-meter hurdles, and winning a silver medal (by decision) in the high jump. She returned to Texas a star, riding in the firechief's car in the parade held in her honor and receiving the key to the city.

During the Olympic games, something else had happened that would change Babe Didrikson's life—she had been invited to play golf with a group of sportswriters. Her remarkable two-hundred-and-fifty yard drives impressed them greatly. "She is the longest hitter women's golf has ever seen, for she has a free, lashing style backed up with championship form," wrote sportswriter Grantland Rice. From that day on, Babe Didrikson knew she wanted to pursue championship golf.

Wrestler George Zaharias, who Didrikson married in December 1938, helped her pursue her dream. She practiced sixteen hours a day and played rounds of exhibition golf, trying to improve her game. Didrikson's career as an amateur and professional golfer has become legendary. She won the U.S. Women's Amateur Tournament in 1946 and then went on to win seventeen amateur tournaments in a row. She was also the first American to win the British Ladies Amateur Tournament. Dissatisfied with the lack of opportunities for women in professional golf, she founded the Ladies Professional Golf Association to sponsor more tournaments for women. She won the U.S. Women's Open in 1948 and in 1950, but cancer interrupted her career. Didrikson said, "All my life I've been competing—and competing to win. I came to realize that in its way, this cancer was the toughest competition I'd faced yet. I made up my mind that I was going to lick it all the way."

After an operation, Didrikson did recover enough to win the U.S. Open in 1954, but she succumbed to the disease a few years later. Golf made "Babe" Didrikson Zaharias rich and famous, but it was her versatility that made her unique. Today, she remains a shining symbol of what women can achieve in the world of sports.

Bonnie Eisenberg and Mary Ruthsdotter

Mary Leakey

(1913–   )

*"What I have done in my life I have done because I wanted to do
it and because it interested me. I just happen to be a woman, and
I don't believe it has made much difference."*
—*Disclosing the Past*, 1984

Largely self-educated, Mary Leakey made numerous contributions to
the field of anthropology during her extraordinary fifty-year career.
Some of her discoveries have changed the theory of human
evolution.

Mary Nicol was born in London, England. Her father, who was an artist,
taught her to draw and read and sparked her interest in anthropology with
his stories about prehistoric humans. Mary was very close to her father and
was deeply affected by his death when she was thirteen. Until this time,
Mary had not received any formal education. Though her mother enrolled
her in a series of convent schools, her free spirit and disregard of school
rules always got her expelled. Finally, Mary's mother gave up, leaving her
daughter to pursue drawing and her investigations of prehistoric life.

At the age of twenty, Mary applied to Oxford University to study anthropology, but she was rejected because of her lack of formal education. Still
determined, she began sitting in on lectures at universities and museums
and attending summer archaeological digs. To Mary, searching for remains
from the past was pure joy. From 1930 to 1934, she assisted at a dig in
the south of Britain. In her spare time, she drew pictures of the stone tools
that were unearthed. These drawings soon came to the attention of scholars
in the field of archaeology who asked Mary to illustrate their publications.

One of these scholars was Louis Leakey. Not long after they met, Mary
found herself working in Africa with Louis, digging sites in the Great Rift
Valley in northern Kenya. By the time she returned to England in 1935,
she had found her vocation. "Africa had cast its spell on me," she said. In
December 1936, Mary and Louis were married, and a few weeks later, they
set out again for Africa.

Between the years 1937 and 1948, Mary Leakey worked diligently at sites, finding Late Stone Age implements, a cremation ground, Iron Age pottery, and a Neolithic settlement. In 1959, she made a major discovery when she found a fragmented skull at Olduvai Gorge on the edge of Tanzania's Serengeti plains.

At the time, the skull was thought to have belonged to the "missing link" between the great apes and humans, though today this is uncertain. Analysis revealed that the skull, nicknamed "Nutcracker Man," was 1.75 million years old. This was exciting news for scientists, since most believed that the first hominid (humanlike creature) had lived in Asia only a few hundred thousand years ago. Mary Leakey's discovery provided proof of a much older hominid existence in Africa.

Between 1975 and 1981, Mary made even more remarkable discoveries, finding new mammal species and hominid footprint fossil remains. When analyzed, the footprints proved to be 3.7 million years old, proving that early hominids walked on two legs. This discovery was another breakthrough in the field of paleoanthropology.

Mary Leakey's career spanned than fifty years and yielded numerous books and articles. In 1982, Leaky lost sight in her left eye and turned over her research site to the Tanzania Department of Antiquities. She has since received numerous awards and honorary degrees. Her work, consisting of thorough geological, archaeological, and fossil analyses, has provided a history of the oldest human creatures known.

S. Suzan Jane

Indira Gandhi

(1917–1984)

"We have promises to keep to our people of work, food, clothing, and shelter, health, and education."
—Radio broadcast, January 26, 1966

Inspired by her parents' political activism to free their country from British domination, Indira Gandhi became India's first woman prime minister. Dedicating her life to political and social progress and peace in India, she rose to become one of the most powerful and respected leaders in the world.

Indira, the only child of Jawaharlal and Kamala Nehru, was greatly influenced by her parents—as well as by stories about Joan of Arc. By the age of twelve, she had established the Monkey Brigade, a children's organization engaged in the struggle for independence. Since British government officials were less likely to suspect children of being spies, the Monkey Brigade could operate virtually undetected.

Indira Gandhi speaks to army troops in Joshimath, India, 1984.

Indira's schooling was often interrupted by her parents' imprisonment for their political activities and because of her own frail health. Perhaps the most important element of her education was the lively correspondence she received from her father while he was in prison. Indira studied briefly at Oxford University in England, but illness and her political aspirations brought her back to India.

Once home, Indira resumed her involvement in the independence movement, accepting the risks despite being imprisoned and beaten. In 1942, she married journalist Feroze Gandhi, with whom she had two sons. Although Feroze was elected to Congress, Indira decided to live with her father, who needed a hostess after his wife died in 1936.

Vijaya Lakshmi Pandit

In the first half of the twentieth century, Indira Gandhi's family helped lead India's fight against long-standing British rule. Her aunt, Vijaya Lakshmi Pandit (1900-1990), was one of the leaders of the independence movement and was jailed three times for her public defiance of the imperialist government. In 1946, Pandit led the Indian delegation to the United Nations and later became the first woman president of the United Nations Assembly. She also represented India as its ambassador to several countries: the former Soviet Union, the United States, Great Britain, Mexico, Spain, and Ireland.

In 1947, India won its independence from Great Britain, and Jawaharlal Nehru became the country's first prime minister. Indira Gandhi acted as "first lady," accompanying her father on international travels, attending coronations, summits, and meetings with world leaders.

In 1959, Gandhi was elected president of the Indian National Congress party, the second highest political position in India. She assisted her father in leading the country until his death in 1964. At that time, Nehru's successor, Lal Bahadur Shastri, appointed Gandhi minister of information and broadcasting. In a land of widespread illiteracy, radio and television played an important role in disseminating information to the public. Gandhi encouraged the manufacturing of inexpensive radios, doubled broadcasting time, and started broadcasting a family planning program. She opened television and radio facilities to members of the opposition and independent commentators. For the first time, people were free to voice their ideas publicly—even if they were opposed to the government.

When Shastri died in 1966, Gandhi was selected to serve as prime minister until another election was held. The following year, she became the first woman ever elected to lead a democracy. As prime minister, Gandhi enhanced India's political power and improved its relations with the Soviet Union. She led India to a decisive victory in its war with Pakistan in 1971, and in the same year, sent India's first satellite into orbit. During the elections in 1971, Gandhi's campaign slogan was "Abolish Poverty." Although she won, her opponents accused her of violating election laws, and her leadership became vulnerable.

In her next term, Gandhi instituted a voluntary sterilization program to limit population growth. Her political opponents attacked the program as compulsory, and criticism of her administration grew. Riots and protests ensued in 1975, forcing Gandhi to declare a state of emergency, which limited personal freedoms and called for the imprisonment of political opponents. She was voted out of office in 1977 but made a comeback in 1979.

Gandhi continued to institute reforms that would improve the quality of life in her country. She tried to revitalize agriculture, improved Indo-American relations, won increased American financial aid, and encouraged the importation of grain from the United States to alleviate famine.

Although support for Gandhi was strong, India's population grew, education standards plummeted, and strikers protested inflation. Gandhi also still faced opposition from the right wing as well as from two Communist parties. During another state of emergency in 1984, Indira Gandhi, who had dedicated herself to improving the quality of life in India, was assassinated by her opponents.

S. Suzan Jane

Jessie Lopez De La Cruz

(1919–   )

"Growing up, I could see all the injustices and I would think, 'If only I could do something about it!'"
—Interview, 1980

Jessie Lopez De La Cruz's experiences as a poor wife, mother, and migrant farmworker made her determined to fight injustice. Knowing that farm laborers had to organize to change the miserable conditions in which they lived and worked, Jessie became a moving force in the unions and the migrant community.

Union organizer Jessie Lopez De La Cruz speaks in Washington, D.C., 1980.

Jessie was born into a poor migrant family in California, and it was there that she learned the importance of teamwork. Her family traveled throughout the state, following the crops that were ripe for harvesting, and everyone—even the youngest child—had a job. This migrant life meant that Jessie stopped going to school in the sixth grade. At the age of thirteen, she worked picking cotton, often lifting sacks that weighed more than a hundred pounds.

In 1933, her family settled in the San Joaquin Valley and worked in labor camps in that area. It was the Depression, and conditions in the camps were horrible, with families of ten living in twelve-by-fifteen-foot cabins and having to use filthy outhouses. Children often suffered from malnutrition and illness, and there was no money for medical care. Jessie married Arnold De La Cruz in 1938, and between 1939 and 1947, she gave birth to six children. She continued to work in the fields with just a few months off for each birth.

De La Cruz thought that this was the life she was meant to live, until she met labor leader Cesar Chavez in 1962. He inspired her to work for the migrant unions by saying, "The women have to be involved. They're the ones working out in the fields with their husbands." De La Cruz began talking to women, convincing them to attend meetings of the United Farm Workers Union (UFW) and to join the picket lines. The UFW took notice of De La Cruz's work, and in 1967, she became an official union organizer.

De La Cruz, like other UFW members, was often hosed with pesticides when employers caught her rallying the workers. She persevered nonetheless, organizing workers to picket some of the largest growers in California. When the growers tried to recruit illegal aliens as scabs (nonunion workers) to take the picketers' jobs, De La Cruz helped the border patrol stop incoming aliens.

In 1967, De La Cruz was appointed to the Fresno County Economic Opportunity Commission. The following year she headed the UFW hiring hall near Fresno, where growers could contract with union members. In her spare time, she taught English to Mexican Americans. De La Cruz was one of the founding members of the National Land for People, a farm cooperative in the San Joaquin Valley, in 1974. Three years later, she was honored by the League of Mexican-American Women for her work on behalf of women laborers.

In 1977, De La Cruz returned to school at the Farmworkers' Free University. Since then, she has been devoted to the farm co-op and has done a lot of public speaking about food and farming at colleges, conferences, community meetings, and government hearings. When she is not working outside of her home, De La Cruz spends her time on domestic chores like cooking and sewing. "I can't be with my hands idle," she says. "There is always something to do."

Dinah Dunn

Eva Perón

(1919–1952)

"Almsgiving tends to perpetuate poverty; aid does away with it once and for all.... Charity separates the rich from the poor; aid raises the needy and sets him on the same level with the rich."
—Speech at American Congress of Industrial Medicine, 1949

Eva Perón, known to her followers as Evita, rose from a humble childhood to become a powerful politician in Argentina. Although she and her husband, Juan Perón, were devoted to raising the status of the poor, they fulfilled their own political ambitions and ruled the country with an iron hand.

Eva was the youngest of five illegitimate children born to Juana Ibarguren in the small provincial town of Los Toldos. Their poverty was so great that Juana hired out her children as cooks to wealthy families.

When Eva landed a small part in a school play, she quickly became starstruck and decided to pursue a career in acting. She moved to Buenos Aires, and after seven years of struggling, finally succeeded as a radio and film actress.

In 1944, Eva met Colonel Juan Domingo Perón, one of the strongmen who controlled the military-run government. Juan Perón claimed to be fed up with government corruption, and he wanted to organize a military coup. At forty-eight, he was twice Eva's age, but they both came from working-class roots, and she was attracted by his intelligence and charm.

Eva's relationship with Juan boosted her acting career, and by mid-1944, she was earning a fortune by Argentine standards. The couple married in 1945, and Eva not only supported her husband but became the driving force behind his—and eventually their—rise to power.

Eva insisted that Juan had to become leader of the poor in order to advance his political career. Together, they traveled throughout the countryside and working-class neighborhoods urging the people to oppose the current government. Juan advocated minimum wages, decent working conditions, and regular wage raises.

Eva Perón and husband on their way to a gala, 1951.

By 1946, Eva's talents as an orator had won over thousands of Argentineans. She roused the labor unions to support Juan's presidential bid, and he easily won the election. Although Juan espoused democracy and social betterment, his desire for power was great—as was Eva's. Juan was less well-liked than Eva, however, and his rule came to depend on her popularity.

Eva maintained working-class support by going to the slums and distributing gifts to the people. She appeared to keep the wealthy in their place by "reprimanding" employers who treated workers or servants with cruelty. The Peróns created an atmosphere of fear and repression for anyone who criticized them or opposed the government's wishes. They controlled information by censoring radio and newspapers throughout the country.

As the unofficial minister of health and labor in her husband's cabinet,

Eva formed a charitable foundation to support social and labor reform, women's rights, and education. The funds she collected built hospitals, schools, orphanages, and homes for the elderly and unmarried mothers, and they provided medical services, food, and clothing to those in need. Although her charity did help "redistribute" the money of the wealthy to the poor, Eva skimmed funds from the coffers for herself and her husband.

Eva also became the voice of the feminist movement. She campaigned successfully for women's right to vote, equal pay for equal work, divorce rights, and civil equality. In 1951, as her power peaked, she sought the office of vice president, but despite her popularity with the public, the military opposed her, and her bid failed. Soon after this political blow, Eva suffered an emotional and physical collapse. Less than two months after her husband's second victory in 1952, she died from cancer. Her death, coupled with a plummeting economy, caused Juan Perón to be ousted from power.

Although Eva Perón found personal glory in wealth and power, she did institute reforms that improved the lives of women and the working class in Argentina. Her colorful and controversial life has inspired the writing of many books as well as the musical *Evita*.

S. Suzan Jane

Betty Friedan

(1921–   )

"The problem that has no name—which is simply the fact that American women are kept from growing to their full human capacities—is taking a far greater toll on the physical and mental health of our country than any known disease."
—The Feminine Mystique, 1963

Even though Betty Friedan called it "the problem that has no name," thousands of women across America understood exactly what she was talking about. In her best-selling book *The Feminine Mystique*, Friedan described the frustration of trying to live up to the image of "the ideal housewife and mother" of the 1950s. Educated women who were dissatisfied with the limitations of being a housewife read her book and

realized that they were not alone. As they began to seek ways to change their individual lives, they initiated the women's liberation movement of the 1960s and 1970s.

A bright and outgoing child, Betty Goldstein was born into a wealthy family in Peoria, Illinois. In high school, she started a literary magazine and graduated as class valedictorian. In her junior year at Smith College,

Betty Friedan

where she studied psychology, she became editor of the college newspaper, where she earned a reputation for writing daring and feisty editorials. The skills she learned at Smith turned out to be invaluable for her life's work.

After graduating in 1942, Betty took a job in New York City as a labor journalist. The research she conducted heightened her awareness of the discrimination women faced in the workforce and in society in general. During this time, she met and married Carl Friedan, also a journalist. When their first son was born, she decided to continue to write. Her family needed the money she earned, and she needed the intellectual activity to balance her responsibilities at home.

For her fifteen-year college reunion, Friedan was asked to poll her classmates about their life experiences. What she learned amazed her. The two hundred women who responded clearly were no more satisfied with the limited roles of wife and mother than Friedan herself. Friedan wrote an article about the survey, but magazine after magazine refused to print it. Finally, a publisher agreed to advance her a thousand dollars to expand her research into a book.

NOW

The largest contemporary feminist organization in the United States, NOW was founded by Betty Friedan in 1966. Its purpose is to take "action to bring women into full participation in the mainstream of American society *now*, exercising all the privileges and responsibilities thereof in truly equal partnership with men." For the past thirty years, NOW has continued to lobby for all issues concerning women's rights: the still-unpassed Equal Rights Amendment, reproductive rights, lesbian and gay rights, and antiviolence and antidiscriminatory legislation.

After five years of interviewing, researching, and writing, *The Feminine Mystique* was published in 1963. The book showed how the direction of women's lives is shaped by social conditioning, and how they are denied independence, opportunities, and equality with men. The book's sales were enormous. *The Feminine Mystique* was eventually translated into thirteen languages, touching and changing women's lives everywhere with its call for female equality.

The popularity of her book significantly changed Betty Friedan's own life too. Her talents for public speaking and organizing were suddenly in constant demand. In 1966, she helped found the National Organization for Women (NOW), which works to achieve equal rights for women. She testified before Congress on behalf of women's equality, lobbied for passage of the Equal Rights Amendment to the Constitution, and helped build a network of NOW organizations across the country. She served as NOW's president until 1970.

In the years that followed, Friedan's international reputation as a founder and leader of the modern feminist movement in the United States continued to grow. Recognizing the changing role and goals of the women's movement over time, she expressed a reformist view of feminism in *The Second Stage*, published in 1981. In this book, she states, "Today the problem that has no name is how to juggle work, love, home and children." Through her numerous magazine articles, books, lectures, and speeches, Betty Friedan has continued to promote the concept of women's equality with men in all areas of life.

Bonnie Eisenberg and Mary Ruthsdotter

Diane Arbus

(1923–1971)

"I take photographs because there are things nobody would see unless
I photographed them."
—Interview, 1968

The American photographer Diane Arbus took pictures no one had ever taken before: of giants and dwarfs, transvestites, nudists, and tattooed men. Not only did she forever change what was permissible in photography, she also gave us a new view of human behavior in all its unexpected variety.

Born into a wealthy Jewish family in New York City, Diane was the second of the three children of David and Gertrude Russek Nemerov. Her family owned Russeks Fifth Avenue, a fashionable fur and clothing store. Pampered and isolated in their huge apartment, the children were reared by a succession of nannies. Diane's brother, the poet Howard Nemerov, later remembered that the nannies forbade the children to remove their white gloves even while playing in Central Park sandboxes.

In her privileged childhood, Diane was sheltered from anything "abnormal," yet she had a perverse fascination with what she wasn't supposed to see. When she was a teenager, Diane and a girlfriend traveled around the city on subways in search of unusual-looking people.

The Nemerov children attended New York's exclusive Fieldston School, where they were encouraged to study the creative arts. After graduating from high school, Diane married a young man named Allan Arbus, with whom she had fallen in love when she was fourteen. Five years older than Diane, Allan was working in the advertising department at Russeks when they met. Allan bought Diane a camera, and she eagerly took up photography. The couple worked together as fashion photographers from 1946 to 1957.

The Arbuses gained a reputation for their photographs of models for magazines such as *Glamour, Vogue*, and *Harper's Bazaar*. They also raised two daughters: Doon, born in 1945, and Amy, born in 1954. Despite the Arbuses' business success, after ten years Diane began to feel constricted by fashion photography. In 1957, she left the business and began freelancing.

Diane studied photography for two years with Lisette Model, a documentary photographer. With Model's encouragement, she gained the confidence to take photographs of "the forbidden"—subjects who both scared and excited her. She made a chalkboard list of people to shoot—midgets, hippies, beauty contestants, twins—and overcoming her intense shyness, took her bicycle and the subway at all hours of the day and night, camera in hand.

Diane Arbus had not only great persistence but an unusual ability to relate to her subjects. Because she was both curious and empathetic, her subjects would reveal themselves in unexpected ways. Yet her stark photographs invariably depict people's isolation from one another. Even her pictures of ordinary people somehow nearly always look just as odd and alienated as her "freaks."

Diane and Allan separated in 1960. To support herself and her daughters, Diane sold her photographs to magazines such as *Newsweek* and *Esquire*. She also taught photography courses at nearby colleges and researched photography for New York's Museum of Modern Art. She won two Guggenheim fellowships to support her photography in the mid-1960s, when some people wouldn't even buy her photos. But in 1967 an exhibit of her work opened at the Museum of Modern Art. Her photographs evoked powerful responses from the public. "Diane Arbus is the wizard of odds!" wrote one critic.

For years, Diane Arbus had suffered from bouts of severe depression and hepatitis. On July 28, 1971, her body was found in her apartment, where she had committed suicide one or two days before.

A year later, a major posthumous exhibition opened at the Museum of Modern Art. At least two hundred and fifty thousand people admired and criticized the collection of her most famous portraits. Some saw her work as an exploitation of the unusual people she photographed. Others praised her for daring to pursue her own vision. Diane Arbus might have summed up her work best when she said, "A photograph is a secret about a secret. The more it tells you, the less you know." Despite their often shocking content, her photographs have kept the secrets of her subjects—and her own as well.

Deborah Gore Ohrn

Shirley Chisholm

(1924–   )

"Women should perceive that the negative attitudes they hold toward
their own femaleness are the creation of an anti-feminist society, just
as the black shame at being black is a product of racism."
—*Unbought and Unbossed,* 1970

Shirley Chisholm once heard a politician say, "Black people will advance someday, but black people are always going to need to have white people leading them." Determined to prove that politician wrong, Chisholm became the first African-American woman elected to Congress, where she devoted her life to promoting equal rights for women and people of color.

Shirley Anita St. Hill was born on November 30, 1924, in Brooklyn, New York. During the Depression, she and her three younger sisters went to live with their grandmother on a farm in Barbados so their parents could

*Shirley Chisholm gives the V for Victory sign to her supporters
before the Florida primary, 1972.*

save money for their education. Shirley loved living on a farm that had
chickens, ducks, goats, lambs, and a big garden. She also loved her grandmother, who was warm and loving to the quiet Shirley, and who taught
her "pride, courage, and faith."

Shirley returned to the United States when she was eleven years old.
After graduating from Girls High School in Brooklyn, she received her
degree in sociology from Brooklyn College. Throughout her academic career, Shirley was known to be shy and studious. She discovered she was
not shy, however, when it came to school politics, and she learned a lot
working on the campaigns of other female students who ran for office.

After earning a master's degree in education from Columbia University,
Shirley taught school and worked in the day care system in New York. During
this time, she became increasingly angered by the inequalities that African-
Americans, women, and children faced. She wanted to give a voice to groups
who were not represented by elected officials. Chisholm decided to make
changes within the system, and in 1964, she entered politics. Her husband,
Conrad, whom she had married in 1949, was one of her staunchest supporters.

Chisholm's first bid for office was successful, and she became the second African-American woman to serve in the New York State Assembly. As a legislator, she promoted child welfare and introduced a state law to fund the creation of day care centers. People liked Chisholm's direct, honest style, and in 1968, she became the first black woman elected into the United States Congress.

From the outset, Chisholm had tough battles to fight in Washington. During her fourteen years in Congress, Chisholm lobbied for critical causes: employment, education,

Women in Congress

Shirley Chisholm may have been the first black woman to serve in Congress, but she is only one of many women in America who have been elected to national office.

The first woman elected to the House of Representatives was Jeannette Rankin (R-MT), who served from 1917 to 1919 in the Sixty-fifth Congress and again from 1941 to 1942. The first woman to be elected to the Senate was Rebecca Latimer Fleton (D-GA), in 1921.

In the One Hundred and Third Congress (1993–1995), there were forty-eight woman representatives in the House of Representatives. Seven women also served in the Senate: Barbara Boxer (D-CA), Dianne Feinstein (D-CA), Kay Bailey Hutchison (R-TX), Nancy Landon Kassebaum (R-KS), Barbara Mikulski (D-MD), Patty Murray (D-WA), and Carol Moseley-Braun (D-IL), the first woman of color ever to serve in the Senate. Olympia Snowe, a Republican from Maine, won a Senate seat in the 1994 election.

Information from the Center for the American Woman and Politics

welfare reform, health care, housing, endowments for the arts, job training for the handicapped, and school safety. She outspokenly criticized American involvement in the Vietnam War at a time when it wasn't politically prudent to do so. She supported the Equal Rights Amendment and women's right to safe abortion.

Chisholm made many speeches to her constituents. She especially loved speaking to college students, claiming that they "kept my hope alive—and they did not take no for an answer." Once, a student asked her when someone other than a white male was going to be president. The question stuck in her mind, and in 1972, she made an unprecedented move: *she* ran for president. The bid was unsuccessful, but it was proof of the increasing political power of women and African-Americans.

Chisholm remained in Congress until 1982, when she decided to return to private life. Since retiring from politics, she has been a professor at

Mount Holyoke College, a scholar-in-residence at Spelman College, and the first president of the National Political Congress of Black Women.

Shirley Chisholm continues to teach, lecture, and promote causes in which she believes. Her advice is simple and direct: "What we need is more women in politics because we have a very special contribution to make. I hope that the example of my success will convince other women to go into politics—and not just to stuff envelopes, but to run for office."

Judy Gitenstein

Margaret Thatcher

(1925–   )

"If you want anything said, ask a man. If you want anything done, ask a woman."
—Interview, 1989

Margaret Thatcher, the first woman prime minister of Great Britain, has been called the Iron Lady and Attila the Hun by her detractors. However, she never allowed criticism to keep her from becoming one of the most powerful leaders in the modern world.

Margaret was the oldest daughter of Alfred Roberts, a grocer and mayor, and Beatrice Roberts, a dressmaker. As a child, she attended political gatherings with her father, who had a great influence upon her.

Thatcher graduated from Oxford University with a degree in chemistry, and while working as a research chemist, she attended law school. For several years, she pursued her interest in politics while working as a taxation lawyer. She ran unsuccessfully for Parliament in 1950 and 1951 but was finally elected in 1959. In 1970, Thatcher became the first and sole woman to enter the cabinet of Prime Minister Edward Heath. Serving as his secretary of state for education and science from 1970 to 1974, she faced sharp criticism when forced to cut the budget and eliminate free milk in the schools. A huge protest ensued, characterized by the cry "Thatcher,

Thatcher, the milk snatcher." Thatcher did not budge on the issue, vowing, "I'm not going to be beaten by this."

When Heath resigned from office in 1974, Thatcher succeeded him as leader of the Tory party. In the general elections four years later, she led the Conservatives to a majority in the House of Commons. Thatcher was named the first female prime minister, breaking a seven-hundred-year-old tradition of male domination. Little did she know that she would become the longest-serving prime minister in England, and the longest-serving leader in modern Western Europe.

Thatcher forged ahead with a program called Popular Capitalism, which promoted a free-enterprise economy and strict monetary policies to control

Margaret Thatcher making a point at a news conference, days before the 1983 elections.

inflation. Not everyone benefited from her economic reforms, however. Unemployment doubled between 1979 and 1980, and public approval of the Tory party fell sharply. Knowing that her position was weakened, Thatcher capitalized on the British victory in the Falkland Islands by calling for an early election in 1983. She won her second term as prime minister and became known as the Iron Lady, both for her unwillingness to give in to labor unions and for successfully ending the Argentine invasion of the Falkland Islands.

During her second term, Thatcher continued her Popular Capitalism program. She decreased the budget deficit as well as inflation and curbed the power of labor unions. Wishing to restore England's economic strength and pride, she advocated hard work and entrepreneurialism, solid family values, and a strong national defense.

Thatcher won a third term in 1987, but in 1990, her "poll tax," levied on all British citizens, sparked controversy, as did her resistance to full British participation in the European Monetary System. Forced to resign because of dwindling support, she said, "I shall always keep a close association with the people.... It is my purpose to continue to be a strong ally and friend."

In November 1990, Thatcher supported John Major as her successor. She remains a member of the House of Commons and travels on lecture tours abroad. She has also written her autobiography.

Margaret Thatcher's accomplishments have been numerous and far-reaching. Not only did she reorganize Britain's economic policies and redefine the shape of the Conservative Party, but she rekindled in the people of England an enduring sense of pride.

S. Suzan Jane

Nguyen Thi Binh

(1927–   )

"If you asked us who is the winner, we would like to say,
'peace is the winner.'"
—After the signing of the Paris Peace Accord, 1973

During the Vietnam War in the 1960s, political activist Nguyen Thi Binh was affectionately known as the Flower and Fire of the Revolution.

Nguyen was born into a middle-class political family in Saigon. At the time, Vietnam was governed by France, and as a college student, Nguyen became aware of the effects of French occupation. "I profoundly resented the fact that we were taught Vietnamese as a secondary language to French," she stated. She participated in anti-France movements, organizing demonstrations to protest the continued French occupation of Vietnam and the presence of an American naval fleet.

In 1951, Nguyen's political activities led to her arrest. She was finally released in 1954 after the signing of the Geneva peace accord, which called for a cease-fire and the division of Vietnam into two zones: North and South. The two regions, to be governed by the Communist Viet Minh and the French respectively, were to remain neutral until national elections took place in 1956. After her release, Nguyen married and worked as a teacher.

The conflicts between North Vietnam and South Vietnam escalated in 1960 as the South refused to hold elections. Nguyen joined the newly formed National Liberation Front of South Vietnam (NLF), which called for a nationwide uprising against President Diem's regime in the region. The NLF won widespread support throughout the countryside, and Nguyen became a top diplomat and negotiator for the organization.

From 1963 to 1966, Nguyen chaired the Women's Liberation Association, recruiting women to act as spies, political agitators, and soldiers in support of the NLF cause. During this time, the United States increased its involvement in the Vietnam War, and Nguyen headed the NLF delegation in negotiations to end the war with both American leaders and representatives from the North Vietnamese government. She demanded the withdrawal of American troops and the recognition of South Vietnam's right to settle its own affairs.

While at first many believed that Nguyen would not be taken seriously (one French newspaper dismissed her as "a sort of Joan of Arc of the rice paddies"), she persisted in powerfully articulating the demands of the NLF. Although the talks involved many subtle compromises, Nguyen refused to settle for less than full withdrawal of American troops. By 1969, Nguyen had marked a deadline for American troops to leave, and she made agreements with the United States for the release of American POWs. After years of stalled talks, this was a significant step forward. Finally, on January 27, 1973, a final agreement was reached in Paris, which ended the Vietnam War.

In 1975, Nguyen was named minister of foreign affairs for the Revolutionary Government of South Vietnam. When North and South Vietnam united as the Socialist Republic of Vietnam, she became the minister of education.

A skillful and tireless negotiator, Nguyen Thi Binh hastened the end of a long war which had taken millions of lives. She once said of her thirty-year political career, "People ask why I am in politics. . . . If you mean by politics, the fight for the right to live, then we do it because we are obliged to. But fighting for that is not politics. It is much more fundamental."

S. Suzan Jane

Jacqueline Kennedy Onassis

(1929–1994)

"Throughout my life I have tried to remain true to myself. This I will continue to do as long as I live."
—Quoted in *Scranton Times*, May 25, 1972

Her qualities of independence and inner strength would make Jacqueline Kennedy Onassis one of the most admired women of the twentieth century. Throughout her life, she was debutante, reporter, activist, wife, mother, first lady, fund-raiser, and book editor. But she is best remembered for her courage in the days after her husband, President John F. Kennedy, was assassinated in November 1963.

Jacqueline and her younger sister, Lee, grew up on Long Island in a privileged but unhappy family of French Catholic descent. Her father, "Black Jack" Bouvier, was a handsome ne'er-do-well who lost most of his money in the stock market crash of 1929. Her parents divorced when she was eleven, and her mother remarried a wealthy stockbroker.

At boarding school in Connecticut, where Jackie (as she was called) was sent at age fifteen, she loved to read and was an accomplished rider. Named Debutante of the Year at the age of eighteen, she was unmistakably a beauty. But it was Jackie's independence, intelligence, and spirit of adventure that set her apart from her peers from an early age.

During a year abroad in Paris as a junior in college, Jackie discovered what would be a lifelong passion for the arts. She later recalled the experience as "the high point in my life, my happiest and most carefree year." At twenty-one, she won *Vogue* magazine's Prix de Paris contest, beating out 1,279 other contestants with an essay entitled "People I Wish I Had Known." Her subjects were the writer Oscar Wilde, poet Charles Baudelaire, and ballet master Sergei Diaghilev.

Upon graduating from college, Jackie took a job as the Inquiring Reporter for the *Washington Times-Herald*. She met Senator John Kennedy at a dinner party when she was twenty-three. A year later, they were married. For a few years, Jackie focused on supporting her husband's career and starting a family, giving birth to a daughter, Caroline, and a son, John. But her life changed forever when Kennedy was elected president in 1960.

Though the Kennedy administration lasted less than three years, Jackie made an indelible impression as first lady. She set out at once to restore the White House. Working with a team of experts, she scoured the United States for art and period antiques. When the project was finished, she gave a nationally televised tour of the newly refurbished White House that was watched by eighty million people.

Jackie Kennedy's personal style set trends as well—millions of American women copied the "Jackie look" of elegance and simplicity in fashion. For many women, her intelligence, energy, style, and youth made her a role model. Her popularity rivaled that of her husband. During a 1961 state visit to France, crowds lined the

The graceful Jacqueline Kennedy Onassis

road chanting, "Vive Jackie!" Kennedy remarked, "I am the man who accompanied Jacqueline Kennedy to Paris—and I have enjoyed it."

Then, in November 1963, tragedy struck. President John Kennedy was assassinated as he and Jackie rode in a motorcade in Dallas, Texas. Jackie set an example of courage and fortitude in the days that followed. Her suit and stockings were stained with her husband's blood, but she refused to change before the flight back to Washington, saying, "I want them to see what they have done." Refusing sedatives, she worked through the night, sending aides to look up archives on Lincoln's funeral. She orchestrated every detail of Kennedy's funeral—the riderless horse, the muffled drums, and the eternal flame at the tomb—intending it to be both a memorial to her husband and a ceremony that would restore the nation's dignity. Her courage inspired the grieving nation.

In the years following Kennedy's death, Jackie charted her own course, focusing on raising her children and on defining a new role for herself. In 1968, she astonished the world by marrying the Greek shipping magnate Aristotle Onassis. The marriage was an unhappy one, and the couple was planning a divorce when Onassis died in 1975. She would never marry again. Jacqueline Kennedy Onassis spent the rest of her life living in New York City, where she pursued a rewarding career as a book editor. She was also active in the cause of historic preservation and spoke out to preserve New York City's famous Grand Central Station. In her final years, she seemed to have found the balance she had always sought between her personal and public lives—a balance that included her love of art.

Elisabeth Keating

Violeta Chamorro

(1929–   )

"Behind this war—a civil war between Sandinista soldiers
recruited against their will and Nicaraguan "contras" on the
other side—there is a profound tragedy in which a whole people
is impoverished by the loss of a great treasure: their freedom."
—Foreign Affairs, Winter 1986

With little political experience but much popular support, Violeta Chamorro became the first female president of Nicaragua in 1990. Her election ended an eight-year civil war and brought democracy to this Central American country.

Violeta was born into a family of wealthy cattle ranchers. Her father insisted she attend women's colleges in the United States, but after his death, she dropped out of school and returned to Nicaragua. In 1950, she met and married Pedro Joaquín Chamorro Cardenal, publisher of the controversial newspaper *La Prensa*.

Violeta worked at *La Prensa*, which served as a voice of opposition to the dictatorship of the Somozas, the family that ruled Nicaragua from 1933 to 1979. When the Somoza government began arresting people who disagreed with them, Pedro Joaquín was imprisoned. In 1978, he was assassinated by Somoza's supporters.

As chair of the board of directors of *La Prensa*, Chamorro continued the paper's oppositional stance. She also began contributing funds to the Sandinista National Liberation Front (FSLN), a Marxist organization that opposed the dictatorship. In July 1979, the FSLN succeeded in overthrowing the Somoza regime and bringing Sandinista leader Daniel Ortega Saavedra to power.

Ortega had advocated democracy, but it soon became apparent to Chamorro and others that his administration was not much different from the dictatorship they had just toppled. Ortega forbade "counterrevolutionary" activities and began to nationalize privately owned land and companies. *La Prensa* mounted an attack against Ortega, and people started to protest the new administration. Civil war once again erupted across the country.

On July 29, 1986, Chamorro wrote a "Letter to Ortega" that appeared in the *New York Times*. She denounced the political repression of Ortega's regime and charged that "the Sandinista party has already created a great concentration camp in Nicaragua. But the Nicaraguan people are not losing their liberating spirit and will never lose it even in the worst of the gulags your mind is able to conceive."

Because of her vocal denouncements of the government, Chamorro

Woman Leaders

In 1994, nine countries around the world were headed by women:

Violeta Chamorro, president of Nicaragua

Mary Robinson, president of Ireland

Vidgis Finnbogadottir, president of Iceland

Gro Harlem Brundland, prime minister of Norway

Eugenia Charles, prime minister of Dominica

Benazir Bhutto, prime minister of Pakistan

Tamsu Ciller, prime minister of Turkey

Chan Drika Bandaranaike Kumaratunga, president of Sri Lanka (her mother, former President Sirimavo Bandaranaike, was appointed prime minister)

Khaleda Zia, prime minister of Bangladesh

Information from the Division for the Advancement of Women, UN

265

quickly became the popular choice for Democratic candidate of the National Opposition Union (UNO). Despite threats and censorship of *La Prensa*, she was determined to end the civil war and Ortega's rule. With the promise of democracy, Chamorro secured American support in the election race against Ortega. Becoming a political candidate had never been a goal in her life, but now Chamorro had a mission. "Nicaragua must win its freedom once again," she stated at a rally. "All across the world, people are burying communism and proclaiming democracy."

By 1989, Ortega had agreed to join the Central American peace accord, which called for a free press, disarmament, and free elections. On February 25, 1990, in the first democratic election in 170 years, Chamorro defeated Ortega to become the first women president in Central America.

Chamorro inherited a country plagued by inflation, unemployment, and a large foreign debt. She negotiated a truce to end the civil war and worked quickly to stop the military draft, reduce the size of the army and police force, grant amnesty to political prisoners, and restore private property rights and a free-market economy.

As of this writing, Chamorro continues to lead a nation suffering from high unemployment and a bankrupt economy. Yet Chamorro's achievements have been great. She ended years of bloodshed, brought unity to opposing political forces, and helped give birth to a democracy.

S. Suzan Jane

Toni Morrison

(1931–   )

*"I would like my work to do two things: be as demanding and
sophisticated as I want it to be, and at the same time be
accessible in a sort of emotional way to lots of people, just like jazz.
That's a hard task. But that's what I want to do."*
—*New York Times Magazine* interview, 1994

For as long as she can remember, Toni Morrison has loved to read
books. As an adult, she has combined her enjoyment of reading
with her powerful verbal skills to write captivating and forceful
stories about the lives of African-Americans.

Toni Morrison grew up Chloe Wofford in the integrated neighborhood
of a small Ohio town. Even be-
fore she started school, she spent
many happy hours lost in stories
and books. The Woffords' home
was filled with black folklore,
song, and family storytelling.
Chloe particularly liked detailed
descriptions of characters and
their lives.

After graduating from high
school with honors, Chloe went
to Howard University in Washington, D.C., where she became known by the nickname
"Toni." This was her first experience of what life was like for
African-Americans living in the
segregated South.

After graduate work in English literature at Cornell Uni-

Toni Morrison

versity, Toni married Harold Morrison, an architect. When the marriage ended in 1964, she supported her two sons as a book editor, first in Syracuse, New York, and then in New York City. As an editor for Random House publishers, she worked with black authors to create a body of literature "where black people are talking to black people." One of her major projects at Random House was editing *The Black Book*, an African-American history composed of news articles, photographs, songs, slave bills of sale, and other printed materials.

Morrison's first novel, *The Bluest Eye*, received favorable reviews, and her second book, *Sula*, won equal praise. Both novels explored the difficulties that African-American girls face growing up in white society. Her next novel, *The Song of Solomon* (1977), became her first best-seller, earning the National Book Critics' Circle Award for best fiction. The recognition she received for her powerful and lyrical writing helped propel her career. "What [we black people] have to do now," she noted, "is reintroduce ourselves to ourselves. We have to know what the past was so that we can use it for now."

Morrison published *Tar Baby*, her first book with white characters, in 1981. Set in the Caribbean, the novel depicts the ways in which colonialism affects native culture and family relationships. *Beloved* (1987), a novel about a runaway who confronts her painful history as a slave, won Morrison the Pulitzer Prize for fiction. In 1993, she became only the second American woman to receive the Nobel Prize for literature.

Alice Walker, whose novel *The Color Purple* also won a Pulitzer Prize, said, "No one writes more beautifully than Toni Morrison. She has consistently explored issues of true complexity and terror and love in the lives of African-Americans."

Morrison is now a professor at Princeton University. In addition to her novels, she has written a play and two volumes of essays. Undoubtedly, readers have not seen the last of this prolific and powerful author.

Bonnie Eisenberg and Mary Ruthsdotter

Corazon Aquino

(1933–   )

"No one can say Cory did not give it her all."
—*Time* interview, 1986

Corazon Aquino, a Philippino housewife and mother who was transformed by her husband's political plight, led a people's revolution to end the twenty-year dictatorship of Ferdinand Marcos.

Corazon was born into a wealthy family in the Philippines. Because of her family's status and political connections, she frequently met foreign dignitaries who visited their home. By listening to their discussions, she learned about politics and events occurring around the world.

Corazon attended college in New York, then returned to the Philippines to study law. In 1954, she married Benigno Aquino, a journalist with political aspirations. After serving in various local and national positions, Benigno became the youngest mayor, governor, and senator ever elected in the Philippines. He also led the movement to oust President Ferdinand Marcos.

In 1972, Marcos declared martial law to stop student unrest and prolong his presidency. He also ordered the arrest of Benigno, who posed a threat as the most likely candidate to succeed him. Corazon remained in the shadows until Benigno's imprisonment, when she began to deliver his messages to the press. In 1980, she accompanied him into exile in the United States.

When he tried to return to the Philippines in 1983, Benigno was assassinated at the airport. Corazon was thrust into the limelight immediately, and Benigno's supporters urged her to continue her husband's role in leading the opposition movement against Marcos. Invitations for Corazon to speak poured in daily, and being fluent in five languages, she was able to communicate well with people in the multilingual Philippines.

In late 1985, when Marcos called for presidential elections, a movement to draft Corazon Aquino emerged. The opposition was divided internally and saw Aquino as the only person who could win unified support. She admitted that she didn't know much about being a president but advanced her campaign as the moral alternative to the corrupt and repressive Marcos government.

Violence had often accompanied elections in the Philippines, and 1986 was no exception. When the National Assembly declared Marcos the winner, Aquino charged him with election fraud. She launched a campaign of nonviolent resistance, and unwilling to fire on civilians, Marcos's soldiers retreated. Under pressure from the United States, Marcos resigned and fled the Philippines. Aquino became the seventh president—and the first woman—to head the country.

Aquino released political prisoners, reinstated an elected Congress responsible for making laws, enacted a temporary constitution with a bill of rights, and appointed a commission to draft a new constitution. To revive the ailing economy, she broke up sugar and coconut monopolies, reduced fuel, utilities, fertilizer, and seed taxes, and boosted the confidence of foreign investors.

Despite major obstacles such as national poverty and several coup attempts, Aquino became a very popular president. She remained in office until June 30, 1992, when she was replaced by Fidel Ramos, her handpicked successor. Although she was a political neophyte, Corazon Aquino courageously led her country toward greater democracy and freedom. One of her last achievements as president was the peaceful transfer of power to Ramos, a sharp contrast to the violent elections of previous years.

S. Suzan Jane

Barbara Jordan

(1936–   )

*"What the people want is very simple. They want an America as
good as its promise."*
—Commencement address, Harvard University, 1977

Barbara Jordan always knew she was going to "be something special"
and that she wanted an interesting and challenging career. But it
wasn't until she heard Edith Sampson, a black attorney from Chicago, speak at her high school's "career day" that she began to consider
law. Once Barbara became a lawyer, she soon decided that she wanted to
help make the laws that govern
the nation.

As a young girl growing up in
Houston, Texas, Barbara was encouraged by her family to learn as
much as she could and always to
do her best. She graduated in the
top five percent of her high school
class and went on to study at
Texas Southern University. There,
she joined the debate team, becoming champion of the school
by the time she graduated. After
graduating from the university,
she earned a law degree from Boston University.

*Barbara Jordan speaks at the 1992
Democratic National Convention.*

Returning to Texas in 1959,
Jordan began practicing law from her kitchen, working long hours to help
poor people solve their legal problems. Always eager for challenges and
wanting to make the country more fair to all citizens, Jordan decided to
run for public office. First, she ran for the state house of representatives
and lost twice; then she ran for the state senate and won. She was the first

African-American since 1883, and the first African-American woman ever, to serve in the Texas Senate.

As an African-American woman in government in the 1960s, Jordan's dream of becoming "something special" began to come true. During her term, she helped create the Texas Fair Employment and Practices Commission and fought for her state's first minimum wage requirement. She promoted voting rights for African-Americans and worked to end racial discrimination in the workforce. By the end of her first term, she was so well respected that she was named Outstanding Freshman Senator.

With her reputation established, Jordan ran successfully for the United States House of Representatives in 1972. She helped win an extension of the Voting Rights Act of 1965 and fought for congressional passage of the Equal Rights Amendment. She supported the creation of the Consumer Protection Agency and advocated free legal services for the poor. In 1976, Jordan dazzled a national television audience with her keynote address at the Democratic National Convention, becoming the first woman ever accorded that honor.

Recognizing the importance of her own education, Jordan consistently voted to increase funding to schools. As recently as 1990, she remarked, "Education remains the key to both economic and political empowerment. That is why the schools charged with educating African-Americans have, perhaps, the greatest, the deepest challenge of all."

When she retired from politics in 1978, Jordan became a professor at the Lyndon Baines Johnson School of Public Affairs at the University of Texas. "Now I find teaching extraordinarily satisfying," she said. "I'm teaching young people who will move into local, state, and federal positions of power." In 1990, Barbara Jordan was inducted into the National Women's Hall of Fame.

Bonnie Eisenberg and Mary Ruthsdotter

Valentina Tereshkova

(1937–   )

In an era when scientists questioned the effects of space flight on women, Valentina Tereshkova proved that a woman could successfully complete the rigorous astronaut training and travel through space without harm.

Valentina was born on a farm in the central Soviet Union. Her father, a tractor driver, was killed in World War II, and her mother worked in a textile mill. Opportunities for young women were few. Valentina began working at age sixteen in a tire factory and later worked in a cotton mill.

Yet Valentina's real interests lay far from mundane factory work. In her spare time, Valentina enjoyed swimming, water skiing, and playing badminton, but her true passion was parachuting. She became an expert in this sport and founded the Textile Mill Workers Parachute Club.

Tereshkova later said that the day in 1961 that Yuri Gargarin became the first man in space was the most exciting day of her life, for Gargarin's flight inspired her to become a cosmo-

Valentina Tereshkova at the controls of a Concorde airliner in London, 1984.

naut. Acting on impulse, she wrote about her parachuting skills to the space center in Moscow and asked if she could train for space flight. To her surprise, she soon received word that she had been selected for the training program. In the spring of 1962, Tereshkova went to Star City, a complex similar to Cape Canaveral where cosmonauts study and learn about space flight. There, she underwent rigorous training in isolation, weightless flights, jet piloting, and parachute jumps wearing a space suit. She also studied rocket and spacecraft systems.

On June 16, 1963, Tereshkova blasted off in a one-person capsule, becoming the first woman in space. During her first orbit, she made radio contact with a fellow cosmonaut: "It's beautiful up here. I can see the horizon. What beautiful colors." That night the two cosmonauts sang songs together to fall asleep.

After three days and forty-eight orbits of the earth stretching 1.2 million miles, Tereshkova ejected herself and parachuted to earth. Her flight had been scheduled for the week before an international women's conference was to take place in Moscow. At the conference, prominent figures such as Queen Elizabeth II and Nikita Khrushchev congratulated her and celebrated her achievement. Tereshkova was named Hero of the Soviet Union and received the Order of Lenin and Gold Star Medal.

A few months later, Tereshkova married fellow cosmonaut Andriyan Nicolayev, and they had a daughter in 1964. In the years following her historic flight, she continued to work as an aerospace engineer and graduated from the Zhukovsky Military Air Academy in 1969. Tereshkova traveled abroad to lecture on her flight and on women's issues, and she received numerous awards and honors.

At a time when scientists were performing animal testing to determine the effects of space flight on women, Tereshkova courageously and enthusiastically allowed them to study the real thing. Her pioneer flight paved the way for future generations of women astronauts to participate in space study and exploration.

Elisabeth Keating

Marian Wright Edelman

(1939–   )

"The legacy I want to leave is a child-care system that says that no kid is going to be left alone or left unsafe."
—Essay from *I Dream a World*, 1989

"Service was as much a part of my upbringing as eating breakfast and going to school," Marian Wright Edelman recalled of her childhood. "It was clear that it was the purpose of life." The Wrights taught their daughter Marian and her siblings—including twelve foster children—that neither poverty nor racism were insurmountable obstacles. They encouraged their children to set high goals, and they instilled in them a belief that education and determination would help them achieve their goals. Growing up in Bennettsville, South Carolina, in the early 1940s, Marian needed to believe in herself, for she lived in a racially segregated society.

Public places, transportation, and even restrooms were sectioned off by race. When the black children of her neighborhood were not allowed to play at the community playground, Marian's father, a Baptist minister, built a playground for them behind his church.

Marian Wright Edelman with two young friends.

Marian's father died in 1954, just one week before the Supreme Court passed down its landmark decision *Brown* v. *the Board of Education*, which declared segregation in education illegal. Marian knew how much this milestone in racial equality would have meant to her father, and she decided that she would continue the fight for civil rights.

Marian attended Spelman College, the first college for black women in the country. At daily chapel services, she heard the values instilled by her parents echoed in the words of prominent civil rights leaders, including Whitney Young, president of the National Urban League, Dr. Martin Luther King, Jr., and Fannie Lou Hamer, who founded the Mississippi Freedom party.

CDF

Since 1973, the Children's Defense Fund has lobbied in Washington and across the country for the safeguarding of the rights of children. CDF, a nonprofit organization funded by individual donations, foundations, and corporations, has pushed for laws providing for adequate health care and child care, alleviating child poverty, preventing teen pregnancy, and creating programs for troubled youths. CDF's goal is to make sure that no child grows up without food, shelter, health care, a stable home environment, and a good education.

Some of CDF's triumphs:

•Head Start grew from serving 376,000 children in 1980 to serving more than 700,000 in 1993.

•With CDF's help, the first comprehensive child care and family support legislation was passed in 1990, allocating about five billion dollars for low- and middle-income families receiving child care.

•CDF assisted in passing the Education for All Handicapped Children Act of 1974.

In 1959, the civil rights movement was just gaining momentum with student protests and sit-ins. Marian was arrested in 1960 for her participation in the largest sit-in at City Hall in Atlanta. While working for the Atlanta office of the National Association for the Advancement of Colored People (NAACP), she realized the great need for civil rights lawyers and decided to become an attorney.

Marian graduated from Yale Law School in 1963 and in 1965 became the first black woman to pass the bar in Mississippi. She defended many civil rights cases, mostly getting student protestors released from jail. During her years as a lawyer, she was threatened, jailed, and denied entry to a state courthouse, but she did not let any obstacle stand in the way of achieving justice.

In 1967, Marian met Peter Edelman, a lawyer who had come to Mississippi while working for Robert Kennedy. Though they were from different backgrounds—he was Jewish and from the Midwest—they shared similar values. They were married in 1968.

In the following years, Marian Edelman realized that she had to go to

Washington to defend the interests of the poor, especially children. "I've been struck by the upside-down priorities of the juvenile justice system. We are willing to spend the least amount of money to keep a kid at home, more to put him in a foster home, and the most to institutionalize him," she said. "Every thirty-five seconds, an infant is born into poverty." The result of Edelman's efforts is the nonprofit organization called the Children's Defense Fund, which she founded in 1973 to provide a voice for children. By lobbying for children's rights—including accessible and safe child care, youth employment, family support systems, and education—the CDF has become a powerful vehicle for gaining child-welfare reforms.

Still active as the president of the CDF, Edelman has received numerous awards and honorary degrees and written many articles and books, including the autobiographical *The Measure of Our Success: A Letter to My Children and Yours.*

The legacy of caring and public service that Edelman received from her parents she has now passed along to future generations.

Judy Gitenstein

Wilma Rudolph

(1940–1994)

"I loved the feeling of freedom in running, the fresh air, the feeling that the only person I'm really competing with is me."
—*Wilma*, 1977

It wasn't until Wilma Rudolph was in the sixth grade that she was finally able to walk without a leg brace. More than anything else, she wanted to be able to run and play with the other children. Little did she know that within a few years she would be considered "the fastest woman in the world."

While growing up in Clarksville, Tennessee, Wilma Rudolph caught every childhood disease that came around: measles, mumps, chicken pox, double pneumonia, scarlet fever, and polio. These illnesses left her body weak and one leg paralyzed. Two things made all the difference for her: she was

Wilma Rudolph running for the gold in the 1960 Olympics.

determined to live a normal life, and she had a loving family that was willing to do anything to help her recover. "The doctors told me I would never walk, but my mother told me I would, so I believed my mother."

In the 1940s, the South was still racially segregated. Because the Rudolphs were African-Americans, the only hospital they could use was fifty miles away. Wilma's mother drove her there twice a week for physical therapy. Her brothers and sisters took turns massaging her legs several times a day. Wilma did her school work at home until she was strong enough to attend classes.

All of this hard work and dedication paid off. Wilma could eventually walk, and by the seventh grade, she was strong enough to play basketball. At a tournament, she met Ed Temple, coach for the women's track team at Tennessee State College. He invited her to participate in a summer track program. This training, combined with her natural ability, helped Wilma earn a place on the 1956 United States Olympic track team. At sixteen, she was the youngest member of the team.

The American team won a bronze medal at the Olympic Games that year, and at the 1960 Olympics Games in Rome, Rudolph became a star. She was the first American woman runner to come away with three gold medals in the hundred-meter dash, the two-hundred-meter dash, and the four-hundred-meter relay. Rudolph was showered with attention by the press and public throughout the world. Not only did she win the races, she also won the hearts of the fans with her grace and charm, her joyful smile, and her incredible triumph over the odds she had overcome to achieve such victories.

When she returned to Clarksville, Rudolph was given a hero's welcome, including a parade that was the first integrated event in the town's history. The Associated Press named her Woman Athlete of the Year.

Rudolph hung up her running shoes in 1962 to finish college and raise a family. She worked periodically as a teacher, track coach, and director of youth athletic programs. In 1981, she founded the Wilma Rudolph Foundation in Indianapolis to train and encourage young athletes in their chosen sport. Wilma Rudolph told a reporter that the Olympics had enriched her life, and in turn, she was now "trying to develop other champions."

In November 1994, Rudolph died of a malignant brain tumor. Her name lives on through her foundation.

Bonnie Eisenberg and Mary Ruthsdotter

Billie Jean King

(1943–   )

"When I was five or six . . . [I] told my mother I'd be the best in something; by the time I was twelve, I knew what I'd be the best in."
—Billie Jean, 1982

One of Billie Jean King's goals as a professional tennis player has always been to win. Another has been to make tennis and other professional sports more equitable for women athletes. King has accomplished both of these goals, becoming a star tennis player and helping to create more opportunities for women in tennis and in other sports.

Growing up in Long Beach, California, Billie Jean always loved sports, though there was little encouragement for female athletes in the late 1940s and early 1950s. Her mother suggested she try tennis, and she entered her first tournament when she was eleven years old. By the age of seventeen, Billie Jean was playing at Wimbledon, and she won her first tournament there when she was twenty-two.

Billie Jean King winning the first round of the Toray-Sillook Tennis Tournament, 1973.

As a history student at Los Angeles State College, King earned a reputation as the best athlete on campus. Still, she was not eligible for an athletic scholarship because she was a woman. As she won tournaments, she found that prize money for women was much less than that awarded to men. She also noticed that the media paid less attention to women's tennis, often ignoring it entirely. The discrimination she experienced early in her career motivated King to work toward equity between men's and women's sports, in terms of both financial rewards and opportunity.

In 1967, King won the triple crown at Wimbledon, taking the women's singles, doubles, and mixed doubles titles. For the next ten years, King reigned as queen of women's tennis. She accepted a "battle of the sexes" challenge from former men's champion Bobby Riggs, who bragged that men were better players than women. Her highly publicized defeat of Riggs empowered her to work for and achieve more lucrative tournaments for women players. King became the first woman tennis player to win more than one hundred thousand dollars in a year, and she took home twenty titles from Wimbledon alone—more than any other player.

After retiring from tennis, King organized the first women-only tennis tour, insisting on prize money equal to that earned by men. She founded and was first president of the Women's Tennis Association, and she cofounded *womenSports* magazine. She also established the Women's Sport Foundation to encourage future generations of female athletes.

Since 1984, King has served as commissioner of the Team Tennis League, organizing boys and girls into competitive teams in five hundred cities nationwide. The league also sponsors professional teams and tournaments with more than four hundred thousand dollars in prize money.

Although King has been succeeded on the court by numerous outstanding women tennis players, perhaps no one has done more to promote and advance women's tennis and female athletics in general than Billie Jean King.

Bonnie Eisenberg and Mary Ruthsdotter

Mairead Corrigan

(1944–   )

Betty Williams

(1943–   )

"We have not yet brought peace to Northern Ireland. We have created a climate for peace to be respectable."
—Betty Williams, interview, October 11, 1977

In a country still battling civil unrest, Mairead Corrigan and Betty Williams won the 1976 Nobel Peace Prize for their efforts in bridging the religious and national divisions that have fueled violence in Northern Ireland for centuries.

Mairead Corrigan was born to working-class parents in a Catholic section of West Belfast, Northern Ireland. A secretary and volunteer with the Catholic welfare organization the Legion of Mary, she strongly opposed the violence that permeated Northern Ireland, the only portion of the country still under British rule.

In 1968 and 1969, protests erupted over a decision to increase Catholics' political power. (Catholics constitute one-third of the population in the Protestant-controlled region.) Corrigan was horrified by the violence between the two religious groups, and she saw increasing fear on both sides. Working with the Legion of Mary, she sheltered children and visited prisoners at British camps.

On August 10, 1976, Corrigan was directly affected by the violence when an IRA (Irish Republican Army) getaway car crashed, killing her sister's three

Mairead Corrigan and Betty Williams rally a crowd in Belfast, c. 1975.

children. One onlooker to this violent accident was Betty Williams. Williams was born in Andersonstown, another Catholic section of Belfast, to a Catholic mother and Protestant father. Her father had advocated tolerance and had taught her that bigotry only fosters more violence.

Corrigan and Williams each began independent protests against the violence in Belfast. Corrigan appeared on local television condemning IRA tactics, and Williams solicited signatures for a peace petition. She read the petition on television, calling on all Protestant and Catholic women to pressure the IRA to end its reign of violence.

After watching Williams's public address, Corrigan invited her to attend the children's funeral. There, they decided to join forces and form the Community for Peace People. They staged three peace marches in one month, gathering thousands of followers. The Peace People distributed pamphlets advocating tolerance and an end to violence, and they arranged for the escape of Protestants and Catholics who were on terrorist hit lists. Their actions drew worldwide attention and proved that people from both sides could come together in the name of peace. Corrigan and Williams also went abroad to raise funds and muster moral support for their cause.

Their activism brought much opposition. The slogan "Shoot Betty" was painted on buildings in Belfast, and IRA members tore placards from the hands of marchers. Despite the threats and criticism, violence in Northern Ireland declined by fifty-four percent, and by 1977, killings had decreased to fewer than two a week, as compared to four a week in 1969. In 1977, Corrigan and Williams became the first women to win the Nobel Peace Prize since 1944.

Both women resigned as full-time leaders of the community organization in 1978 but remained "at the disposal of the Peace People." They allocated funds from their prizes and awards for restoring damaged schools, factories, and community centers, and the organization's efforts turned from demonstrations to improving the community.

Two strangers united in tragedy, Mairead Corrigan and Betty Williams joined forces to create the biggest peace movement in Northern Ireland. Although the movement has not had much effect on the current situation in Northern Ireland, it did succeed in reducing violence while it was active, and it drew international support for an end to violence.

S. Suzan Jane

Antonia Novello

(1944–   )

"I hope that being the first woman and minority surgeon general . . . enables me to reach many individuals with my message of empowerment for women, children, and minorities."
—Interview, 1989

As the first woman and the first Hispanic surgeon general of the United States, Antonia Novello focused her energies on promoting better health for women, children, and minorities.

Antonia was born in Fajardo, Puerto Rico, the oldest of three children. Her father died when she was eight years old, and her mother, a junior-high-school principal, supported the family. Antonia was strongly influenced by her mother's belief in the importance of education. She was also greatly affected by the medical problems she experienced as a child. Suffering from a chronic intestinal ailment, she was often hospitalized and didn't receive corrective surgery until she was eighteen. As an adult, she realized that the medical care she had had as a child had been negligent, and she resolved to help others—no matter what their social status—receive the care they needed.

Novello attended college and medical school in Puerto Rico, earning her MD in 1970. As a resident, she specialized in pediatric nephrology (children's kidney diseases). She then earned a master's degree in public health from Johns Hopkins University in Maryland. Novello joined the United States Public Health Service in 1972, where, within eight years, she was promoted to deputy director.

In her new post, Novello worked hard on issues affecting the health of children, minorities, and women, as well as on preventive medicine. Her work paid off, and her skills and talents were recognized on October 17, 1989, when President George Bush nominated her to succeed Dr. C. Everett Koop as surgeon general of the United States.

Novello's first act as surgeon general was to attack cigarette and alcohol manufacturers. She claimed that their advertisements targeted children and minorities and encouraged them to smoke and drink. She may be best remembered for her successful campaign calling for stronger cigarette warning labels that specifically cite the dangers of smoking for pregnant women. She also met with some of the biggest wine and beer companies to ask them to stop aiming advertising at children.

As surgeon general, Novello spent a lot of time on the road promoting health causes and giving speeches. She focused on issues such as breast cancer, America's high infant mortality rate, vaccination of children, and AIDS. "I continue to hear that AIDS isn't my problem . . . it's theirs," she stated. "The truth is that AIDS is everyone's problem. We must face our fears squarely and shed our false beliefs." She worked to increase the public's awareness of the disease, including heterosexual AIDS and the plight of AIDS-infected children.

Since stepping down as surgeon general in 1993, Antonia Novello has written numerous articles and book chapters on pediatrics and public health policy and received many awards and honors. Today, she continues to try to make America a healthier place in which to live.

S. Suzan Jane

Aung San Suu Kyi

(1945–   )

"It is not power that corrupts, but fear. Fear of losing power corrupts."
—Freedom From Fear, 1991

Aung San Suu Kyi, a political activist, is the leader of the prodemocracy movement in Myanmar (formally Burma) and cofounder of the opposition party, the National League for Democracy. For her courageous efforts on behalf of peace and political reform, she was awarded the Nobel Peace Prize in 1991.

Suu Kyi was the third child born to Khin Kyi and Aung San, who was known as the Father of Modern Burma. He led the 1940s nationalist movement that resulted in Burma's freedom from British rule. Three years after Suu Kyi's birth, on the eve of Burma's independence, Aung San was assassinated.

Aung San's legend and legacy greatly influenced Suu Kyi, who learned about her father's role in Burma's struggle for independence through family stories and books that were written about him. "It was only when I grew older . . . [that] I . . . conceive[d] an admiration for him as a patriot and statesman. . . . It is perhaps because of this strong bond that I came to feel such a deep sense of responsibility for the welfare of my country."

While attending college in India, Suu Kyi was inspired by the teachings of Mahatma Gandhi, who advocated nonviolent civil disobedience. Upon leaving India in 1967, she finished her education at Oxford St. Hughs College in London. She lived in Bhutan and Japan before settling in England with her husband, Michael Aris, a British professor.

In 1988, Suu Kyi returned to Myanmar to care for her dying mother. She found that people were beginning to protest the dictatorship of Ne Win, who had governed since 1962, and that Ne Win was having his opponents brutally murdered. Suu Kyi was horrified by the reports of thousands of people being butchered and detained as political prisoners. She said, "As my father's daughter, I felt I had a duty to get involved." She joined the protest movement, cofounding the National League for Democracy.

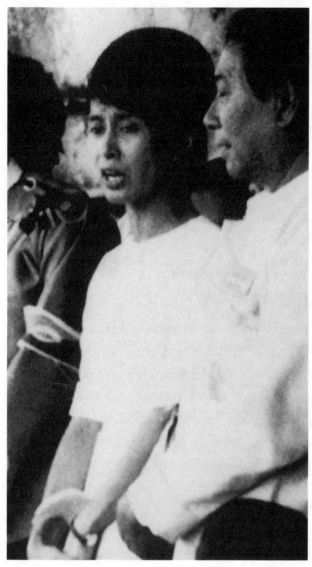

Suu Kyi addressing a rally in Burma, 1988.

The league espoused human rights, most importantly the peoples' right to choose their own government. Suu Kyi condemned the military's political power and felt that its role ought to be to protect the people. She advocated a compromise and reconciliation between civil and military authority, seeing this as necessary for achieving democracy.

Over a period of eleven months, Suu Kyi traveled throughout Myanmar, rallying people to the cause of democratic reform and pressing for a nonviolent revolution. Her popularity soon began to pose a threat to Ne Win. On April 5, 1989, six soldiers acted on orders to kill Suu Kyi, but she narrowly escaped. Three months later, she was arrested for violating a ban on political activity and for criticizing the government.

Suu Kyi was placed under house arrest, where she still remains. Her family compound is surrounded by barbed wire and guarded twenty-four hours a day. Suu Kyi has only been allowed to see her husband and two sons twice since her detainment.

Although the National League for Democracy won the 1990 election, the military regime refuses to cede power. In 1991, Suu Kyi was awarded the Nobel Peace Prize and was praised for her nonviolent resistance to the dictatorship in Myanmar.

Recently, Suu Kyi was granted permission to leave the country, but to do so, she had to promise never to return to Myanmar or to become involved in any political organization. As of this writing, Suu Kyi has rejected the terms of this offer. Today, the National League for Democracy continues its struggle to end Myanmar's brutal military regime.

S. Suzan Jane

Wilma Mankiller

(1945–   )

"You don't have to have a title or a position to be effective."
—At announcement of resignation as Cherokee chief, April 4, 1994

In 1985, Wilma Mankiller became the first woman chief of the Cherokee Nation, and she has used her position to advocate successfully for Native American causes.

Wilma was born in Mankiller Flats, Oklahoma, in a Cherokee family. When the farm failed, the United States Bureau of Indian Affairs relocated the family to San Francisco as part of a program to move Native Americans from rural towns to urban areas. The Mankillers found it hard to adjust to the city, but they tried to make the most of their new life.

Wilma, like many young women in the 1950s and 1960s, graduated from high school, married, had children, and became a homemaker. She thought this was the American dream, but she soon realized that it was not *her* dream. She felt far from home spiritually as well as geographically.

In 1969, Mankiller saw on television the AIM (American Indian Movement) protest at Alcatraz Island, the site of a former federal prison in San Francisco Bay. AIM stated they were taking back land that was rightfully theirs. Wilma visited Alcatraz many times during the eighteen-month seige, and she raised money to support the protestors. This activism inspired her to continue supporting Native American causes.

While studying sociology at San Francisco State University, Mankiller advocated for property and treaty rights for the Pit River Tribe, and she ran Native American education programs. In 1977, she returned to Oklahoma as a college graduate and began working to advance the Cherokee Nation, the second largest tribe in the United States.

In 1979, Mankiller was injured in a near-fatal car crash that led to seventeen grueling operations. Yet she remained optimistic, and after her recovery, she worked even harder for the Cherokee. In 1981, she raised private and government funds for the Bell Community Revitalization Project, which provided jobs, new homes, and a pipeline that brought in running water. Her community development programs received national attention and became models for other tribes to follow.

Mankiller's accomplishments as a leader in the Cherokee community earned her the recognition of Ross Swimmer, the chief of the Cherokee Nation, who appointed her deputy chief. When Swimmer resigned in 1985, Mankiller became the first woman principal chief. She was elected to a four-year term in 1987 and was reelected in 1991.

As chief, Mankiller was an effective spokesperson in Washington, championing health care programs, better housing, job training, and programs for children. She founded the Cherokee Nation's chamber of commerce, which helped link tribal businesses to the larger economic community, and she worked with the Environmental Protection Agency regarding the building of a hydroelectric power plant on Cherokee land. Always concerned with the preservation of Native American language and culture, Mankiller initiated the Institute for Cherokee Literacy.

In 1994, Mankiller announced her decision not to run for reelection, but she will never give up her commitment to her people. By modernizing the economy and education of the Cherokee Nation while preserving its native culture, Wilma Mankiller has left a legacy of change and empowerment to future leaders of her tribe.

Judy Gitenstein

Eka Esu-Williams

(1950–   )

"Working with communities is an incredibly rewarding experience, especially when you see people becoming empowered through understanding."
—Letter to Elisabeth Keating, 1994

An academic, educator, and community leader, Eka Esu-Williams is a highly educated modern woman as well as a wife and mother in the traditional male-oriented society of Nigeria.

Eka grew up in northern Nigeria, the third of eight children. Her mother, who was the community midwife, taught her to care for others. Her father taught his daughter that education was as important for girls as it was for boys. In her girls' school, she learned the value of discipline, self-esteem, and excellence from the missionaries who were her teachers.

Eka received her undergraduate degree from the University of Nigeria and then traveled to Great Britain to study immunology (the science of the immune system). In 1985, she returned to Nigeria and became a lecturer at the University of Calabar. Two years later, when she was passed over for a promotion, she realized that her gender was a handicap: "It was felt that I shouldn't aspire to greater heights since I was already married, had children, and had a good education—everything a lucky woman could hope for! The desire to work hard and push for more was not acceptable in a woman."

Eka Esu-Williams, African AIDS educator

Female Circumcision

Nigeria is just one of twenty-eight African countries where female circumcision is practiced. It is estimated that over one hundred million women and girls in Africa have undergone some sort of genital mutilation. The procedure can range from cutting off just part of the clitoris to the removal of the whole middle section of the vulva. Genital mutilation is meant to preserve female virginity and ensure marital fidelity. It can also cause chronic infection, painful menstruation, and life-threatening health problems. World and African health organizations and African women's groups are trying to educate people about the dangers of this traditional cultural practice.

In response to this setback, Esu-Williams decided to found the Society for Women Against AIDS in Africa (SWAA). To her, founding SWAA was "an instinctive thing to do." Her degree in immunology had made her well informed on the issue of AIDS (a disease of the immune system), while her mother's example had given her a natural interest in community work.

When Esu-Williams founded SWAA in 1988, eighty percent of the world's women who had AIDS were in Africa. Tradition and a lack of education had put African women at a greater risk of contracting AIDS than women anywhere else in the world. SWAA's mission is to halt this trend by educating and empowering African women. It offers workshops, public education, and other support services through which women learn how AIDS is transmitted, how to protect themselves against AIDS, and how to educate others in their families and communities about AIDS.

SWAA also addresses traditions and superstitions that have led to unsafe sexual practices. From infancy, many African girls are taught to be submissive, unassertive, and unprotesting when their husbands prac-

Lesotho girls with concealed faces on their way to a female circumcision ritual.

tice polygamy and wife inheritance. In SWAA workshops, girls and women learn self-esteem and discover that they have control over their lives.

Esu-Williams, who is married with three daughters and one son, applies SWAA's lessons to her own family. She says, "My son does not feel differently from his sisters and seeks no special attention. . . . I encourage [my daughters] to promote values of independence and self-esteem among their peers, to help girls plan their own lives and not be vulnerable because they are female."

Elisabeth Keating

Rigoberta Menchú

(1959–   )

"My commitment to our struggle recognizes neither boundaries nor limits: only those of us who carry our cause in our hearts are willing to run the risks."
—*I . . . Rigoberta Menchú*, 1983

Rigoberta grew up poor in the beautiful northern highlands village of Chimel, Guatemala. Her family was Quiché Indian, one of the twenty-three ethnic groups in the country. Every year, they would spend four months in the mountains and eight months on the coast, working up to fifteen hours a day on coffee or cotton plantations called *fincas*. When Rigoberta was a child, the land her village farmed in the mountains was too poor to support the family year-round.

When finally the land started to produce, big landowners tried to wrest it away from the peasants. Although Indians are in the majority in Guatemala, they have traditionally had no say in the government, which is run by people of Spanish descent, and they lack any of the ordinary rights of citizens. For twenty-two years, Rigoberta's father, Vincente, was a leader in the peasant movement against the Guatemalan government, working to improve the lives of indigenous peoples and to legalize Indian-owned land. In January 1980, Vincente was protesting violations of Indian human rights at the Spanish embassy when he and thirty-eight other Indian leaders died

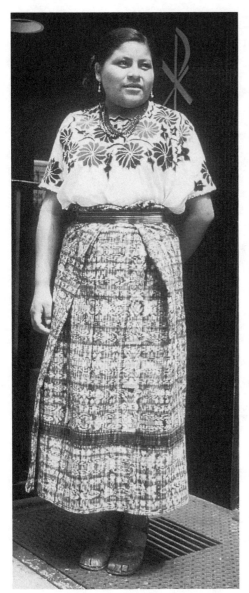

*Nobel Peace Prize winner
Rigoberta Menchú in handwoven
huipil blouse and skirt.*

in a fire. Earlier, Rigoberta's sixteen-year-old brother, Petrocinio, had been kidnapped by soldiers, tortured, and burned alive. Rigoberta's mother, a traditional healer and leader in her community, was later kidnapped, raped, and killed.

After her parents' deaths, Rigoberta learned Spanish in addition to her native Quiché language and helped organize peasant strikes with her father's movement, the United Peasant Committee. In one strike against *finca* owners, as many as eighty thousand supporters protested for fifteen days. Wanted by the Guatemalan government, Menchú went into hiding and then, in 1981, fled to Mexico, fearing for her life. Two of her sisters joined guerrilla forces in the mountains.

In 1983, Menchú dictated her autobiography, *I . . . Rigoberta Menchú,* telling about not only her life but also the lives of her *compañeros,* her fellow Indians, as well. "Life has been our teacher," she wrote. "The horrors I have suffered are enough for me. And I've also felt in the deepest part of me what discrimination is, what exploitation is. It is the story of my life." Menchú's book brought international attention to the thirty-year-long conflict between the Indians and the military government of Guatemala, in which an estimated one hundred and fifty thousand Indians have been killed.

In 1992, Rigoberta Menchú won the Nobel Peace Prize and used its $1.2 million cash prize to set up a foundation in her father's name to aid indigenous peoples. "I hope this is a contribution so that we Indian peoples of America can live forever," she said, "and so that we demonstrate that the wound we feel is a wound of all humanity."

Rigoberta Menchú has continued to work for her people, giving speeches in the United States, Latin America, and Europe to focus international pressure on the Guatemalan military rulers. Because of continual death threats, guards travel with her at all times. As a result of her efforts, the United Nations declared 1993 as the International Year for Indigenous Populations.

Deborah Gore Ohrn

Selected Bibliography and Suggested Further Reading

(suggested further reading indicated by *)

Adamson, Peter, and Petra Morrison, eds. *The Progress of Nations.* New York: United Nations Children's Fund (UNICEF), 1994.

*Addams, Jane. *Twenty Years at Hull House.* James Hunt, ed. Urbana, IL: University of Chicago Press, 1990.

Ahmed, Leila. *Women and Gender in Islam.* New Haven, CT: Yale University Press, 1992.

Albertson, Chris. *Bessie.* New York: Stein and Day, 1972.

Alexander, John T. *Catherine the Great: Life and Legend.* New York: Oxford, 1989.

*Anderson, Bonnie S., and Judith P. Zinsser. *A History of Their Own.* 2 vols. New York: Harper & Row, 1988.

*Archer, Jules. *Breaking Barriers: The Feminist Revolution from Susan B. Anthony to Margaret Sanger to Betty Friedan.* New York: Viking, 1991.

*Baker, Rachel. *The First Woman Doctor: The Story of Elizabeth Blackwell, M.D.* New York: Scholastic, 1994.

Banner, Lois. *Elizabeth Cady Stanton.* Boston: Little, Brown, 1980. ·

*Barton, Clara. *The Story of My Childhood.* Salem, NH: Ayer, 1980.

Bell, Quentin. *Virginia Woolf.* 2 vols. London: The Hogarth Press, 1973.

Bosworth, Patricia. *Diane Arbus: A Biography.* New York: Knopf, 1984.

*Bourke-White, Margaret. *Portrait of Myself.* New York: Simon and Schuster, 1963.

Bridenthal, Renate, Claudia Koontz, and Susan Stuard. *Becoming Visible: Women in European History,* 2nd ed. Boston: Houghton Mifflin, 1987.

*Brownmiller, Susan, and William H. Matthews. *Shirley Chisholm.* New York: Doubleday, 1970.

Bull, Angela. *Florence Nightingale.* London: Hamish Hamilton, 1988.

*Callahan, Sean, ed. *The Photographs of Margaret Bourke-White.* New York: Bonanza Books, 1972.

*Cantarow, Ellen. *Moving the Mountain.* Old Westbury, NY: The Feminist Press, 1980.

*Castiglia, Julie. *Margaret Mead.* Englewood Cliffs, NJ: Silver Burdett Press, 1989.

Chesler, Ellen. *Woman of Valor: Margaret Sanger and the Birth Control Movement in America.* New York: Simon and Schuster, 1993.

Chisholm, Shirley. *Unbought and Unbossed.* New York, Houghton Mifflin, 1970.

Chissel, Joan. *Clara Schumann: A Dedicated Spirit.* London: Hamish Hamilton, 1983.

Cliff, Tony. *Rosa Luxemburg.* London: Bookmarks, 1983.

*Cosman, Carol, Joan Keefe, and Kathleen Weaver. *The Penguin Book of Women Poets.* New York: Penguin Books, 1978.

*De Beauvoir, Simone. *The Second Sex.* New York: Bantam, 1952.

De Mille, Agnes. *Martha: The Life and Work of Martha Graham.* New York: Random House, 1991.

*Drucker, Malka. *Frida Kahlo: Torment and Triumph in Her Life and Art.* New York: Bantam, 1991.

*Dubois, Jill. *Women in Society: Mexico.* New York: Marshall Cavendish, 1993.

Duby, Georges, and Michelle Perrot, et. al., eds. *A History of Women in the West.* 5 vols. Cambridge, MA: The Belknap Press 1992–1994.

Duley, Margot I., and Mary L. Edwards. *The Cross-Cultural Study of Women.* New York: The Feminist Press, 1986.

*Edelman, Marian Wright. *The Measure of Our Success: A Letter to My Children and Yours.* Boston: Beacon Press, 1992.

*Ehrenberg, Margaret. *Women in Prehistory.* Norman, OK: University of Oklahoma Press, 1989.

Ehrenreich, Barbara, and Deirdre English. *Witches, Midwives, and Nurses: A History of Women Healers.* New Westbury, NY: Feminist Press, 1972.

*Emboden, William. *Sarah Bernhardt.* New York: Macmillan, 1974.

Etienne, Mona, and Eleanor Leacock, eds. *Women and Colonization: Historical Perspectives.* New York: Praeger, 1980.

*Evans, Sara. *Born for Liberty: A History of Women in America.* New York: Free Press, 1989.

*Fantham, Elaine, et. al. *Women in the Classical World.* New York: Oxford, 1994.

Fauset, Arthur. *Sojourner Truth: God's Faithful Pilgrim.* New York: Russell, 1971.

Flexner, Elinor. *Century of Struggle: The Woman's Rights Movement in the United States.* Cambridge, MA: Harvard University Press, 1915.

Flexner, Elinor. *Mary Wollstonecraft.* New York: Penguin, 1975.

Fraser, Antonia. *Mary Queen of Scots.* New York: Delacorte, 1969.

*Fraser, Antonia. *The Warrior Queens.* New York: Knopf, 1989.

*Fraser, Rebecca. *The Brontës: Charlotte Brontë and Her Family.* New York: Fawcett Columbine, 1988.

*Freedman, Russell. *Eleanor Roosevelt: A Life of Discovery.* New York: Clarion Books, 1993.

*Freeman, Lucy, and Alma Bond. *America's First Woman Warrior: The Courage of Deborah Sampson.* New York: Paragon House, 1992.

*Friedan, Betty. *The Feminine Mystique.* New York: Dell, 1984.

*Gherman, Beverly. *Georgia O'Keeffe: The "Wideness and Wonder" of Her World.* New York: Macmillan, 1986.

Goldberg, Vicki. *Margaret Bourke-White: A Biography.* New York: Harper & Row, 1986.

*Green, Rayna. *Women in American Indian Society.* New York: Chelsea House, 1992.

Gross, Susan, and Margorie Bingham. *Women in Latin America: The 20th Century.* St. Louis Park, MN: Glenhurst Publications, 1985.

Haedrich, Marcel. *Coco Chanel: Her Life, Her Secrets.* Boston: Little, Brown, 1971.

Hafkin, Nancy J., and Edna G. Bay. *Women in Africa: Studies in Social and Economic Change.* Palo Alto, CA: Stanford University Press, 1976.

*Halasa, Malu. *Mary McLeod Bethune, Educator.* New York: Chelsea House, 1989.

Halperin, John. *The Life of Jane Austen.* Baltimore, MD: The Johns Hopkins University Press, 1984.

Hamilton, Leni. *Clara Barton.* New York: Chelsea House, 1988.

*Haskins, Jim. *One More River to Cross: The Stories of Twelve Black Americans.* New York: Scholastic, 1992.

Hedrick, Joan D. *Harriet Beecher Stowe: A Life.* New York: Oxford University Press, 1994.

*Heller, Nancy. *Women Artists: An Illustrated History.* New York: Abbeville Press, 1987.

*Henderson, James D., and Linda Roddy. *Ten Notable Women of Latin America.* Chicago: Nelson-Hall, 1978.

Henry, Sandra, and Emily Taitz. *Betty Friedan: Fighter for Women's Rights.* Hillside, NJ: Enslow Publishing, 1990.

Herrera, Hayden. *Frida: A Biography of Frida Kahlo.* New York: Harper & Row, 1983.

Hole, Dorothy. *Margaret Thatcher: Britain's Prime Minister.* Hillside, NJ: Enslow Publishing, 1990.

*Hoobler, Dorothy and Thomas. *Cleopatra.* New York: Chelsea House, 1988.

*Hymowitz, Carol, and Michaele Weissman. *A History of Women in America.* New York: Bantam, 1978.

*Jakoubek, Robert E., *Harriet Beecher Stowe.* New York: Chelsea House, 1989.

*Johnston, Norma. *Louisa May: The World and Works of Louisa May Alcott.* New York: Macmillan, 1991.

*Kanematsu, Elizabeth. *Women in Society: Japan.* New York: Marshall Cavendish, 1993.

Keddie, Nikki R., and Beth Baron. *Women in Middle Eastern History.* New Haven, CT: Yale University Press, 1991.

*Kliment, Bud. *Billy Holiday.* New York: Chelsea House, 1990.

Lane, Ann J. *To Herland and Beyond: The Life and Work of Charlotte Perkins Gilman.* New York: Pantheon Books, 1980.

Lavrin, Asuncion, ed. *Latin American Women: Historical Perspectives.* Westport, CT: Greenwood, 1978.

Lerner, Gerda. *The Creation of Feminine Consciousness: From the Middle Ages to 1870.* New York: Oxford, 1993.

Lerner, Gerda. *The Grimké Sisters from South Carolina: Pioneers for Women's Rights and Abolition.* New York: Schocken Books, 1971.

*Levy, Patricia. *Women in Society: Britain.* New York: Marshall Cavendish, 1993.

Longford, Elizabeth. *Queen Victoria: Born to Succeed.* New York: Harper and Row, 1964.

Lutz, Alma. *Emma Willard: Daughter of Democracy.* Boston: Houghton Mifflin, 1929.

*Lyons, Mary E. *Sorrow's Kitchen: The Life and Folklore of Zora Neale Hurston.* New York: Scribner's, 1990.

Magolis, Nadia. *Joan of Arc in History, Literature and Film.* New York: Garland Publishers, 1990.

*McAuley, Karen. *Golda Meir.* New York: Chelsea House, 1985.

*Mead, Margaret. *Blackberry Winter: My Earliest Years.* New York: Harper & Row, 1972.

*Meir, Golda. *A Land of Our Own: An Oral Autobiography by Golda Meir.* New York: G. P. Putnam's Sons, 1973.

*Meltzer, Milton, and Lawrence Loder. *Margaret Sanger: Pioneer of Birth Control.* New York: Crowell, 1969.

Menchú, Rigoberta. *I . . . Rigoberta Menchú: An Indian Woman in Guatamala.* Elisabeth Buros-Debray, ed. Ann Wright, trans. London: Verso, 1986.

*Meyer, Susan E. *Mary Cassatt.* New York: Abrams, 1990.

Miles, Rosalind. *Women's History of the World.* New York: Harper Collins, 1990.

*Morgan, Robin, ed. *Sisterhood is Global: The International Women's Movement Anthology.* New York: Anchor Books, 1984.

*Morrison, Dorothy Nafus. *Chief Sarah: Sarah Winnemucca's Fight for Indian Rights.* Portland, OR: Oregon Historical Society Press, 1990.

Neale, J. E. *Queen Elizabeth I.* London: Jonathan Cape, 1952.

*Nies, Judith. *Seven Women: Portraits from the American Radical Tradition.* New York: Viking, 1977.

Ogilvie, Marilyn Bailey. *Women in Science: Antiquity Through the Nineteenth Century.* Cambridge, MA: MIT Press, 1986.

Oliver, Paul. *Bessie Smith.* South Brunswick, NJ: A. S. Barnes, 1961.

*Otfinoski, Steve. *Marian Wright Edelman: Defender of Children's Rights.* New York: Rosen Publishing Group, 1991.

*Peavy, Linda, and Ursula Smith, *Dreams into Deeds: Nine Women Who Dared.* New York: Scribner's, 1985.

*Petry, Ann. *Harriet Tubman: Conductor on the Underground Railroad.* New York: Crowell, 1955.

Pomeroy, Sarah B. *Goddesses, Whores, Wives, and Slaves; Women in Classical Antiquity.* New York: Schocken Books, 1975.

*Power, Eileen. *Medieval Women.* M. M. Postan, ed. Cambridge: Cambridge University Press, 1992.

*Rappaport, Doreen. *American Women: Their Lives in Their Words.* New York: Harper Collins, 1992.

*Reese, Lyn. *Spindle Stories.* Berkeley, CA: Women in the World Curriculum Resource Project, 1991.

Rissik, Dee. *Women in Society: South Africa.* New York: Marshall Cavendish, 1993.

Robertson, Claire C., and Martin A. Klein, eds. *Women and Slavery in Africa.* Madison, WI: University of Wisconsin Press, 1983.

*Rose, Phyllis, ed. *The Norton Book of Women's Lives.* New York: Norton, 1993.

*Rossi, Alice S., ed. and intro. *The Feminist Papers: From Adams to De Beauvoir.* New York: Bantam, 1974.

*Samaan, Angèle Botros. *Women in Society: Egypt.* New York: Marshal Cavendish, 1993.

*Sanford, William R. *Babe Didrikson Zaharias.* New York: Crestwood House, 1993.

Seagrave, Sterling. *Dragon Lady: The Life and Legend of the Last Empress of China.* New York: Vintage Books, 1992.

Sewell, Richard B. *The Life of Emily Dickinson.* 2 vols. New York: Farrar, Straus and Giroux, 1974.

*Shaarawi, Huda. *Harem Years: The Memoirs of an Egyptian Feminist.* Margot Badran, trans. and intro. New York: The Feminist Press, 1987.

Shikibu, Murasaki. *The Tale of Genji.* Edward G. Seidensticker, trans. and intro. New York: Vintage Books, 1985.

Skinner, Cornelia Otis. *Madame Sarah.* Boston: Houghton Mifflin, 1967.

Sklar, Catherine Kish. *Catherine Beecher: A Study in American Domesticity.* New York: W.W. Norton, 1976.

*Sloate, Susan. *Amelia Earhart, Challenging the Skies.* New York: Fawcett Columbine, 1990.

*Smith, Jessie Carney, ed. *Notable Black American Women.* Detroit, MI: Gale Research, 1992.

*Stefoff, Rebecca. *Women of the World: Women Travelers and Explorers.* New York: Oxford University Press, 1992.

*Steinem, Gloria. *Outrageous Acts & Everyday Rebellions.* New York: Holt, Rinehart, and Winston, 1983.

*Sterling, Dorothy. *Black Foremothers: Three Lives.* Margaret Walker, intro. Old Westbury, NY: The Feminist Press, 1979.

*Sterling, Dorothy. *Freedom Train: The Story of Harriet Tubman.* New York: Scholastic, 1987.

Strage, Mark. *The Life and Times of Catherine de Medici.* New York: Harcourt, Brace, Jovanovich, 1976.

*Sunstein, Emily W. *A Different Face: The Life of Mary Wollstonecraft.* Boston: Little Brown, and Co., 1975.

Suu Kyi, Aung San. *Freedom From Fear.* New York: Penguin Books, 1991.

*Tan, Pamela. *Women in Society: China.* New York: Marshall Cavendish, 1993.

*Taylor, Judy, et. al. *Beatrix Potter 1866–1943: The Artist and Her World.* London: Frederick Warne, 1987.

*Terry, Walter. *Frontiers of Dance: The Life of Martha Graham.* New York: Crowell, 1975.

*Trager, James. *The Woman's Chronology.* New York: Henry Holt, 1994.

*Truth, Sojourner. *Narrative of Sojourner Truth.* Margaret Washington, ed. New York: Vintage, 1993.

Vicinus, Martha, ed. *Suffer and Be Still: Woman in the Victorian Age.* Bloomington, IN: Indiana University Press, 1973.

Welu, James A., and Pieter Biesboer, eds. *Judith Leyster: A Dutch Master and Her World.* New Haven, CT: Yale University Press, 1993.

*Wepman, Dennis. *Helen Keller.* New York: Chelsea House, 1987.

Willard, Charity Cannon. *Christine de Pizan: Her Life and Works.* New York: Persea Books, 1984.

*Winter, Jane Kohen. *Women in Society: Brazil.* New York: Marshall Cavendish, 1993.

Wolf, Margery and Roxane Witke, eds. *Women in Chinese Society.* Palo Alto, CA: Stanford University Press, 1975.

*Wollstonecraft, Mary. *A Vindication of the Rights of Woman.* Carol H. Postin, ed. New York: Norton, 1967.

Woodham-Smith, Cecil. *Florence Nightingale.* New York: Atheneum, 1983.

*Woolf, Virginia. *A Room of One's Own.* New York: Harcourt, Brace & World, 1929.

CONTRIBUTORS:

Ruth Ashby received her bachelor's degree from Yale University and her master's degree in English literature from the University of Michigan. While working toward her doctorate at the University of Virginia, she served on the executive committee of the Women's Studies Program and taught courses on women in literature. She presently teaches part-time at Marymount Manhattan College and works full-time as a children's book editor and writer in New York City.

Dinah Dunn received her bachelor's degree from American University. She is currently an editor concentrating on nonfiction adult trade books in New York City.

Bonnie Eisenberg graduated from Berkeley with a bachelor's degree in social sciences, and from Sonoma State University with a master's degree in both psychology and counseling. Actively involved in the women's movement since 1968, she is now a staff member at the National Women's History Project and has written and edited many of its curriculum units. In addition, she is editor of the newsletter *Sex Equity and Education,* for which she also served as president and member of Board of Directors. She currently lives in Santa Rosa, California.

Judy Gitenstein received her bachelor's degree from New York University's School of Arts. With over twenty years involvement in the field of publishing, she has worked as an editor of children's books for Bantam Doubleday Dell, Random House, and Avon Books. She is currently a freelance writer/editor for middle grade fiction and non-fiction. She lives in New York City.

S. Suzan Jane has a bachelor's degree from the University of Wisconsin and a master's degree in international relations from the United States International University at San Diego. She is currently a doctoral candidate at the University of Hawaii at Honolulu in political science. Most recently, she has presented a paper at the International Conference on Women and Power in Honolulu.

Lisa Keating has a bachelor's degree in social studies from Harvard University. She has written and edited history textbooks for Scholastic Inc. and numerous articles for *Crayola Kids* magazine and *Scholastic Magazine,* and more recently has helped develop educational programming for Channel Thirteen public television. She has also worked on the book *Healing of the Mind* with Bill Moyers. She currently lives in New York City.

Deborah Gore Ohrn has a master's degree in American history with a concentration in women's history from the University of Iowa. She has written and edited articles and books for Scholastic Inc., Macmillan, and Children's Television Workshop. She was also the editor for the award-winning children's history magazine *The Goldfinch* and is currently the editor of *Crayola Kids* magazine, based in Des Moines, Iowa.

Lyn Reese has a master's degree in history from Stanford University and has specialized in creating classroom resources which include *I Will Not Bow My Head: Documenting Women's Resistance in World History; Spindle Stories: Nine Middle School Units in Women's World History; I'm on My Way Running: Women Speak on Coming of Age; Women in the World: Annotated Bibliography of Student Resources.* She also serves on a number of committees concerned with educational equity for girls both nationally and abroad. She currently lives in Berkeley, California.

Mary Ruthsdotter graduated from UCLA with a bachelor's degree in urban geography and a master's degree in urban planning. Her recent projects include *The Women's Almanac,* to be published by John Wiley & Sons, Inc., and the premiere edition of *Women's History Magazine,* available in March of this year. In addition, she and Bonnie Eisenberg helped create a five-part video documentary about the history of U.S. women called *Women in American Life.* She currently lives in Santa Rosa, California.

ACKNOWLEDGMENTS:

Ruth Ashby would like to give special thanks to her parents, Dorothea and Arthur Ashby, and her husband, Ernie Colón, for their support, patience, and countless hours of babysitting.

Bonnie Eisenberg would like to give special thanks to Lisl Smith, who was involved in the initial research and fact-checking for material included in *Herstory*.

Judy Gitenstein would like to give special thanks to her parents for their friendship.

Deborah Gore Ohrn would like to give special thanks to Jennifer Guttenfelder Golay for research assistance, to her husband, Steven Ohrn, for all of his love and encouragement, and to the next generation of young women and men. May the women in this book provide you with the inspiration, hope, and determination to accomplish in life whatever you dream.

S. Suzan Jane would like to give special thanks to the National Women's History Project for their continued work on women in history and for allowing her to work with them while she was in California.

Mary Ruthsdotter would like to give special thanks to the reading public who increasingly appreciate women's contributions to American history.

The editors who worked on this book would also like to thank:

The Division for the Advancement of Women at the United Nations, the Harry Ransom Humanities Research Center, Henry Blanke at the Marymount Manhattan College Library, the International Women's Tribune Center, Marie-Hélène Gold at the Schlesinger Library, the Metropolitan Museum of Art Photograph & Slide Division, Michael Shulman at Archive Photos, the New York Public Library, Tom Gilbert at AP/Wide World Photos.

Acknowledgments continued from copyright page:

Cambridge University Press: Selection from *Medieval English Nunneries* by Eileen Power; copyright © Cambridge University Press, 1975. *Hogarth Press and The Virginia Woolf Estate:* Excerpts from *A Room of One's Own* by Virginia Woolf; copyright © Leonard Woolf, 1957. *New Directions Publishing Corporation:* Excerpt from *Women Poets of China* by Kenneth Rexroth and Ling Chung; copyright © Kenneth Rexroth and Ling Chung, 1967. *Penguin Books:* Selection from *The Penguin Book of Women Poets* edited by Carol Cosman, Joan Keefe, and Kathleen Weaver: poem translated by D. M. Pettinella; copyright © Carol Cosman, Joan Keefe, and Kathleen Weaver, 1978. *Penguin Books, UK:* Excerpt from *The Canterbury Tales* by Geoffery Chaucer: copyright 1951 by Nevill Coghill, copyright © renewed Nevill Coghill, 1977. *Persea Books:* Excerpt from *The Book of the City of Ladies* by Christine de Pizan, translated by Earl Jeffery Richards; copyright © Persea Books, 1982. *Charles Scribner's Sons:* Excerpt from *Sorrow's Kitchen: The Life and Folklore of Zora Neale Hurston* by Mary E. Lyons; copyright © The Zora Neale Hurston Estate, 1990. *The University of California Press:* Selections from *Sappho: A New Translation* by Mary Barnard; copyright © The University of California Press, 1958. *W. W. Norton & Company* (U.S. and Canada) and *Victor Gollancz Ltd.* (UK, Australia, New Zealand): Excerpt from *The Feminine Mystique* by Betty Friedan; copyright 1963 by Betty Friedan, copyright © renewed Betty Friedan, 1974.

PHOTO CREDITS:

Section I:

p. ii & 26: Bronze statue of Boudica and her daughters. By Thomas Thornycroft, cast in 1902. Photo by Margaret Ehrenberg; p. viii: Gloria Steinem. AP/Wide World Photos; p. 1: Woman leading a little boy. Greek vase, fifth century, B.C. Metropolitan Museum of Art, Rogers Fund, 1964. (64.11.7); p. 2: Prähistorische Abteilung Naturhistorisches Museum, Wien; p. 5: Metropolitan Museum of Art, Museum Excavations, 1919-20, Rogers Fund and contribution of Edward S. Harkness (20.3.7); p. 7: Metropolitan Museum of Art, Fletcher Fund, 1931 (31.11.10); p. 10: Metropolitan Museum of Art, Gift of J. Pierpont Morgan, 1916 (16.30); p. 12: Peabody Essex Museum, Salem, Mass; p. 15: Courtesy Department Library Services, American Museum of Natural History, negative #15115; p. 17: Metropolitan Museum of Art, Rogers Fund and Edward S. Harkness Gift, 1929 (29.3.2); p. 20, 30: Alinari/Art Resource; p. 22: Antikensammlung SMPK/bpk, Berlin 1994; p. 24: Maurice Durand Collection of Vietnamese Art, Southeast Asian Collection, Sterling Library, Yale University; p. 37: © cliché Bibliothèque Nationale de France, Paris; p. 38: AP/Wide World Photos; p. 42: Bettmann Archive; p. 45: Scala/Art Resource; p. 50: Detroit Institute of Arts, Gift of Mr. Leslie H. Green; p. 52: Judith Leyster, "Self Portrait," Gift of Mr. and Mrs. Robert Woods Bliss, © 1994 Board of Trustees, National Gallery of Art, Washington.

Section II:

p. 57: Women bearing arms during the French revolution, October 1789. © cliché Bibliothèque Nationale de France, Paris; p. 60: Tate Gallery, London/Art Resource, NY; p. 62, 63, 69, 97, 109, 111, 117, 142, 150: courtesy of the Library of Congress; p. 64: *Punch* magazine library; p. 76: © Archive Photos; p. 78, 85, 91, 125, 146: courtesy of the Schlesinger Library, Radcliffe College; p. 80: Oregon Historical Society, negative #OrHi-27715; p. 89: Smithsonian Institution/Art Resource, NY; p. 93: Metropolitan Museum of Art, Gift of I.N. Phelps Stokes, Edward S. Hawes, Alice Mary Hawes, Marion Augusta Hawes, 1937 (37.14.40); p. 101: courtesy of National Portrait Gallery, London; p. 103: courtesy of Special Collections, Vassar College libraries; p. 106, 129, 138: AP/Wide World Photos; p. 119: courtesy *Mother Jones* magazine; p. 120: Victoria & Albert Museum, London/Art Resource, NY; p. 127: courtesy of Fogg Art Museum, Harvard University Art Museums, Bequest of Grenville L. Winthrop; p. 131: George Eastman House; p. 133: Metropolitan Museum of Art, Bequest of Edith H. Proskauer, 1975 (1975.319.1); p. 135: Nevada Historical Society; p. 139: Kansas Historical Society; p. 148: Jane Addams Memorial Collection, Special Collections, University Library, University of Illinois at Chicago; p. 153: Pierpont Morgan Library, New York. MA, negative #2009.

Section III:

p. 155: Rally at the United Nations-sponsored Declaration of American Women Conference, Houston, 1977. Courtesy of International Women's Tribune Center/Anne Walker; p. 156, 157, 158, 178, 205, 221: courtesy of the Library of Congress; p. 160, 165, 171, 176, 187, 190, 192, 203, 207, 209, 212, 216, 218, 223, 226, 239, 243, 246, 249, 251, 256, 259, 263, 271, 273, 278, 280, 282, 286: AP/Wide World Photos; p. 161: International Women's Tribune Center/Adela Alonso; p. 174: Bettmann Archive; p. 180: drawing by Nin Chi; p. 193, 228, 235: © Archive Photos; p. 197: © Archive Photos/Camera Press/Cecil Beaton; p. 198: © Archive Photos/Express Newspapers; p. 200: United Nations photo; p. 231: reproduction authorized by the Instituto Nacional de Bellas Artes and the Harry Ransom Humanities Research Center at the University of Texas at Austin; p. 267: © Kate Kunz; p. 275: courtesy of Children's Defense Fund/Katherine Lambert; p. 289: photo courtesy of Eka Esu-Williams; p. 290: United Nations photo/John Isaac; p. 292: © Maryknoll/J. Hahn.

GEOGRAPHICAL INDEX

ALPHABETICAL INDEX

OCCUPATIONAL INDEX